Praise for

ENOUGH

by Roger Thurow and Scott Kilman

"In the twenty-first century, the world has no excuse for tolerating the existence of a billion people going without food. *Enough* is a passionate and clearly-reasoned call for action to finally end forever the age-old scourge of hunger for any human being."

—MUHAMMAD YUNUS, **winner of the Nobel Peace Prize and author of** *Creating a World Without Poverty*

"For a general wrap-up of how we got into this mess and what we need to do about it, you can't do better than *Enough* by Roger Thurow and Scott Kilman. . . . [A] very readable book."

—*New Scientist*

"How, in a world of plenty, can people be left to starve? We think, 'It's just the way of the world.' But if it is the way of the world, we must overthrow the way of the world. Enough is enough."

—BONO

"Devastating yet hopeful. . . . There are heartbreaking stories of how failed policies and misguided approaches led to scenarios where African children died of starvation while surplus food rotted in warehouses only miles away."

—*Minneapolis Star-Tribune*

"A page turner. Unless you simply don't give a damn, this is a must read, and it is a must read now."

—DAN SILVERSTEIN, *The Huffington Post*

"Every person connected to the food industry should read it."

—*AG Week*

"Thurow and Kilman lead the reader on a journey across continents, explaining the complexities of economic dysfunction and reminding us that there is a symbiosis of wealth and poverty that explains why starvation endures in an age of plenty."

—*USA Today*

"Thurow and Kilman are journalists who have covered famines in Africa, agricultural policy in the corridors of Washington and Brussels, and food commodities markets in Chicago. Yet their book is more than just a rough first draft of history. While grounded in colourful, entertaining reportage, *Enough* also displays a depth of thought and research more commonly found in academic studies. Well-chosen anecdotes bring the issues to life."

—*Financial Times*

"*Enough* is by no means a tragedy. The second half recounts stories of what people are trying to do to change the nature of foreign assistance and humanitarian relief. It tells the story of a movement of people throughout the U.S. who want something different and better."

—*The Christian Century*

FOR KELSEY—

RAISE THE CLAMOR!

[signature: Roger Thurow]

GO GET 'EM!

4/10/2011

ENOUGH

Why the World's Poorest Starve in an Age of Plenty

ROGER THUROW and **SCOTT KILMAN**

THE CHICAGO COUNCIL
ON GLOBAL AFFAIRS

PUBLICAFFAIRS
New York

The Library of Congress has cataloged the hardcover as follows:
Thurow, Roger.
    Enough : why the world's poorest starve in an age of plenty / Roger Thurow and
Scott Kilman.
        p.   cm.
    Includes bibliographical references and index.
    ISBN: 978-1-58648-511-5 (alk. paper)
    1. Poverty—Africa.   2. Poverty—Africa—Prevention.   3. Poverty.   4. Poverty—
Prevention.   5. Starvation.   6. Starvation—Prevention.   7. International
cooperation.   I. Kilman, Scott.   II. Title.
    HC800.Z9P6285 2009
    363.8—dc22

                                                                    2009009638
Paperback ISBN: 978-1-58648-818-5

10 9 8 7 6 5 4 3

From Roger:
For Anne, Brian, and Aishling,
who nourish the vision and the spirit

From Scott:
For Trish, Helen, and Rosemary,
who show how individuals can make a difference in the world

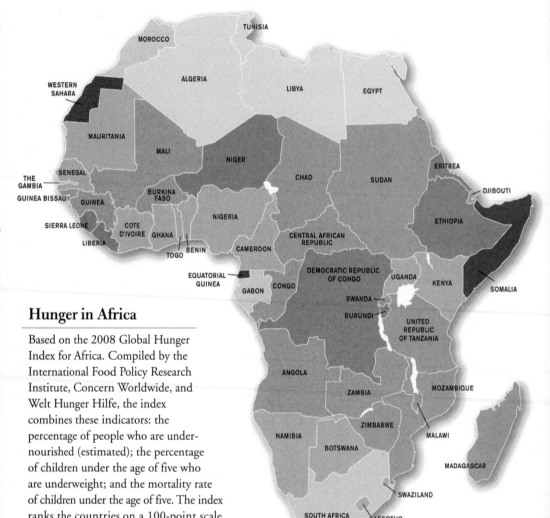

Hunger in Africa

Based on the 2008 Global Hunger Index for Africa. Compiled by the International Food Policy Research Institute, Concern Worldwide, and Welt Hunger Hilfe, the index combines these indicators: the percentage of people who are under-nourished (estimated); the percentage of children under the age of five who are underweight; and the mortality rate of children under the age of five. The index ranks the countries on a 100-point scale, with 0 being the best score (no hunger).

≥ 30.0 Extremely alarming

20.0–29.9 Alarming

10.0–19.9 Serious

5.0–9.9 Moderate

≤ 4.9 Low

No data

CONTENTS

With Pious Regret

Boricha, the Ethiopian Highlands, 2003

In the searing heat of late spring, before anyone realized that what was happening here was just the beginning of something much bigger, a tiny girl stumbled through a field of rocks toward a group of international aid workers. She was barefoot and limping. Flies dotted her face, craving the moisture of her eyes, lips, and nostrils. A shabby gray dress smudged with dirt hung limply from her shoulders. Though she was no more than eight years old, she carried her baby sister on her back, a turquoise blanket binding them together. Without speaking, for that would have required too much energy, the girl weakly stretched out her arms, one hand supporting the other. Her dark, frightened eyes were desperate. Please, they beseeched, something to eat, anything at all. In a famine, the starving speak with their eyes.

Beyond the girl, on the edge of the rocky field, was a warren of olive-green tents. Inside them, 166 children were dying of starvation.

Emmanuel Otoro, the director of Ethiopia's Disaster Prevention and Preparedness Commission for the Boricha region, gently stroked the girl's cheek. A second of comfort was all he could spare. Then he parted the flaps of one of the tents and entered a scene nearly incomprehensible to the modern mind.

Starvation is death by deprivation, the absence of one of the essential elements for life. It's not the result of an accident or a spasm of violence, the ravages of disease or the inevitable decay of old age. It occurs because people are forced to live in the hollow of plenty. For decades, the world has grown enough food to nourish everyone adequately. Satellites can spot budding crop failures; shortages can be avoided. In the modern world, like never before, famine is by and large preventable. When it occurs, it represents civilization's collective failure.

Just inside the canvas walls of the tent, Emmanuel came upon two infants receiving nourishment through nose tubes. He swatted away the flies buzzing around their heads. "We've never seen a disaster like this before around here," he whispered to a group of nurses and aid workers.

It was an astonishing statement, given Ethiopia's history. In 1984, more than 12 million people had teetered on the verge of starvation, and nearly 1 million of them died. The suffering was so intense, so vast, and so pitiable that the world swore such famine would never happen again. Yet not even twenty years later, "never again" was happening again, in Boricha and many of Ethiopia's blighted regions. And this time, even more people—14 million—were desperate for something to eat.

Emmanuel made his way to a corner of the tent where five-year-old Hagirso sat like a rag doll on a flimsy mattress, propped up between the spindly legs of his father, Tesfaye Ketema. A few days before, Tesfaye had cradled his emaciated son for an hour and a half as they rode in a donkey-drawn wagon over rutted dirt roads to this makeshift famine clinic. Hagirso was starving to death. He weighed just twenty-seven pounds when he arrived. His arms and legs were bone-thin, his head swollen from the effects of protein deficiency. He did not cry or plead for help. His eyes were deep, dark, empty holes. Farewell, they said.

The year before, Tesfaye, along with many other Ethiopian peasant farmers, had reaped his best harvest ever. Then he trekked happily to the market town of Boricha carrying heavy sacks of grain. But the historic bumper harvest overwhelmed the country's underdeveloped markets with a surplus, and prices collapsed. What Tesfaye received from the merchants of Boricha was barely enough to cover his planting and harvesting costs. At the end of the day, including labor and transportation expenses, he reckoned he actually lost money.

The next planting season, he cut back on costs by sowing cheaper, lower-quality corn seed on his three-quarters of an acre and abandoning the use of expensive fertilizer. He knew this would result in a smaller harvest, but he calculated he would still reap enough to feed his family. Farmers all across Ethiopia reacted in the same manner. Some who worked the country's largest farms took thousands of acres out of production. Others shut off their simple irrigation systems to reduce expenses.

Then all of Ethiopia looked heavenward for rain. But in many places the rains never came. With drought choking the land, Ethiopia's, and Tesfaye's, harvest shrank even further than expected. Tesfaye's family soon ate through their reserve from the previous year. As the pain of hunger gnawed relentlessly, Tesfaye began selling off his few possessions to buy food. First he sold his ox, which pulled his plow. Then he sold the family cow, which provided milk. Then he sold the goats. With nothing left, Tesfaye watched Hagirso waste away. Instead of lugging bags of surplus corn to the market town as he had the year before, he now carried his dying son.

In the emergency feeding tent, he stared at the starving little boy slumped between his legs. "He is our youngest," he mournfully told the nurses and aid workers. Surrounded by the dying children of other peasant farmers, Tesfaye was heavy with worry and guilt. What, he wondered, had he done to his son?

As Emmanuel Otoro moved from starving child to starving child, from horrified parent to horrified parent, he heard the same lament over and over. A thought began to form: This wasn't just a disaster scene. It was a crime scene, for what was happening to these families had not been their own doing.

Four decades before, the Green Revolution had introduced scientific and technological breakthroughs, such as new wheat and rice strains and new farming methods, that ultimately succeeded in conquering famine throughout Asia and Latin America. Millions upon millions of lives were saved as the Green Revolution rolled through India and Pakistan and then across Asia. Basket cases became breadbaskets. Norman Borlaug, a dogged plant breeder from small-town Iowa, hailed as the father of the Green Revolution and the savior of more lives than perhaps any other human being in history, had won the Nobel Peace Prize.

These scientific and technological breakthroughs were also introduced to Africa. In Ethiopia's Great Rift Valley highlands, as fertile a place as any on the continent, food production steadily increased. The Boricha region, a plateau overlooking a chain of Rift Valley lakes, declared itself food self-sufficient at the dawn of the new millennium. Ethiopia, so hungry for so long, was closing in on the goal of feeding itself.

Yet something was terribly wrong. The record harvests brought only more misery to the farmers, as the surpluses led to price collapses. Beyond the harvest gains, certain vital aspects of the Green Revolution never made it to Africa. There had been no investment in rural infrastructure to enable the movement of crops from where they were plentiful to where they were scarce, no development of markets so farmers could get fair prices, no financing to support farmers, no subsidies to cushion them against price drops, no crop insurance to compensate them for weather disasters. The political will to finish the job of ending famine had evaporated in Africa.

African agriculture and the Ethiopian peasants and their children were left to die. For Emmanuel Otoro, this neglect was the unprecedented disaster. "First, the market failed," he observed as he turned away from Tesfaye and Hagirso to leave the tent. "And *then* the weather."

In the Ethiopian capital, Addis Ababa, Volli Carucci of the United Nations' World Food Program (WFP), which had the task of feeding the hungry, unfurled a map of Africa across the shiny expanse of a conference table. Ethiopia, he demonstrated to a visitor with a sweep of his hand, was only the tip of the iceberg. Hunger was raging across the continent. Up and down the east coast, from the Horn of Africa to the Cape of Good Hope, and west across the hem of the Sahara, from the Red Sea to the Atlantic Ocean, crops were failing and more than 40 million people were starving, saved only by food aid pouring in from North America, Europe, Japan, and Australia. Beyond the zones of full-blown famine and starvation, there was the everyday grind of chronic malnutrition that was leaving several hundred million more Africans with gnawing, half-empty stomachs. Countries were growing as weak as their people, for hunger also eats away at economies. Hungry children can't study, hungry adults can't work, malnourished people die more quickly when other diseases strike. You're hungry and malnourished and get malaria, you're a goner. Diarrhea, cholera, measles: You have no strength to fight them. Tuberculosis, gone. Pneumonia, AIDS, gone. Everywhere people were blind and lame, too small for their age, too old looking for their years. That too, Carucci explained, was hunger and malnutrition—deficiencies of micronutrients such as vitamin A, iron, and zinc—at work.

Hunger in all its forms was spreading, not retreating, despite all of the scientific advances and the decades of intense effort by so many people. "Starvation is an ancient emotion. It is something people in Europe and the United States have forgotten about," Carucci, an Italian, lamented. "Looking into the eyes of someone dying of hunger becomes a disease of the soul. You see that nobody should have to die of hunger."

Since the time of the Green Revolution, the world has known how to end famine and tame chronic hunger. We have the information and tools. But we haven't done it. We explored the heavens. We wired the world for the Internet. We embarked on quests to conquer AIDS and assail global warming. We lifted hundreds of millions of people out of poverty and into the middle class. Yet somehow we haven't eliminated the most primitive scourge of all.

Norman Borlaug had warned of the consequences of such failure, pleading in his 1970 Nobel lecture in Oslo, "Man can and must prevent the tragedy of famine in the future instead of merely trying with pious regret to salvage the human wreckage of the famine, as he has so often done in the past. We will be guilty of criminal negligence, without extenuation, if we permit future famines."

The 14 million Ethiopians starving in 2003 bore silent witness on behalf of the world's hungry—850 million of them around the globe at the time—to the missteps and neglect that allowed famine to invade the twenty-first century and persist in a world that produces more than enough food for everybody. And they warned of an even more dire worldwide food crisis yet to come. Within a few years, surging demand, soaring prices, and spreading hunger would trigger food riots in a number of countries, prompting panicky governments to temporarily ban exports of their grain and rattling economies across the globe. The desperate supplication of the barefoot girl in Boricha was only the beginning.

By 2008, the number of undernourished people in the world had swelled to nearly 1 billion, the largest number since the early 1970s, when the full impact of the Green Revolution was just kicking in. After dropping in the 1970s and 1980s, the size of the world's hungry population changed little in the 1990s as the new millennium approached, though the proportion of the population in hunger declined due to an expanding population. Now, though, the cost of grain, having settled at a new plateau after gyrating wildly in 2007 and 2008, is once again increasing the ranks of the hungry. Many of the new hungry are in sub-Saharan Africa, where 457 million were undernourished in 2007, an amount that was up 53 percent since the U.S. Department of Agriculture began calculating these numbers in 1992. The region could soon be home to half of the world's hungry, even though it has just about one-tenth of the world's population.

UN health and food organizations calculate that 25,000 people throughout the developing world die every day from hunger and malnutrition and related diseases. That's three times as many daily deaths as occurred during the 1994 genocide in Rwanda, when an average of 8,000 people were slaughtered each day during a one hundred–day orgy of killing. Or as officials of the United Nations World Food Program have grimly noted, it's the equivalent of sixty jumbo jets crashing each day.

Hunger's grip on children is particularly cruel, contributing to about 6 million young deaths annually at the beginning of this century. Of the children who survive, 300 million are classified as "chronically hungry," which means that night after night they go to bed with an empty stomach; 150 million children under the age of five are stunted from malnourishment, which means they likely never will reach their full potential, physically or mentally.

The failed momentum of the Green Revolution deprives some places of the world, particularly Africa, from maximizing their agricultural potential. This denies global markets a tremendous source of food; Africa, after all, has almost twice as much arable land as the European Union, and much of that land, as Ethiopia proved, could be just as productive. Africa is agriculture's largely untapped final frontier.

This neglect is battering consumers around the world. For most years of this young century so far, the world has consumed more grain than it has produced, draining reserves and elevating prices. Borlaug had put us out front in the race to keep food production ahead of the rate of population growth, but now the food supply has become less secure. We're falling behind not so much because of a population increase but because of the population's increased prosperity. As the formerly hungry of India and China move toward the middle class, they are eating better, escalating the demand for grain-fed meat and dairy products. Meanwhile, volatile oil prices this decade have pushed politicians in a number of countries, chief among them the United States and nations of the European Union, to promote alternative sources of fuel that are made from food. In the United States, ethanol-fuel makers were devouring about 30 percent of the nation's corn crop by 2009, roughly double the amount they used in 2006. Many farmers reduced their plantings of some crops, such as soybeans, wheat, peas, and lentils, to grow more corn for cars instead. Biofuel companies are now competitors of the hungry.

The consequences of this growing demand are dwindling supplies and greater vulnerability to natural disasters that could lessen harvests. Global grain reserves plummeted in 2007 and 2008 to their lowest levels in three decades, ending a long period of gluts that had steadily pushed down the inflation-adjusted, or real, price of food. Between 2006 and 2008, prices of many of the world's staples doubled. Rioting erupted in dozens of nations in 2007 and 2008, escalating global security concerns. A prime minister resigned in Haiti as hungry people clamored for more rice.

Even countries where the Green Revolution advanced the furthest couldn't escape impact. In Mexico, where Borlaug first bred the seeds of the revolution, rising tortilla prices triggered protests. In India and Pakistan and across Asia, complacency over the rising production had sapped the political will to keep the momentum of agricultural development going. They paid for their shortsightedness in soaring rice prices, which more than doubled in the first half of 2008. It all left the World Food Program scrambling to keep up. The WFP traditionally fed those in rural areas who didn't have access to enough food because of crop failures. Now suddenly it also had to feed swelling numbers of urban residents unable to afford the food available. At the same time, its own costs for food aid were escalating.

The global financial crisis that began in late 2008 doused crop prices like everything else. But hunger fighters are bracing for the situation to get worse once the economy recovers. Deserts are expanding, lakes in Africa are drying up, water tables in China and India are sinking, and climate change is expected to complicate the growing of staple crops in the tropical zones around the equator. Africa is perhaps the most vulnerable, as the majority of its farmers are dependent on rainfall. Bringing more land into production would take a long time, for that opportunity, too, was squandered. Dire predictions are pouring in from many quarters. In July 2008, the U.S. Department of Agriculture predicted that the number of malnourished will rise to 1.2 billion by 2017. The world is on course to give back many of the gains of the Green Revolution.

For a decade we have covered hunger and world agriculture for *The Wall Street Journal,* reporting from the famine zones of Ethiopia and the overflowing silos of Iowa; from the lush fields of Ghana and Malawi and the desert sands of Niger and Chad; from the amber waves of grain in North Dakota, Russia, and India and the cotton fields of Mali and Mississippi; from the peaceful green hills of Washington State's Palouse and France's Normandy and the blood-soaked, tear-stained soil of Zimbabwe and Sudan; from the world-trade negotiating tables in Geneva and the corridors of power in Washington, D.C., London, and Brussels.

Along the way, we have met many well-meaning people who believe that hunger in the world is a given; that, like the poor, it will always be with us. They think hunger is a natural disaster, as it was in the wake of the Asian tsunami of 2004. Or that it is a tool of political control wielded by desperate dictators like Robert Mugabe in Zimbabwe and Omar al-Bashir in Sudan. Or that it follows as a consequence of war, as in Biafra and the Congo. They believe that beyond their donations to the United Nations Children's Fund (UNICEF) or the World Food Program, there is nothing else they can do about it; they can alleviate the suffering but not prevent it.

The truth is that natural disasters will occur and unconscionable dictators will ruin their countries. But so much of the chronic, everyday hunger in the world is now a man-made catastrophe, caused one anonymous decision at a time, one day at a time, by people, institutions, and governments doing what they thought was best for themselves or sometimes even what they thought at the time was best for Africa.

Even now, many of the people making those decisions—among them renowned economists, development experts, politicians, preachers, farmers, humanitarians—have no idea what impact they had or what part they played in reversing decades of progress. Farm subsidies in the United States and Europe, for instance, started out as a vehicle for helping poor farmers recover from economic calamity or war. But over the years they have grown to be a matter of addiction. By 2007, the world's rich, developed countries were paying $260 billion in support to their own farmers, making it impossible for competing unsubsidized farmers to grow strong in places such as sub-Saharan Africa. On top of that, the international financial institutions controlled by the United States and Europe have long forbade African governments from subsidizing their own farmers if they are to receive any loans. So it is, too, with American food aid, which began as warmhearted generosity toward the hungry and evolved into a jealously protected entitlement *for those providing the aid*. A Band-Aid for the poor is now an industry for the rich. In Ethiopia in 2003, the United States provided more than $500 million in American-grown grain to feed the hungry but only $5 million in agricultural development aid to help them avoid becoming hungry in the first place.

The hunger that grows from these decisions—the catastrophe that is man-made—is preventable. And there is more to do than donate money. There is the need for informed people to advocate for policy reform and new practices that work for the world's poorest, to be aware of the global consequences of self-interested decisions, to roll up sleeves and get to work in the fields. Fighting hunger isn't hopeless. It is a battle that can be won, for this generation has more weapons at its disposal than any other.

To that end, a new movement founded on a new will to conquer hunger is rising once again among people proclaiming "enough is enough." It is coming from the well-fed in America and Europe whose eyes have been opened to the problem, from philanthropists, from churches and synagogues and mosques and temples, from corporate boardrooms, from universities, from small towns and big institutions, from farmers, from entrepreneurs, from the meek and the mighty. And it is coming from the hungry Africans themselves, from peasants and presidents alike, who are fed up with begging for food. But unless we are clear about what went wrong, we risk making the same mistakes, or, as happened before, letting a year or two of plenty sap our will to construct a system that works in fallow years.

This book tells the story of the squandered promise of the Green Revolution and the neglect that brought hunger and famine into the twenty-first century. It is the story of Africa and the missed opportunities, the wars and the megalomania, the folly and the good intentions gone bad that have left its agricultural potential largely unrealized, its people hungrier than ever before, and the entire world aching for more and cheaper food. It is a tale of self-interest and hypocrisy in the United States and Europe, how subsidies and food aid have gone awry, how geopolitics influenced by remnants of colonial-era policies and practices of the old European powers determine that some countries should bloom and others should starve, how markets failed, how warnings went unheeded, how the present crisis is engulfing us.

This is also, in Part II, the story of the new movement to reclaim the revolution's lost promise and restore its momentum. It follows the trail from Borlaug to Bono, the Irish rock musician haunted by the chorus of the hungry he first heard in Ethiopia in 1984. From Bill Gates and his foundation colleagues, who realized that the medicine they were bringing to Africa was useless in a malnourished body, to Joe Mamlin, an Indiana doctor who became a farmer in Kenya so his AIDS patients would have something to eat. From Eleni Gabre-Madhin, who kept tilting at windmills until she brought a commodities exchange to her native Ethiopia, to Francis Pelekamoyo, whose Bible led his conversion from Malawi's central banker to humble microlender. From a small town in Ohio to a tiny village in Kenya. From European CEOs to a couple of American sitcom-watching moms to a son of billionaire investor Warren Buffett. From British church activists to former UK Prime Minister Tony Blair to statesmen in Ireland working to ensure that their country's dark history of famine isn't repeated elsewhere in the future.

We don't promote one brand of politics over another, unless it is the politics of common sense and doing what is right for the poorest of the poor. We don't favor one religion over another; the major faiths all command their followers to feed the hungry. If we bring any personal baggage to this issue, it is that we are journalists. Although newspaper reporters are often viewed as a cynical bunch, in truth we are a profession of optimists. We believe that finding the solution to a problem often begins with people reading about it. We trust that reasonable people will feel compelled to act. So we write.

In amplifying our reporting for *The Wall Street Journal* into a book, which is based on our own interviews and research unless otherwise noted, we have had the generous assistance of the Rockefeller and William and Flora Hewlett foundations and the Chicago Council on Global Affairs. None of these organizations, however, had any influence over the writing or editing of this book.

Our purpose is to help stir a constituency of people who will reverse the neglect and build on the new momentum. The hungry are watching, and waiting.

PART I

The Unfinished Revolution

CHAPTER 1

Seeds of Change

MEXICO, 1944

Norman Borlaug didn't set out to feed the world's hungry. His ambition as a young scientist was more modest: defeat rust blight. That, and secure a steady job where he could work outdoors.

The world was at war for a second time, and in America college graduates were being drafted into an array of special operations to gather intelligence, break codes, and otherwise confound and outsmart the enemy. Borlaug, fresh from the University of Minnesota with a doctorate in plant pathology, was fulfilling his patriotic duty at the Wilmington, Delaware, laboratories of chemical giant DuPont Co. Though he had been hired to develop agricultural chemicals, the war altered his mission: He and his unit of fellow scientists were testing military supplies, including condoms, for their durability in the tropical conditions of the Pacific theater. Borlaug was toiling in his lab one day in the spring of 1944 when the Office of Special Studies tapped him on the shoulder. His services were needed in Mexico.

Borlaug was new to the world of foreign adventure. In fact, he was new to the world, period. He was an Iowa farm boy from the Norwegian-influenced countryside near the village of Cresco up by the Minnesota border. Educated in a one-room schoolhouse, he had idly dreamed of playing second base for the Chicago Cubs. When he applied to the University of Minnesota, he flunked the entrance exam. The university sent him to its new general college for a chance to earn a two-year degree. Disappointed but determined to make good, Borlaug improved his grades and transferred to the big university, where he excelled in wrestling and the study of forestry, two passions that matched his stoic disposition. One summer he worked for the U.S. Forest Service as a fire lookout on Idaho's Cold Mountain. Alone for several weeks at a time, a two-day horse ride from the nearest ranger station, he savored the solitude and embraced it as his calling. Confident of a full-time job with the Forest Service upon graduation, Borlaug proposed to his college sweetheart, Margaret Gibson. Together, he pledged, they would find happiness in the wilderness.

Budget cuts, though, felled the forestry job. Crestfallen and facing an aimless future, Borlaug sought advice from his university mentor, eminent plant pathologist Elvin Charles Stakman. The professor suggested his young charge take up his own work; a plant pathologist, he told him, had good job security, for crop diseases always found a way to circumvent man's cures. With a new wife to support, Borlaug knew he would need a reliable job. Plant pathology it would be. He even enlisted in Stakman's lifelong assault on rust blight, one of the biggest destroyers of cereal crops around the world.

The quasi-governmental Office of Special Studies had been established in 1943 at the suggestion of Stakman and two other scientists. The mission: increase production of corn, wheat, and beans in Mexico to prevent hunger and instability south of the border. The special project needed a crusader against a most insidious enemy: wheat rust. Stakman knew just the man.

In September 1944, Borlaug left his pregnant wife and infant daughter in Wilmington and drove off to Mexico, an unlikely revolutionary.

From the beginning, the Green Revolution was the unintended outcome of unlikely work by determined individuals. Henry Wallace, who blazed Borlaug's trail to Mexico, simply wanted to practice his Spanish.

In 1940, before he took office beside Franklin D. Roosevelt, Vice President–elect Wallace headed to Mexico. An intellectually restless scion of an Iowa family that published the influential rural magazine *Wallaces' Farmer*, Wallace had served as Roosevelt's activist agriculture secretary since 1933. Wallace recognized that the farmers of that era were, as small commodity producers, economically weak relative to their suppliers and customers. His Agriculture Department created many of the farmer-friendly programs that he had trumpeted in his magazine: farm subsidies, food stamps, federal crop insurance, and soil conservation. He also instituted an "ever-normal granary" policy, whereby the federal government began to buy crops during surplus years as insurance against poor future harvests. The strategy was designed to help farmers by slowing any drop in grain prices during years of excessive production, and it later would keep food on the table when the country's entry into World War II triggered the rationing of many household goods.

Wallace told the president he wanted to visit Latin America before starting his official duties. Roosevelt, eager to develop closer Pan-American ties amid growing global tensions, dispatched Wallace to Mexico to represent the United States at the December 1940 inauguration of Manuel Ávila Camacho, who was friendly to the United States and whose election had been bitterly fought.

As it turned out, Wallace and Mexico shared a common passion. Wallace's hobby was breeding corn, and Mexicans loved eating it. Corn, known as maize in Mexico, was the country's staple food and was grown in every conceivable nook and cranny, from mountain slopes to the floating islands of Xochimilco.

Wallace's fascination with plants dated back to his childhood. George Washington Carver, the future famous botanist, was then the first black student at Iowa State University in Ames, where Wallace's father was teaching. Carver took young Wallace on walks to study plants and shared his own passion for growing things. In his teenage years, Wallace began growing corn in his backyard for study. He couldn't have picked a racier subject, so far as vegetation goes. Corn is an unusually promiscuous grain due to the fact that its sex parts are unusually distant from each other. The male tassel, which sheds pollen, is often several feet above the female ear, which holds the ovules for fertilization into kernels. Unlike a self-pollinating plant such as the soybean, which has its reproductive parts packed tightly together, corn's cross-pollination design encourages the species to swap wind-blown pollen—which easily can travel hundreds of yards.

Corn's architecture makes it a favorite of crop breeders, who sell seed to farmers with the promise of ever-improving plants. Breeders do this by picking promising parents and mating them in hopes of creating a plant with better genes. Wallace was a young man when breeders experimenting with forcing corn plants to self-pollinate discovered a peculiar phenomenon: When they forced self-pollination for several generations, the inbred line seemed to lose some of its ability to produce grain as a dominant trait took hold. But if they took one inbred line and crossed it with another, it ignited an extraordinary leap in the yield of their offspring, a dynamic known as hybrid vigor. Just as mysteriously, the explosion in yield occurred for just one generation.

Wallace, long an advocate for using science to help farmers, saw a way to use it to make money as well. He made a fortune as one of the first to tap the business potential of hybrid corn. Farmers paid a premium for such high-yielding seed. And they kept coming back to the breeder year after year since they couldn't simply save some of their harvest as seed and get the same results. In 1926, Wallace and a group of friends founded what would become corn-seed giant Pioneer Hi-Bred. Hybrid corn's appeal to farmers was so strong that it swept across the Midwest even as the Great Depression unfolded and farmers pinched pennies. By the time the United States entered World War II, much of Iowa's corn crop came from hybrid seed.

The productivity of U.S. corn farmers exploded. Before hybrid seed, an acre of Iowa farmland had been producing about the same amount of corn for roughly sixty years. In 1930 the average corn yield in Iowa was thirty-four bushels an acre. By 1940, the average Iowa yield had jumped to fifty-two and a half bushels an acre. Wallace's company became a Farm Belt icon alongside the John Deere tractor as U.S. corn yields continued to climb.

So when he visited Mexico in 1940, Wallace carried with him a unique perspective. He frequently stopped his Plymouth alongside the rough roads and waded into fields to talk with farmers. Most Mexicans depended on farming. The Mexican Revolution, a bloody struggle that had ended twenty years earlier, ousted a dictatorship and then seized land from a wealthy few and redistributed it among the poor. The new government slowly parceled out land to 1.7 million landless peasants in hopes that they could grow their own food. But land reform wasn't enough.

Hunger and poverty were widespread by the time Wallace arrived. Little had been done to educate small farmers. Agricultural scientists were scarce and most of the rural population illiterate. Mexican farms were yielding only one-third the corn and beans of U.S. farms, and even that productivity was slipping. The soils were depleted of nutrients and heavily eroded. Tractors were rare. Many farmers still did all their work with hand tools, limiting how much they could grow. While wheat farmers were among Mexico's most sophisticated growers, their yields were just two-thirds that of U.S. farmers. Diseases often wiped out the wheat crop, forcing Mexico to import half of its needs.

The hunger situation seemed hopeless to most. But Wallace saw the solution: raise crop yields. If poor Mexican farmers could produce more from their land—and Wallace had admired their work ethic—they could feed themselves and then have something left over to sell for income. At the time, Wallace's idea was radical. With U.S. farmers mired in the Depression and an expensive war on the horizon, there was little support in Washington for spending money to help somebody else's poor farmers. Indeed, the obligation to fight hunger outside U.S. borders was just a fledgling concept pioneered by another Iowan, Herbert Hoover, before his stint in the White House. A wealthy mining engineer, Hoover organized private food-aid drives that fed millions of Europeans during World War I. It wasn't until after the second global conflagration that the U.S. government would see the diplomatic value of food aid and development aid.

When Wallace moved into the office of vice president in 1941, he called upon the Rockefeller Foundation, which was fighting infectious diseases such as malaria and hookworm in many poor countries. Some of the foundation's medical staff already were coming to the view that poor nutrition was eroding the health standards of poor countries.

Wallace asked Rockefeller Foundation President Raymond B. Fosdick to study how to increase Mexican harvests; Fosdick, in turn, dispatched a trio of experts to scour the countryside. By the summer of 1941, Harvard plant breeder Paul Mangelsdorf, Cornell agronomist Richard Bradfield, and University of Minnesota plant pathologist E. C. Stakman were picking their way across thousands of miles of Mexico in a green GMC Suburban Carryall station wagon.

Like Wallace, the professors were big believers in "scientific farming." For the first time in history, farmers in the United States produced more crops without putting more land under the plow. Why not Mexico? they wondered. Their report convinced the foundation to set up a joint research program with the Mexican government in 1943, to be christened the Office of Special Studies. A platoon of U.S. scientists was hired to run the program with the idea that they would eventually work themselves out of jobs by training Mexican scientists to do their work of breeding ever-higher-yielding varieties of corn, wheat, and beans.

Poor Mexican farmers couldn't afford to buy hybrid corn seed each year, so Rockefeller scientists resorted to teaching them how to plant a few varieties of inbred seed—the precursor to hybrid seed—and allow them to cross-pollinate naturally. Although yields didn't jump as dramatically as they could with hybrid plants, this so-called synthetic seed grew into corn plants that produced a tenth to a quarter more corn than the best varieties around. What's more, farmers could continue their practice of saving kernels from their highest-yielding plants as seed for the next season.

What interested Professor Stakman was Mexico's second-biggest crop: wheat. Stakman, who spoke fluent Spanish, was an expert on the fungal disease called stem rust, which was turning Mexico's golden wheat fields into a gray tangle of dead plants. The epidemics erupted so frequently that many Mexican farmers stopped growing wheat, an important source of protein in a country where meat was often hard to come by.

Stakman had battled the rust blight ever since he was a young high school teacher, when he traveled by horse and buggy across the Great Plains studying outbreaks. In Mexico, he had the disease in his sights, and he drafted two protégés from the University of Minnesota to lead the assault. J. George "Dutch" Harrar took charge of the Mexico mission and would later become president of the Rockefeller Foundation. The second hire was a young man fresh out of college by the name of Norman Borlaug.

The working conditions in Mexico were far more primitive than anything Borlaug had encountered as a researcher in the United States. Because of the war, supplies of everything from farm equipment to gasoline were tight.

The only way Borlaug could stop the rust epidemics was to scour the world for wheat plants with natural immunity and breed the trait into his Mexican crop. It meant growing hundreds of different varieties of wheat in rust-infested areas and then waiting to see if any didn't get sick from the windblown fungal spores. When he found survivors, Borlaug bred them for living in the Mexican environment.

Creating a variety of wheat was a tedious process. Bending over in fields baked by a relentless Mexican sun, Borlaug worked with surgical precision to bring together the parents of his choosing. Using tweezers, he emasculated one parent by removing its stamen—the male part of a young flower—and then deftly applied the pollen he had collected from the other parent to the pistil, or ovary. He put a bag over the flower to block any other source of pollen.

Then he waited, and waited, for nature to take its course. Months passed. Borlaug harvested the seed. More months passed before the next growing season arrived. Borlaug planted the seed. More often than not, the results weren't satisfactory and another match had to be tried. Finding a resistant strain for Mexico could easily take a decade.

Borlaug wasn't that patient. The rust organism mutated so quickly that the one-crop-a-year process would never allow him to catch up with it and stay ahead with new strains. Then he heard a farmer talking about the Yaquí Valley in Mexico's Pacific Northwest, where the wheat was planted in October and harvested in the spring—the opposite cycle from Mexico's main wheat-growing belt in the central highlands. Borlaug booked a seat on a trimotor plane for the two-day, 2,000-kilometer flight to Ciudad Obregón, roughly 800 miles away. Once he arrived, he hitchhiked through the valley, visiting farms and prospecting for wheat seeds.

Borlaug's idea: shorten the time to create varieties by shuttling newly harvested seed between the Yaquí Valley and his experimental plots near Mexico City. That effectively squeezed two growing seasons out of one year. The idea challenged the conventional wisdom of plant breeders, who had long believed that crops had to be bred where farmers would raise them. Many crops are very sensitive to their surroundings, which limits where they can grow.

Harrar, Borlaug's boss, repeatedly rejected his idea. Harrar worried that shuttle breeding would exhaust the project's scarce resources. Breeding wheat in two places year-round would double Borlaug's expenses and separate his staff from their families in Mexico City for months at a time. If Borlaug's unconventional idea proved wrong, his venture would squander the time that could have been spent breeding plants the conventional way.

It took the intervention of their common mentor, Professor Stakman, to settle the fight. Borlaug got what he wanted, but the pressure to succeed consequently grew heavier.

When Borlaug returned to the Yaquí Valley, his bare-bones budget relegated him to a government-owned experiment station that had fallen into disrepair. He cooked beans over an outdoor stove and kept a double-barrel shotgun nearby to bag ducks and scare off any bandits. At night he slept on the second floor of the grain storehouse to avoid rats.

At first the farmers didn't know what to think of the American who had dropped into their midst. Borlaug looked as if he had stepped out of a Grant Wood painting: square jaw, broad shoulders, blue eyes. The little Spanish he spoke was pronounced with the Norwegian accent of his parents back in Iowa. He had less equipment than the neighboring farmers he was there to help. But his childhood on an Iowa farm had prepared him to work as hard as they did. He borrowed a mule-drawn plow to prepare the plots and harvested his first experimental wheat with a sickle. Soon curious neighbors invited Borlaug to dinner and Sunday bullfights.

Rodolfo Elías Calles, a local boy captivated by this foreigner, was impressed with how Borlaug devoured a thick steak for supper and that he challenged men to wrestling matches. "Farmers liked him. He was a big man but he talked to farmers directly," Calles remembered. "He was sincere and simple, and that was amazing to us."

Borlaug dictated a frantic pace for himself and his assistants. After planting in the Yaquí Valley in November, they walked miles of wheat rows looking for plants that seemed impervious to rust. During the flowering season, they were stooped over in the fields crossbreeding the healthiest plants. Borlaug helped harvest the plumpest grain in April, which he then carried south by truck over rough roads to his test plots in Toluca, near Mexico City, for planting in early May.

Borlaug's impatience was at times a ticket to trouble, imperiling his entire endeavor. In 1948, he was driving a truck full of supplies and seed for a new growing season in the Yaquí Valley. A flood had knocked out a bridge in the Copper Canyon system, which is nearly as rugged as the Grand Canyon. A makeshift raft was attached to a cable strung across the river, but the operator had quit for the weekend. When Borlaug learned that a truck successfully forded the river earlier in the day, he tried his luck.

He didn't realize that the river was rising until he drove into it. Soon the water was over the driver's seat, forcing Borlaug to swim to safety. He hiked back to where he had passed a road construction crew, which helped him pull the truck out of the muck. Luckily, his supplies and precious seed had stayed dry. "If I had lost the truck," Borlaug later recalled, "I figured Harrar could fire me."

In just four years, Borlaug's frenetic shuttle breeding began to pay off. Using wheat lines from four countries, he generated his first rust-resistant plants. Many scientists would have declared success at that point and left it to others to worry about getting his inventions into the hands of farmers. But Borlaug realized that in a poor country, it was up to him to get enough farmers interested in his seeds so that government officials and entrepreneurs would take notice. He prepared demonstration plots and served free beer and barbecued beef.

One of the first farmers to try Borlaug's new seeds was Calles's father, Don Rodolfo Elías Calles, a former Sonora governor and son of former Mexican President Plutarco Elías Calles. He planted some of Borlaug's first rust-resistant wheat varieties. His farm yield climbed so rapidly that neighbors quickly followed suit, as did their neighbors. Borlaug's wheat swept across Mexico. Unlike with hybrid corn, farmers could save seeds from the best of their wheat harvest and plant them the next year to get the same results. By 1951, about 70 percent of Mexico's wheat came from Borlaug, who was hailed by some farmers as "Super Sabio": Super Sage.

The high-yielding plants sucked so much out of the soil that fields had to be replenished with plenty of water and synthetic fertilizer. But farmers were able to produce far more grain from their land than ever thought possible, ending Mexico's dependence on foreign wheat at the time and igniting an economic boom in the region.

Several new forms of rust battered Mexico throughout the early 1950s. Each time, shuttle breeding allowed Borlaug and his fellow researchers to find resistant plants quickly, and ramp up production of new seed for farmers. As a result, Mexico's wheat shortage ended by the mid-1950s. And as the Yaquí Valley's production grew, so did the political power of its farmers. The Mexican government built roads and irrigation projects.

Mexico's wheat farms soon became so productive that Borlaug faced a new problem. With bigger crops, many farmers could afford to buy synthetic fertilizer for the first time, boosting their harvests even more. Mexico's wheat fields became so heavy with grain that the plants had to be redesigned so they wouldn't topple over. Borlaug solved that problem by using a dwarf Japanese variety to develop a shorter, sturdier plant. By 1960, the wheat farmers of the Yaquí Valley were reaping fifty to seventy-five bushels an acre, compared to about eleven bushels an acre when Borlaug first arrived.

Borlaug's unorthodox way of breeding wheat changed his creations in ways he didn't foresee. Wheat, like many plants, is sensitive to seasonal changes in day length. The amount of time between dawn and dusk is a signal to start certain biological changes. Spinach, for example, can't be bred near the equator because the days there are never long enough to initiate the internal sequence that leads to flowering. U.S.-grown spring wheat was hard to transplant to Mexico because it needed the lengthy daylight of the northern summer to trigger the ripening process. Photoperiodism was a big reason crop breeders believed that they had to do their work in the places where the crops were meant to grow.

Borlaug's wheat varieties, however, were the offspring of parents selected for their ability to thrive in two very different environments. In the Yaquí Valley, which is near sea level, the crops depended on irrigation during the growing season, which started as the days grew progressively shorter. In the Toluca Valley far to the south, the wheat fields were about 2,500 meters above sea level and relied on rainfall. There, planting began in the spring, as the days lengthened.

The constant commuting desensitized Borlaug's wheat plants to daylight, making them easy to plant across Mexico—and the world. "We did shuttle breeding to cut the time in half," Borlaug noted years later. "But what we discovered is that it made crops more flexible."

By 1960, much of the developing world seemed destined for starvation. The European powers had neglected investments in their colonies' food production, and the populations of newly independent countries were growing at historic rates. Then back-to-back droughts struck parts of Asia. The United States shipped one-fifth of its entire wheat crop to India to stave off mass hunger. It seemed that humans were outstripping the earth's capacity to produce enough food to feed everyone. Stanford University biologist Paul R. Ehrlich helped stir a doomsday panic with his predictions of mass starvation in his book *The Population Bomb.*

Borlaug's wheat came to the rescue. His unorthodox breeding methods had created a plant capable of flourishing quickly in strange lands—a trait that surprised many plant scientists, and saved Asia many years of looking for a solution. India and Pakistan bought tens of thousands of tons of seed from the farmers in the Yaquí Valley.

In India, where the population was growing by 10 million annually, farm fields were producing roughly one-third to one-half the yields of developed countries. That meant most of its labor force was tied up trying to grow food, preventing its economy from modernizing. At the time, by comparison, only about 10 percent of the U.S. population lived on the farm.

Applying lessons learned in the Yaquí Valley, Borlaug and his fellow researchers used demonstration plots to show poor Indian farmers what they could accomplish on their own land with the Mexican wheat. Farmers clamored for his Mexican seeds after seeing chemically fertilized plots produce five times as much grain as the same amount of land using traditional seeds and old methods.

Borlaug's seeds made him a celebrity in Asia, which he exploited to grab newspaper headlines in order to cajole government officials into helping farmers get fertilizer, credit, and subsidies. He warned political leaders of a public backlash if they didn't encourage construction of fertilizer factories and guarantee profitable prices for growers. It was unusual for an American scientist to play such a role in the domestic affairs of Asian countries, but Borlaug had powerful people in his corner: American President Lyndon Johnson threatened to withhold food aid from India unless New Delhi adopted farmer-friendly policies.

In short order, Prime Minister Indira Gandhi ripped up a flower bed in front of her residence and planted Borlaug's wheat. Her government replaced price limits on grain with price supports, and it called for a proliferation of fertilizer factories. Donors ranging from the governments of the United States and Europe to private philanthropies and humanitarian organizations poured money into building irrigation networks, constructing roads for bringing crops to market, and sending educators into the fields to teach modern farming techniques.

India's wheat harvest doubled in just four years. Schools temporarily closed so the buildings could be used to store it all. By the mid-1970s, India was growing enough grain both to be self-sufficient in feeding its own people and to build vast national reserves. The growth of Pakistan's farm sector wasn't as smooth, but it eventually became a wheat producer equal in size to Canada. The threat of famine in both countries retreated. Borlaug's wheat soon spread to Turkey, Afghanistan, Tunisia, Morocco, Lebanon, and Iraq, and then sprouted in China and elsewhere in Asia. Mexican seeds and their descendants were planted on tens of millions of acres around the world.

Asia's agricultural revolution was stunning: Cereal production between 1970 and 1995 grew far faster than the region's population. In addition to pushing back the food shortages, the Green Revolution gave hundreds of millions of poor farmers extra crops to sell for money to pay for education, medicine, and a better life. In India, the remarkable jump in agricultural productivity raised farm incomes enough to help slash the rural poverty rate from 64 percent in 1967 to 34 percent in 1986, according to the World Bank. The real—that is, inflation-adjusted—price of farm commodities sank steadily, making food more affordable to the poor.

Everybody, it seemed, wanted to get in on the Green Revolution. Encouraged by Borlaug's success with wheat, the Rockefeller and Ford foundations had established a small laboratory in the Philippines in 1960 to try to make similar improvements to rice, Asia's most important crop. The first breakthrough was a fast-maturing, high-yielding variety called IR8. Because Asia's diet hinged on rice and wheat, scientists working on just these two crops were able to save untold millions of people from starvation.

So many donors wanted to fund Green Revolution–style research that the World Bank and its prime backers in the United States and Europe created a new science organization, which inherited the work started by the foundations. The Consultative Group on International Agricultural Research (CGIAR) spawned more than a dozen centers around the world to specialize in everything from agroforestry to fish. A trickle of money for research became a torrent.

Borlaug, though, was happiest in his fields, far away from the hubbub. That's where he was on October 20, 1970, working with a handful of young scientists in his muddy Toluca test plots, collecting seeds for the trip north to the Yaquí Valley nursery. Out of nowhere, his wife appeared, as excited as he had ever seen her. Margaret had driven from Mexico City over rugged roads to deliver big news. The phone at home, she said, was ringing with callers wanting to congratulate the newest Nobel Peace Prize laureate.

Her husband thought it was a joke, someone playing a trick on him. He was just a breeder, after all, not a statesman. "No. No. That can't be," he told his wife. "Someone's pulling your leg." He turned and hurried back to the harvest. Thousands of plants needed his close attention.

Then a pickup truck ferrying local reporters appeared on the horizon. This was no joke. A solitary, stubborn, impatient, brilliant scientist was about to become an international hero, and an example of what an individual can accomplish in the quest to end hunger.

CHAPTER 2

Flow and Ebb

OSLO, NORWAY, 1970

The optimism that famine would soon be consigned to the history books lifted Norman Borlaug from his test fields in Mexico onto the stage of the University of Oslo auditorium on December 10, 1970. There was no Nobel Prize for agricultural science. But the Nobel committee of the Norwegian Parliament deemed a crop breeder worthy of the Peace Prize for defusing an ancient scourge of mankind.

"The world has been oscillating between fears of two catastrophes: the population explosion and the atom bomb. Both pose a mortal threat," said Aase Lionaes, the head of the Nobel Committee, in presenting the award. "In this intolerable situation, with the menace of doomsday hanging over us, Dr. Borlaug comes onto the stage and cuts the Gordian knot. He has given us a well-founded hope, an alternative of peace and of life—the Green Revolution."

What Borlaug had done, in addition to rescuing millions of people from hunger, was to give politicians, social planners, and economists a few more decades to defuse the population crisis. In what ranked as one of the greatest technological achievements of the twentieth century, per capita food supplies grew even as the population expanded. Borlaug, said Lionaes, had "turned pessimism into optimism in the dramatic race between population explosion and our production of food." She exhorted the world to follow his lead and, above all, to adopt his urgency: "Dr. Borlaug cannot afford to wait. There is an important cause weighing on his mind, something that must be carried out and must be carried out now."

Winning the world's most prestigious honor changed Borlaug and the way he regarded his work. The sunburned scientist who felt most at home kneeling beside his plants in muddy boots and jotting down the details of their intimate lives in his notebooks became a celebrated humanitarian. The recognition stole time from his research; his biggest discoveries were behind him, and he would grumble plenty about it. But he now had a bigger job: rattling the world's conscience. If famine and hunger were to be conquered, it was up to him to inspire, outrage, shame—anything so the world wouldn't squander the promise of his Green Revolution.

"The obligations imposed by the honor are far greater than the honor itself," Borlaug observed in his brief acceptance speech after receiving the Peace Prize, "for the Green Revolution has not yet been won. . . . It is true that the tide of the battle against hunger has changed for the better during the past three years. But tides have a way of flowing and then ebbing again. We may be at high tide now, but ebb tide could soon set in if we become complacent and relax our efforts."

The very next day, delivering the Nobel lecture, Borlaug talked about his purpose in life in a new way. He was accustomed to giving science lectures, and he had always approached his work with an entrepreneurial zeal. He measured success by breeding rates, yields, how many farmers adopted his methods. On December 11, 1970, he revealed a spiritual and emotional side of himself that had been forming during his years working with poor farmers.

The world's powers, he insisted, had a *moral* duty to support the Green Revolution and to recognize a universal right to food. A person who is starving has lost everything. Without nourishment, there is no life. Without food for all, there can be no justice and all other rights are meaningless. "Food," Borlaug argued, "is the moral right of all who are born into this world."

That was the cornerstone of his philosophy: Do what is best for the hungry, be it giving poor farmers the tools to feed themselves or building an international grain reserve for lean times. Whatever problems that would come of such efforts would be problems of abundance, which he argued were better than problems caused by shortage. His success—civilization's success—should now be measured by how many people were moved out of hunger and poverty. "The underprivileged billions in the forgotten world" deserved a universal Green Revolution, he said. "Hunger has been a constant companion, and starvation has all too often lurked in the nearby shadows."

As a scientist, Borlaug avoided taking sides politically. He couldn't be seen as an advocate for American interests or of favoring one party within a developing country over another. His work required the cooperation of leaders of all sorts of political persuasions. In Oslo, he invoked a higher power.

Raised in the Lutheran Church, Borlaug let the Scriptures speak for him for the first time. He cited Genesis, and the Old Testament prophets Isaiah, Amos, and Joel, and the Lord's Prayer: "Give us this day our daily bread."

He issued a prophesy of his own. His and future generations would be judged harshly if they squandered the opportunity that the Green Revolution presented. "We will be guilty of criminal negligence, without extenuation, if we permit future famines," Borlaug warned. "Humanity cannot tolerate that guilt."

Although Borlaug's fame was greater overseas than at home, soaring food prices in America began boosting his efforts to draw attention to the hungry. At the beginning of the decade, officials in Washington were wringing their hands over what to do with a price-depressing mountain of surplus crops. But Washington abruptly shifted fears when the Soviet Union, attempting to compensate for the staggering inefficiencies of centrally planned farming, quietly began buying massive amounts of grain from around the world. Moscow cleverly took advantage of a U.S. export-subsidy program in 1972 to acquire roughly one-third of the entire U.S. wheat crop. The press dubbed the shopping spree the "Great Grain Robbery." The Nixon White House didn't comprehend the implications of the Soviet purchases. Only later would the U.S. government force secretive U.S. grain exporters to disclose more about their deals to move American food overseas.

Suddenly, what had been going on for years in the poorest recesses of the world hit home, and that finally made it a crisis for many Americans who had barely paid attention to the work of the latest home-grown Nobel Peace laureate. The price of wheat tripled in the twelve-month period ending in August 1973. Prices of corn and soybeans, meanwhile, more than doubled, greatly increasing the costs of fattening cattle, hogs, and chickens.

The commodity-price shock rippled through the aisles of American grocery stores. The Consumer Price Index for food soared 14.5 percent in 1973. By some estimates, the Soviet purchases directly increased the food bill of American consumers by $2 billion in a single year. U.S. food prices climbed another 14.3 percent in 1974.

The food-price hikes hit at the same time as the 1973 Arab oil embargo forced gasoline prices higher. Many American households were forced to economize. Fights over food broke out in supermarket aisles. Panic hoarding proliferated. The federal government applied haphazard price controls. Soybean supplies shrank so low that the White House imposed an export embargo.

Many of the same forces were rattling European governments and consumers. Grain and oil prices were climbing in Europe as well. With memories of food shortages during World War II still sharp, the European Economic Community also sought to limit its wheat exports in an effort to husband supplies and protect its farmers.

A bushel of gloomy pundits captivated consumers around the world by retracing the views of British economist Thomas Robert Malthus, whose 1798 publication *An Essay on the Principle of Population* helped to earn the field of economics the moniker "the dismal science." He famously argued that the human race was condemned to live in the shadow of famine because it reproduces far faster than it can eke more food from the earth.

On that point, Malthus was wrong, of course. He underestimated the potential for agricultural productivity and didn't understand that people tend to have fewer children when their economic circumstances improve. But 175 years later, Malthusian gloom once again spread. Hollywood capitalized on that sentiment with the 1973 release of the Charlton Heston sci-fi movie *Soylent Green,* in which an overpopulated city depends on a gigantic corporation for food wafers. The secret ingredient: corpses.

While some argued that there wasn't enough food for everybody, others focused on sharing. Schoolchildren in America and Canada went door-to-door at Halloween collecting coins in little orange boxes for UNICEF, reaping millions of dollars for hungry kids overseas. Trick-or-treating for UNICEF, which grew from humble beginnings in the 1950s, became an icon of North American childhood. In Western Europe, as prosperity returned after the devastation of the postwar years, churches and social groups assumed greater responsibility for nourishing people in Africa, where poverty pricked the former colonial consciences. Caritas International chapters flourished across Europe following the Second Vatican Council and the Pope's encyclical calling for a greater focus on development and social justice. Children in Ireland canvassed neighborhoods and shopping areas for donations to the national humanitarian agency Concern; families in Britain fasted and donated their food savings to the Catholic Fund for Overseas Development. On the Continent—in Germany, Austria, Switzerland, and other countries—television and radio documentaries of poverty and famine in the developing world often spawned nationwide money-raising appeals. The Washington-based World Bank, the main financier of development projects in poor nations, capitalized on this greater grassroots attention to the food needs of the developing world to rally a surge in agricultural investment by its backers in the United States, Europe, and Japan; it also nurtured the expansion of the first international network of research stations aimed at helping the world's poorest farmers.

In the United States, a new wave of political activism emerged. Working from a Lutheran church on the Lower East Side of Manhattan, Pastor Arthur Simon founded the Christian citizens' group Bread for the World to lobby politicians to end hunger. Bread's first appeal in May 1974 drew thousands of eager volunteers who readily forked over the ten-dollar membership fee; it became a Christian force on the American political scene, inspired by the call of Jesus to feed the hungry. "We were all giving some money in the collection plate," Pastor Simon said, "but nothing was being done to challenge Christians to see what they could do to bring love and justice to others through political action." Within a year, Bread's foot soldiers had convinced Congress to adopt the Right to Food resolution.

It was, as Borlaug noted in Oslo, high tide in the fight against hunger. Such a level of interest in feeding the hungry hadn't been seen since the end of World War II, when the United States and its Allies were brimming with bold ideas for rebuilding Europe as well as attacking the sources of human misery that fuel conflict and undermine democracy.

The idea of food as an essential human right was popularized at a World Food Conference in Rome in November 1974, convened by the United Nations at the prodding of U.S. Secretary of State Henry Kissinger. There, delegates from 135 nations decreed that "every man, woman and child has the inalienable right to be free from hunger and malnutrition." Striking an optimistic tone, the delegates concluded that political will was all that stood in the way of achieving this goal. Civilization already possessed the resources and technology to end hunger; there could be enough for everybody. Norman Borlaug had illuminated the way. The conference's biggest accomplishment was creating a UN agency, the International Fund for Agricultural Development, to funnel some of the windfall profits racked up by Arab oil powers into rural farming projects in developing countries. The Rome conference even inspired Werner Erhard, the New Age creator of the human-potential program called *est*, to establish the Hunger Project to rally attention for ending famine.

Famously, Kissinger declared in Rome that within a decade no child should go to bed hungry. Several of the attending nations did indeed commit themselves to donating more grain for feeding the hungry. But despite Kissinger's grand pronouncement, the Ford administration wasn't one of them. The volume of U.S. aid shipments had shrunk dramatically due to soaring grain costs, and much of what was still in the pipeline went to a few politically sensitive customers, such as South Vietnam.

President Ford convened a panel of eminent scientists to recommend what role the United States could play in the battle against hunger: It, too, concluded that political will was the key. But in those days the White House's priority was restraining federal spending amid economic turmoil at home. Food aid shipments wouldn't grow significantly until grain costs fell.

Geopolitical considerations also shot down several potent schemes for fighting hunger. A group of scholars, businesspeople, and scientists championed the creation of an international agency that would control vast grain reserves for the purpose of responding to emergencies and feeding hungry children—an idea that had been around for decades and one that Borlaug had articulated in his Nobel lecture. But a multilateral organization of this type would reduce opportunities for the world's agricultural powers to use their homegrown food aid as a tool for furthering their own diplomatic aims. The proposal never got off the ground. Instead, the UN's hunger-relief agency, the World Food Program, was forced to perpetually hold out the begging bowl for financial contributions whenever emergencies materialized.

The global food crisis soon left the stage for reasons that had little to do with the Rome summit. Amid all the speech making, farmers got busy— at least those with the proper means did. Surpluses replaced shortages. In the West, farmers responded to the high prices and sweetened government subsidies by planting more crops. In Asia and Latin America, the Green Revolution continued to spread its roots. Armed with improved seeds and fertilizer, many nations sprinted down the path to self-sufficiency. India would become a major exporter of wheat and rice. The Cerrado, a vast stretch of barren land in Brazil, was reborn as one of the world's richest Farm Belts in part because scientists figured out how to use fertilizer, lime, and micronutrients to counter problems such as toxic levels of aluminum in the soil. China sowed the seeds of a farming boom that would lift millions from hunger.

World production of corn, wheat, and rice grew more than twice as fast as the population between 1975 and 1985, once again generating price-depressing gluts in the United States and Europe. The rich countries tried to shove the surpluses overseas. But thanks to the Green Revolution, several old customers such as Mexico and India had become far less dependent on the West for their grain. The U.S. government suddenly found itself in the maddening position of spending $1 billion annually on export subsidies to pump surplus American wheat overseas so that it didn't depress prices at home. Similarly, the European Community heavily subsidized exports of everything from wheat and beef to butter and milk to whittle down its huge surpluses and protect its farmers. The escalation of the subsidies race between the United States and Europe severely distorted world markets and drove down prices as big multinational commodities firms played the United States and Europe against each other for the cheapest grain. Both of these developments—rising rich-world subsidies and cheaper commodities—hit the farmers in the developing world particularly hard; without similar levels of subsidies from their impoverished governments, they absorbed the full impact of the low prices.

Mankind hadn't conquered hunger, but the new surpluses and low grain prices created a false sense of accomplishment and security in the rich world. The phrase "Malthusian optimism," coined by economist Amartya Sen, described this trap. When food output once again exceeds population growth, and the fear of widespread famine eases, the people who are still too poor to eat enough seem to evaporate from public consciousness. To be sure, the total number of hungry people around the world was falling from roughly 1 billion in the early 1970s, but hundreds of millions were still in desperate straits.

Everything was moving away from the push to grow as much food as possible: The religious zeal, the social buzz, the development philosophy, the financial institutions that had been Borlaug's allies in the Green Revolution retreated from the side of the hungry. Aid agencies shifted their attention to social programs like education and health, leaving fewer resources for agricultural development. Complacency—what Borlaug feared most—threatened to undermine his life's work. The ebb tide had set in.

Even organizations that should have been in tune with Borlaug's concerns turned a deaf ear to him. The World Economic Forum in Davos, Switzerland, which began meeting in the 1970s, was supposed to tackle just the sort of sweeping global problem that Borlaug was fighting. The best and the brightest and the richest and the ritziest gathered in the Alps each January. Their grandiose motto: "Committed to improving the state of the world." But Norman Borlaug, Super Sage, was never invited to speak. (The state of the hungry wasn't high on the agenda at the first Davos summit in 1971, when the number of malnourished in sub-Saharan Africa was about 90 million. Nor was it until 2006, when the region's hungry had grown to more than 400 million.)

On the religious front, meanwhile, Pastor Simon and Bread for the World soon found their admonitions about hunger and poverty competing with the exhortations and scolding of evangelists like Jerry Falwell. Ascending the new pulpit known as cable TV, these leaders spent their energy cultivating political influence rather than inspiring humanitarian achievement. They set out to forge a "moral majority" that focused more on what you were doing *with* your brethren—gay marriage, abortion, pornography—than on Jesus's Judgment Day question of what you would do *for* your brethren, especially "the least of these my brethren." Clearly, the least of all were those who didn't have enough to eat. But ending hunger was hard to find on this "moral" agenda. Hunger wasn't a useful "wedge issue" for church leaders seeking to mobilize their followers to vote for Ronald Reagan for president—and to increase their own political influence.

In a world seemingly awash in cheap food, Borlaug's simple idea of helping hungry countries feed themselves became more and more complicated. Many environmentalists distrusted the Green Revolution because it introduced fertilizers and pesticides to hundreds of millions of acres of land. Indeed, a new sort of pollution had come to the developing world: Pesticides and nitrates were poisoning some drinking water and threatening some beneficial species—just as had happened in the Farm Belts of the well-fed nations. In the Philippines, for example, farm chemicals were killing the fish that lived in rice paddies and waterways. In many cases, eager farmers poured too much fertilizer onto their land. Farmers knew that more fertilizer equaled more crops, so they used as much as they could afford. They didn't understand that their crops couldn't use all of it and that what they couldn't use often ended up in the water supply. Farmers in the developed world often made the same mistake. Over the decades scientists would get better at figuring out how to prescribe fertilizer in smaller amounts so that less was wasted, but at the time, chemical pollution created negative press for the Green Revolution.

Some social scientists, meanwhile, fretted that the Green Revolution was upending the harmony of rural villages. Although subsistence-farming communities were often haunted by hunger, academics marveled at how these villages endured hard times by sharing. The hungry could exchange their labor for food from more fortunate neighbors or could help themselves to communal land. Critics blamed the Green Revolution for altering the balance of power in rural communities. The ability of farmers to generate crop surpluses made profit possible, which created an incentive for the most efficient farmers to acquire more land, squeezing out others. Those who stayed had to borrow to buy the ingredients of the Green Revolution: seeds, fertilizer, and weed killer. Having a bad crop got riskier. Just as in the West's modern breadbaskets, banks were unforgiving with farmers who missed loan payments.

Green Revolution–style research dwindled. Although the budget for the Consultative Group on International Agricultural Research had grown since its founding, what many of its donors were willing to fund reflected the desires of well-fed nations for safer food produced in environmentally friendly ways. The CGIAR's traditional priority of pushing crop yields ever higher had faded, though that remained the overriding goal of poor farmers.

The neglect and criticism stung Borlaug. In 1979, at the age of sixty-five, he semiretired. He left the International Maize and Wheat Improvement Center in Mexico for a teaching post at Texas A&M. He had a small windowless office crammed with his papers and photographs of himself with farmers from around the world. But with his legacy now under siege on multiple fronts, and increasingly anxious that the world wasn't using the time he had given it to step up production in places like Africa, he barnstormed the globe, using his celebrity as a Nobel laureate to attack the West's complacency about hunger in the developing world.

In speeches, letters to editors, and press interviews, he argued that helping poor farmers squeeze more crops from their land would protect fragile habitat by eliminating the need for more farmland. Environmentalists should applaud, he insisted. And he sang the praises of synthetic fertilizer. Hauling out charts and jabbing a finger in the air, Borlaug noted that the human race obtained 40 percent of its calories from crops grown with synthetic fertilizer. Organic agriculture simply wasn't enough to sustain most of the population of the developing world. For heaven's sake, he fumed, the poorest countries had been organic for centuries, and what had that gotten them? Hungrier and hungrier, that's what.

It was the Green Revolution that had set the stage for Asia's manufacturing boom. Before Borlaug's wheat came along, most of the people in Asia were fully occupied with feeding themselves. The Green Revolution's high-yielding crops made labor available for factories. Indeed, Western economies, including the mighty engine of the United States, hadn't taken off until they had achieved food security. Since many of the world's malnourished were small farmers, Borlaug maintained that the surest way to get enough food in their mouths was to help them grow it.

Borlaug's lobbying didn't change many minds. His temper often got the better of him. He called environmentalists "elitists," even as the movement grew in popularity. "They can talk in their dreamy theoretical sense," he said. "But they never live in poverty. They live in ivory towers. They never live around hunger and misery and poverty. I have."

Much of his wrath, though, was trained on the World Bank, which had been turning away from funding agricultural development. He scolded the bank's mandarins for sounding retreat in the war on hunger. He railed at officials who discouraged poor governments from subsidizing their farmers the way India did to make the Green Revolution possible. He ridiculed their philosophy that treated poor farmers as the problem rather than the solution. "Idiots," he called them.

Elliot Berg, a Harvard-trained economist, was a smart man. But he saw the world through a different lens than Borlaug. He was an economics professor at the University of Michigan and former director of its Center for Research in Economic Development in 1980 when the World Bank commissioned him to compose a new strategy for dealing with Africa. Berg had lived in Africa for a couple of years and was considered an expert on policy reform and privatization programs.

He produced a 1981 report optimistically titled *Accelerated Development in Sub-Saharan Africa.* In it, Berg insisted that an agricultural revolution was crucial for turning around the economic struggles of the region, which he blamed, in part, on the heavy taxation of crops for export and the region's growing dependence on imported food. He called on the wealthy nations that funded World Bank programs to extend even more aid to African farmers.

It was a strategy that could have been ripped from the playbook of the Green Revolution. On paper, it was designed to deliver agricultural growth and food security. But in reality the Berg report was used to shove African agriculture over the cliff. For there was a second set of recommendations in the report that was more attractive to those wealthy nations, which at the time were trying to revive their own teetering finances as well as trying to corral failing economies in Latin America. The West mostly ignored the call to help Africa's farmers and instead latched on only to the report's array of belt-tightening policy prescriptions. Among other things, the World Bank argued that African governments had become bloated from getting involved in too many aspects of their economies that were better left to private enterprise.

When the European colonial powers pulled out of Africa in the 1960s, they generally left the countries devoid of skilled managers and educated entrepreneurs. So the state intervened in the private sector to fill the vacuum. As the Berg report noted, the vast country of Zaire (now the Democratic Republic of the Congo) didn't have a single African physician, lawyer, or engineer at the time of independence. Only 3 percent of the high school–age population was receiving an education in 1960, compared to 20 percent in India. It was that way all across the continent. In Mozambique, independence leaders could count on two hands the number of colleagues who had college educations when the Portuguese colonialists left.

As a result, fledgling governments nationalized many businesses and set up state-controlled monopolies, with civil servants running everything from manufacturing and mining to transportation and utilities. In some African countries, the public sector provided more than 40 percent of the recorded jobs. On the agricultural front, state-run enterprises supplied farmers with seed and fertilizer and bought, processed, and marketed their crops.

The bank's new strategy, which was echoed by the International Monetary Fund (IMF), was this: In exchange for more loans that were vital to spur economic and social development, poor nations had to shrink the size of their governments, disband the inefficient monopolies, and allow a freer hand for private enterprise. The emphasis was on fiscal discipline, cleaning up budgets, reining in currency fluctuations, and scaling down the continent's mountain of international debt. It was sound government policy, laudatory free-market theory. But the reforms, which came to be known as "structural adjustment," assumed a life of their own. African agriculture took a beating.

African governments twisted these loan conditions to justify shaping their budgets in favor of their wealthier, more influential supporters: the urban elite and the military. They set about cutting the size of government bureaucracy by whacking agricultural programs; this had few consequences for those in government since the poor, undereducated rural masses had no political power. Money was cannibalized from government research centers working on new seeds. Agricultural schools for training scientists and agronomists fell into disrepair. Irrigation projects dried up. The extension service, created to distribute the latest scientific advice to farmers, could hardly extend: Agents often didn't even have a bicycle and were forced to walk or hitchhike to make their rounds of farms. As a result, agents visited fewer and fewer farmers. Farm subsidies were cut. And the state withdrew from the business of seeds, fertilizer, and grain marketing, stepping aside for the private sector.

The problem was, in most countries, there *was* no private sector—at least not one capable of taking over these tasks. The intention of structural adjustment was to replace the heavy hand of the government with the "invisible hand" of the markets—the natural force that guides competition for goods and services, as described by Adam Smith in his free-market manifesto, *The Wealth of Nations.* But in much of Africa, market forces weren't merely out of sight, they were nonexistent, particularly in the agricultural realm. What was left was the Hunger of Nations.

In Ethiopia, for example, the government withdrew from and liberalized the grain market in March 1990, lifting all restrictions on private trade after fifteen years in which the state had exercised control over prices and movements of grain within the country. The state-run systems for buying, storing, and marketing agricultural products that proliferated across Africa in the 1970s were, as a rule, poorly run and a huge drain on government budgets. But in the absence of any other system, they provided at least a semblance of support for poor farmers. As it turned out, they were better than nothing.

Under structural adjustment, the government ended its responsibility for these market functions, and left them to the private sector. But in most places the private sector lacked the capital and infrastructure to take on tasks such as marketing fertilizer and seed or buying and transporting grain. Farmers from Ethiopia in the north to Mozambique in the south, from Tanzania in the east to Ghana in the west, fell without a safety net between the withdrawn government intervention and the weak free-market system. These reforms, without a parallel development of new markets and private-sector businesses, were a fatal cure.

To make matters worse, the new loans that were promised with the reforms—and the increased aid urged by Berg—never arrived. Instead, funding levels plummeted. The World Bank, which was the largest player of the bunch and set the example for other donors, would devote just 9 percent of its total lending in sub-Saharan Africa to agricultural development, even though the vast majority of the poor depended on agriculture for their livelihoods. That fact—that so many of the poor were farmers—was evidence to officials in Western capitals that agriculture was the cause of poverty, not the answer to it. They decided that farming couldn't lift the continent out of its poverty, so they turned away from rural development and concentrated on urban engines of growth. Other donors followed suit. Agriculture's share of total development assistance from the rich world to the poor shrank from 17 percent to 3 percent in the closing decades of the twentieth century. "The bank," said one of its mandarins who was involved in African agriculture at the time, "got a bad odor in Africa. We became the bogeyman."

It was a role reversal for the World Bank, which was supposed to be the champion of the world's poor. Created during World War II to help fund the reconstruction of war-ravaged Europe, the bank turned much of its attention to the poor in the developing world when Robert S. McNamara, the former U.S. secretary of defense, arrived as president in 1968.

In his military work, McNamara had come to see that the worsening poverty in the poorest nations was kindling for future wars. In September 1973, as the global food crisis gathered momentum, he used his address at the bank's annual meeting in Nairobi, Kenya—the first ever held in Africa—to ask the world's wealthy nations to funnel more money to the bank. Yes, he said, the United States and other industrial powers had poor of their own who could use the money. But, he argued, the people outside their borders lived in a far worse state of squalor and hunger. "This is absolute poverty: a condition of life so limited as to prevent realization of the potential of the genes with which one is born; a condition of life so degrading as to insult human dignity—and yet a condition of life so common as to be the lot of some 40% of the peoples of the developing countries," McNamara said. "And are not we who tolerate such poverty, when it is within our power to reduce the number afflicted by it, failing to fulfill the fundamental obligations accepted by civilized men since the beginning of time?"

He continued on, echoing Borlaug's admonitions: "There are, of course, many grounds for development assistance, among others, the expansion of trade, the strengthening of international stability and the reduction of social tensions. But in my view, the fundamental case for development assistance is the moral one. The whole of human history has recognized the principle—at least in the abstract—that the rich and the powerful have a moral obligation to assist the poor and the weak. This is what the sense of community is all about."

Seizing on the reality that most of the world's poor lived in rural areas and survived off the land, McNamara argued that the most efficient way to attack poverty was to help subsistence farmers grow more food, enough to have something to sell after feeding their families. His agenda was ambitious, involving everything from irrigation projects and farm-to-market roads to training extension agents and finding ways for small farmers to borrow.

In the next five-year plan, which covered the fiscal years of 1974 to 1978, the World Bank made $9.93 billion in agricultural loans, nearly quadrupling the $2.61 billion loaned during the previous five-year plan (1969–1973). This funding was essential for continuing the Green Revolution in Asia and Latin America. Loans for African agricultural projects rose at nearly the same rate; during the 1974–1978 period, agricultural lending commitments by the bank in sub-Saharan Africa totaled $1.6 billion, or 16 percent of the worldwide portfolio. By the mid-1970s, roughly one-third of the bank's loans were for agricultural development, compared to just 4 percent during the first twenty-five years of its existence.

By the 1980s, however, the mood within the bank had shifted in lockstep with the domestic politics of the United States, which, as the largest source of funds, traditionally selects the bank's president. The election of Ronald Reagan ended the era of McNamara, whose ardent advocacy for the world's poor irritated conservatives. They thought the bank should focus on promoting a free-market philosophy around the world. In July 1981, A. W. Clausen, a former Bank of America president, took over. Later that summer, the Berg report crystallized the new thinking. Consensus for this new philosophy built in Europe as well, as conservative leaders—particularly Margaret Thatcher in Britain and Helmut Kohl in West Germany—grew in stature and power.

Out went the moral prism of the McNamara era, and in came flinty-eyed return-on-investment metrics. In those calculations, which prized sales and profits and exportable commodities, the ability of a farmer to grow enough to feed his family didn't count as much because there was nothing to count. The production was consumed in the household. Through this sort of lens, helping poor farmers feed their families wasn't a sexy investment. It became riskier for an ambitious bureaucrat at the bank to propose an African agricultural project. It wasn't the way up the ladder.

Hypocrisy reigned. While the United States and Europe continued to lavish subsidies on their farmers, they pushed the World Bank to prevent poor countries, particularly African nations, from doling out subsidies of their own. The budgets of most poor nations were financed by outside donations, and those donor nations didn't want their money to help develop competing farmers. They argued that subsidies were wasteful. What is good for us, the rich Western countries said, isn't good for you. They imposed a diet of free trade and free markets on Africa that they themselves weren't willing to stomach. When, during one set of loan negotiations, an African finance official asked, "Why are you hanging so tough on no agriculture subsidies when that's what you do in the U.S.?" an American at the World Bank was heard to reply, "Because we can afford to be stupid and you can't." This imbalance in subsidies put Africa's small farmers at a big disadvantage on the global market, where cheaper subsidized food from the West undermined their production. It wasn't long before cheap imported crops were displacing locally grown food throughout the developing world. Africa's hopes of food self-sufficiency—the best barrier against famine and hunger—crumbled.

The policy certainly helped Western governments by creating a market for their burdensome stockpiles of subsidized crops. John Block, Reagan's agriculture secretary as the U.S. farm economy struggled under the weight of price-depressing gluts, put it bluntly: "[The] idea that developing countries should feed themselves is an anachronism from a bygone era. . . . They could better ensure their food security by relying on U.S. agricultural products, which are available, in most cases, at lower cost."

Given the struggles of those poor small farmers, exacerbated by exhausted soils and fickle climates, some development experts argued that helping them produce bigger harvests would only prolong their penury. They were poor because they were shackled to subsistence farming; they needed to be freed by finding jobs in manufacturing, tourism, or services, jobs from which they could make money to buy food instead of growing it themselves. In the view of the World Bank and other development organizations, food self-reliance became more important than food self-sufficiency: It made more sense for the poorest countries to develop businesses to earn the money needed to import food rather than grow their own.

This was dubbed "comparative advantage." Better to invest in manufacturing where local labor was cheaper, than in agriculture where foreign food was cheaper. In Haiti, for instance, farmers stopped growing rice and instead drifted to factories making underwear. Food production plummeted, but as long as prices remained low, the country could import what it needed, paying for food with money earned from exporting the underwear made by former farmers. "In all my years that we asked for help," said former Haitian agriculture minister Philippe Mathieu, "the answer was: No. Agriculture is not a tool for development."

Led by the World Bank, an increasing number of other institutions and humanitarian agencies also came to doubt that helping the agricultural sector and the peasant farmers of poor nations was the most effective way to fight poverty. They shifted their focus from growing food to delivering improved social services, like health and education. Funding by the community of rich nations—the United States, Europe, Japan, Canada, Australia—for agricultural projects in the developing world collapsed. Official development assistance to agriculture would plummet to $3.4 billion by 2004 from the peak in 1984 of $8 billion, measured in 2004 dollars, according to the World Bank. The world's rich nations spent roughly $4 billion annually on agricultural development aid for Asia in the late 1970s and early 1980s as they threw their weight behind the Green Revolution there. Financial support for Asian agriculture would begin to evaporate in the mid-1980s. Annual spending on development assistance to agriculture in Africa would briefly exceed $3 billion in the mid-1980s, then eventually sink back to the level it was at in 1975, which was $1.2 billion measured in 2004 dollars. The U.S. government's retreat was particularly dramatic. U.S. bilateral aid for agricultural development would shrink by 2003 to just one-tenth of the record $1.98 billion in 1980, measured in 1999 dollars.

Philanthropists also went looking for other holy grails: Intelligent life in outer space and cyberspace. A cure for AIDS. Unlocking the human genome. Holding back climate change. Borlaug had already won the Nobel for hunger. New Nobels were to be won.

Wherever he went, Borlaug continued to fume—if to less and less attention. The opportunity he had given the world was being squandered.

Africa, in particular, was growing hungrier in the 1980s. But instead of boosting agriculture there, Africa was being fenced off from the Green Revolution. Incredibly, it was being ordered out of agriculture. "No one wants to fight with Dr. Borlaug; he is one of the greats," said Kevin Cleaver, who would become the World Bank's director of agriculture and rural development. "But he doesn't bring appropriate technology to Africa."

Borlaug's Green Revolution was out of fashion. The world had moved on.

CHAPTER 3

Into Africa

NORTHERN ETHIOPIA, 1984

Africa was on the move, too, but in the wrong direction. It was heading backward. In the Horn, the cradle of mankind, the poor farmers who didn't count in the world of structural adjustment retreated to a place of primitive misery. Millions of them, abandoned by the emerging development theory and left to fend for themselves as drought choked the region, crawled across the sunbaked wastelands stretching north from Ethiopia's Great Rift Valley, desperately searching for food. Every morning, as 1984 rolled into 1985, the rising sun revealed new multitudes of emaciated bodies pressing against the wire fencing of hastily constructed refugee camps and feeding centers. Parents held out their children, surrendering them to the arms of foreign humanitarian-aid workers who gathered them in with the faint hope of saving just a few lives. By the time the drought broke and the rains returned, 1 million peasant farmers and their offspring had starved to death.

Ethiopia's communist dictator, Mengistu Haile Mariam, had conspired to keep the world from learning about the extent of the disaster as it spread across his country. His military regime enlisted the drought as a weapon in its campaign against government rebels in the north; hunger would kill more people than bullets. Meanwhile, Mengistu spent lavishly in the capital, Addis Ababa, to celebrate the tenth anniversary of communist rule and socialist brotherhood.

It was only when some intrepid international camera crews reached the famine zones that the outside world began to see and feel the tragedy. As the pictures circled the globe, so did the shock: Famine still plagued the world, only now the epicenter had shifted from Asia to Africa. Though initial pictures of starving Africans emerged during the Biafra famine at the end of the 1960s, it was Ethiopia that became the enduring image of starvation post–Green Revolution. Rock musicians orchestrated concerts spanning the continents, uniting the world in hand-holding horror. Money poured into relief agencies old and new; Mazon, a Jewish antihunger organization, was created in response, and formed a broad religious coalition with Bread for the World. Food aid and sympathy rushed to the dying fields in Ethiopia. Once again, the scramble was on "with pious regret to salvage the human wreckage of famine," as Borlaug had prophesied.

The shock, though, did little to spark change in the West's economic medicine for Africa. In fact, the famine emboldened the advocates of the policies of structural adjustment and comparative advantage in the rightness of their course. To them, the vast starvation confirmed the hopeless vulnerability of Africa's farmers to the whims of weather and the cruelty of evil regimes. More than ever, peasant farmers were seen as the problem, not the solution. They should be working in factories, making underwear for export, rather than trying to grow their own food. The free market and global trade would somehow take care of them. And so would food aid; the world had plenty of excess grain. Surely, the generosity of the world would have saved the Ethiopians if only the communists hadn't hidden the problem.

One of the rare challenges to this line of thinking stirred in an unlikely source. Ryoicho Sasakawa, an octogenarian racing-boat magnate and philanthropist, rallied Japan's response to the tragedy. But as he dispatched food and medical supplies to the hungry of Ethiopia, he wondered why the rich world wasn't stoking an African agricultural revolution that could prevent the starving in the first place—like the one he knew had worked miracles in Asia. He dialed the number of the one man who would know, the one man, he believed, who could do something about it.

Norman Borlaug answered the ringing telephone in his office at Texas A&M University. "Why has there been no Green Revolution in sub-Saharan Africa?" the voice from the other side of the world demanded to know.

For Borlaug, the call came straight out of the blue. He was seventy years old, had settled into the role of elder statesman and teacher, and was considering a position at forest-products giant Weyerhaeuser Company. He told Sasakawa he had spent his career working in Latin America and Asia and knew little about Africa.

Sasakawa offered to bankroll Borlaug. But Borlaug doubted he could get enough money and commitment to succeed. He had painfully watched the changing tides slow the momentum of his Green Revolution. Although he fervently desired to banish hunger from the world, the old collegiate wrestler knew Africa would require unrelenting energy and stamina. There were not only fickle soil and pesky bugs and myriad climates to battle but also a whole philosophy aligned against him. Perhaps, he said, it was a job for a young man. "I'm too old to start over," Borlaug told Sasakawa. Then he hung up.

The next day, Borlaug's phone rang again. Sasakawa's voice jumped out of the receiver: "Young man, I'm fifteen years older than you. Let's get to work in Africa and not waste any more time."

One impatient, persistent man lobbied another. Borlaug warmed to the entreaties coming from Japan and found himself stirred by the challenge. His legacy, after all, was at stake. Bringing the Green Revolution to Africa would complete his life's work and prove the naysayers wrong. It could be his crowning achievement.

The two men summoned veterans of the Green Revolution and several old Africa hands to a conference in Geneva in 1985. There, they wrestled with the possibility of doubling or tripling crop yields in Africa. They were joined by former President Jimmy Carter, whose Carter Center in Atlanta was dedicated to incubating solutions to thorny humanitarian problems. The gathering concluded that Africa's vast legion of small farmers had enormous possibility for growth and could succeed with the proper support. Success would be farmers harvesting enough to at least feed their own families; they would move from problem to solution. If a series of pilot projects introducing better seeds and fertilizer and modern farming methods could demonstrate the possibilities and spark a grassroots movement, an agricultural revolution could gain traction. Borlaug believed the food crisis in

Africa was the fault of neglectful political leaders, not its farmers. Africa's farmers, he said often, had great potential. "But you can't eat potential."

In 1986, the Sasakawa Africa Association was established. Sasakawa provided the money. Borlaug brought the expertise. Carter contributed the diplomatic connections and power of political persuasion.

Their first stop was Ghana. Then they ventured into Ethiopia and Mozambique and Mali and a dozen other countries. Borlaug deployed seeds, fertilizer, and technological advice against the hard rock face of structural adjustment, market fundamentalism, and Africa's mercurial geography and politics. Later Borlaug would say: "I had no idea what I was getting into."

The great paradox of Africa confronting the Sasakawa team was how a continent rich enough to serve as the womb of our species could slip so far behind the rest of the world. Why wasn't Africa a farming power; indeed, why hadn't it invented agriculture? Africa had been given the huge advantage of time. And Africans had probably been producing food together longer than anyone else. They gathered the seeds of scores of species of wild grasses on Africa's ancient savannas. But that wasn't farming. Making the leap from hunter-gatherers to farmers would take much longer in Africa than other places.

In part that was because Africans did very well as hunter-gatherers. Another big reason was Africa's geographical bad luck, as evolutionary biologist Jared Diamond has argued. Despite Africa's amazing biodiversity, very few of the plants and animals in the world that ultimately proved most successfully amenable to domestication were native to Africa. The ancestors of modern-day wheat and barley were found in the Fertile Crescent of the Middle East. Rice and soybeans originated in Asia. Corn, potatoes, and tomatoes sprouted in the Americas. While corn, wheat, rice, and soybeans became the staple suppliers of most of humankind's calories—and they all eventually made their way to Africa, carried by traders and colonialists— Africa's historical contribution to farming consisted of minor crops such as sorghum, millet, and teff. The result was that over thousands of years Africa's agricultural development lagged behind that of Europe, Asia, and the Americas, delaying the economic growth that happens when a society grows enough food to free its people from the necessity of using all their time and labor simply to feed themselves.

When Borlaug ignited the Green Revolution in the 1960s, Asia had been the center of global hunger and Africa was brimming with optimism. The independence movement was sweeping the continent. Political aspirations were soaring. The wealth from the region's natural resources, rather than being harvested and sent to Europe, could be deployed at home to the benefit of the local populations. This included the continent's agricultural output. Hopes were high that Africa could feed itself.

But even then, Asia had advantages over Africa. Asian farmers had laid down irrigation systems for their rice fields; African farmers were almost totally reliant on rain. Asia had a network of roads, trains, and rivers that moved farm goods to markets; Africa had few paved roads, and those mainly ran between the ports and the mining areas so the European colonialists could ship the continent's precious natural resources home. Asia had a more open and sophisticated system of traders and markets ready to absorb any boost in production; Africa relied on markets that essentially hadn't changed since the Middle Ages. In much of Africa, goods moved from farmer to consumer on the backs of donkeys. Middlemen set prices in roadside haggling. Merchants literally sat on their piles of grain in outdoor stalls. Also, Asia was simpler, in agronomic terms, than Africa. Asia's consumers depended on rice and wheat, so Borlaug and his colleagues could make a big impact by targeting just two crops. Africa's food supply was far more diverse, with the staples ranging from millet in the Sahel to cassava and rice in the west to corn in the east and south. Corn raised the stakes economically for Africa. Being so naturally promiscuous, its descendants quickly diluted any traits bred into it by scientists. As Henry Wallace knew, farmers who wanted to raise high-yielding corn had to regularly buy seed, an enormous expense for a subsistence grower. In Asia, farmers didn't face such costs; they could save some of their harvest of wheat and rice for seed to plant the next year. Once these self-pollinating crops were changed by breeders like Borlaug, the traits held fast through generations.

Thus did Africa fall further and further behind the rest of the world—even though sub-Saharan Africa had more than enough arable land to feed itself if properly tended. While Africa was blessed with some of the world's most fertile farmland in the eastern highlands and southern savannas, the nutrients in much of the continent's soil had been sapped by ever-more-intensive use of the land. With a growing population, farmers couldn't afford to let fields lie fallow to recharge the soil. Africa's poor farmers applied only 8 kilograms (about 18 pounds) of soil-enriching fertilizer per hectare on average compared to 78 kilograms (about 172 pounds) in Latin America and 101 kilograms (about 222 pounds) in South Asia. The number of tractors working 1,000 hectares of arable land was eight times greater in Latin America and three times greater in Asia than in Africa. Farm-to-market road networks were more than two and a half times greater in Latin America and six times greater in Asia than in Africa. Africa's irrigation systems lagged even more dramatically.

Africa's subsistence farmers had become the poorest of the poor. Without outside assistance, there was no way their harvests could keep up with the continent's growing population. But with lending institutions and aid organizations adhering to the budgetary rigors of structural adjustment, no such assistance would be forthcoming: There would be no subsidies, no rural financing, no price supports, no crop insurance—benefits available, in varying degrees, to farmers almost everywhere else in the world. In those blessed areas, especially in the United States, a crop fails and the government writes a check. In Africa, a crop fails and people die. African farmers were left to bear 100 percent of the risk in a very risky business.

The spread of hunger throughout Africa was relentless. By the mid-1980s, when Borlaug arrived, Africa was home to the largest collection of poor and hungry nations and the most primitive farming conditions in the world.

Africa's farmers didn't get much help from their own leaders. Quite the opposite. As the Green Revolution was taking root in Asia, much of Africa was literally uprooting its agriculture. Independence wars against colonial rulers morphed into postindependence civil wars that killed and maimed millions of farmers, laid waste to large swaths of farmland, and destroyed rural infrastructure like roads and markets. The thirsty fields of Africa were too often quenched with blood instead of water.

Beginning with civil war in Nigeria, which led to the Biafra famine in the late 1960s, armed conflict and hunger had often joined together in a mad tango of death. Up and down the continent they danced. Sometimes conflict led, causing hunger. Other times hunger led, triggering conflict. The United Nations' Food and Agriculture Organization estimated that conflicts cost Africa more than $120 billion worth of agricultural production during the last third of the twentieth century.

While famine spread across the Horn in 1984, for instance, the government of Sudan fueled the crisis in its country by specifically attacking farmers in the restive southern region. That area, coveted in colonial times for its fertile Nile valleys, was the breadbasket of the country. Within a couple of years, millions of acres of farmland were a battlefield of fierce ethnic and religious strife and would remain so for two decades. Philip Majak abandoned his thirty-acre farm in southern Sudan in the mid-1980s, fleeing the fighting that killed his first wife (and would kill 2 million other people), and settled in a dusty refugee camp outside the capital, Khartoum. Seventeen years later he was still there, carving furniture instead of raising food. "My house was destroyed, and my tractor. My seventy cows were stolen, the land has grown wild," he said inside the barbed-wire fence ringing the camp. "It's such a waste. But I'll never go back until there's peace."

In Ethiopia, the tango of famine and fighting had been particularly frenetic. In 1972, as hunger spread in the Ethiopian countryside from drought, so too did the forces of revolution against Emperor Haile Selassie. A cabal of military officers led by Mengistu Haile Mariam toppled the emperor in 1974, accusing him, among other things, of being willfully negligent in combating the famine. Mengistu's new Marxist regime launched a ruthless campaign to smash all opposition, waging counterinsurgency wars against rebels in various parts of the country. When the rains failed and the tyranny of drought tightened, especially in some of the rebel areas that had been cut off by the government, the famine of 1984 exploded. (Another famine would come in 1989–1990 and embolden a new set of rebel forces to move against the communist government; in 1991, they rolled across the country and drove Mengistu into exile. Alas, it wasn't long before the victors of that fight were battling each other over the independence of Eritrea, a strip of land along the Red Sea.)

Not all the brutality in Africa had come from the barrel of a gun or the blade of a machete. Corruption, bad governance, and gross economic mismanagement had also battered the continent and its farmers—at times aided and abetted, or outright ignored, by countries in the developed world using African leaders as pawns during the Cold War.

In some countries where the new postcolonial governments were smitten with Marxist ideology borrowed from their Soviet paymasters, the land was nationalized and collectivized, turning highly entrepreneurial peasant farmers into the lumpen proletariat. Plied with cash loans by both the East and West in return for their allegiance in the Cold War years, Africa's new rulers built grand monuments to themselves and merrily marched their countries deep into debt. They built grandiose cities in the bush from whence they and their ancestors came. They built glossy international airports where no international flights landed. They built cement factories and then great urban concrete structures like hotels and convention centers (Zanzibar sought to build the world's largest cement swimming pool on a swamp; it promptly sank into the muck). They built grand ministerial edifices and filled them with legions of bureaucrats, all of whom ate food but none of whom produced it. By the time they finished building, there was little left in the budgets to aid the vast majority of the population, the peasant farmers who grew the food.

In Nigeria, a string of leaders steered billions of dollars in oil revenues into private bank accounts around the world, some blithely carrying the money out of the country in suitcases and paper bags. Meanwhile, more than half the population lived on less than two dollars a day.

Zaire's Mobutu Sese Seko, an American ally who favored a leopard-skin hat, enjoyed the high life in France and Switzerland while his country, now the Democratic Republic of the Congo, began a descent into a hellish war. He stashed millions in secret Swiss bank accounts and bought a getaway home among the vineyards on the placid shores of Lake Geneva. The sixteen-bedroom mansion featured Louis XIV–style furniture and a swimming pool with a view of the Alps. He had a blue Mercedes in the garage, three hundred bottles of wine in the cellar, and gold-plated faucets in the bathroom. On an office desk sat a marble-framed portrait of President Richard Nixon's family with handwritten "best wishes" for a "prosperous, peaceful and independent" country.

These so-called Big Men of Africa rarely cared about the little people of Africa. And certainly not the peasant farmers.

As he traveled the world as a top UN officer throughout the 1980s and 1990s, Kofi Annan, one of the most prominent sons of Africa who would later become the world body's secretary-general, bemoaned the neglect of

farming—and the hunger that followed—as one of Africa's biggest dis-
graces. "It hits you harder as an African, and even harder as an African who
has traveled the world and seen these problems solved in situations which
may have been equally desperate or been worse than the African situation,"
he would say later in an interview. "Year in and year out, agriculture was
decreasing. And you say, 'But if they can do it here and there, what are my
people doing? What are we doing to the people?' It hits you, it challenges
you." Annan continued, "Some governments really ignored agriculture.
Some wanted to jump immediately to industrial production at the expense
of agriculture and they lost out on both. The rush to industrialize, it happened in Ghana."

Annan, a Ghanaian himself, recalled the early years of postcolonial independence under the nation's first leader, Kwame Nkrumah. Ghana was
one of Africa's most prosperous countries at the time, relying on the revenue of its cocoa farmers. But Nkrumah had a desire to lead a country of
factories, not farms. "[Nkrumah] brought in an advisor from Trinidad,
and apparently [the advisor] recommended a focus on agriculture and to
really push it as far as one could. The story goes that Nkrumah said, 'I'm
not going to turn Ghana into a sugar cane growing country.' So suddenly
you see in the government ministers for light and heavy industry, which is
sort of the socialism model."

Nkrumah had positioned himself as the vanguard of a budding African
union movement, and he insisted he had the superior ideas for the continent's development. So confident was Nkrumah that he agreed to a bet
with Ivory Coast leader Felix Houphouet-Boigny. "Houphouet did lots of
agricultural work and also focused on the open market," Annan recalled.
"So apparently the bet was, 'You go your way in the so-called socialist
outlook, and I'll go my way with a capitalist attitude and in ten years we'll
see who has done more for his country.' Nkrumah was overthrown before that period ended, but for a while the Ivory Coast did much better
than Ghana."

For a while. Houphouet-Boigny called himself "the Number-One Peasant." But as time went on, he profited from the labors of other peasants—
mainly the country's cocoa and coffee farmers—to satisfy his own whims.
One of his pet projects was to transform his humble hometown of Ya-
moussoukro into a shiny oasis of splendor. Deep in the bush, 150 miles

north of the seat of government and business, Abidjan, workers peeled
away banana and mango trees and built wide boulevards lined with street-
lights. A high-rise hotel with a lobby as grand as a European opera hall
towered above a well-manicured, albeit slightly parched, golf course. Government buildings and elite schools, chiseled out of marble and other fine
stone, glistened in the hot sun. Houphouet-Boigny's grand palace was surrounded by a moat stocked with alligators feasting on chickens served up
by a grizzled old curator.

In the middle of all this megalomania rose a magnificent Roman
Catholic basilica designed to rival Saint Peter's in the Vatican. Houphouet-
Boigny envisioned presenting the basilica to the Pope as a gift. To his countrymen, though, "the Number-One Peasant" (who also liked to be called
"the Sage of Africa") presented a foreign debt that at one stage almost
equaled the country's gross domestic product, an economy in ruins, and
misery and dissension in the countryside. It all precipitated a brutal civil
war that left the land in tatters and the people hungry.

Few places, though, matched Mozambique for ruin in the countryside.
The slim country on the Indian Ocean staggered straight from a decade of
war against Portuguese colonial rule into two decades of civil war. By the
mid-1980s, nearly three-quarters of Mozambique's 14 million people, the
vast majority of whom were peasant farmers, had at one time been chased
from their homes by the fighting. For years, the roads were thick with displaced migrants—children carrying sacks, women balancing bundles on
their heads and babies on their backs, men pushing carts. Hunger and malnutrition were rampant. The infant mortality rate of about 20 percent was
the highest in the world. Nearly one-third of Mozambique's children died
before they were five years old. More than 40 percent of the government
budget was spent on fighting the war. Foreign debt of $3.2 billion crippled
an economy that exported only $80 million worth of goods each year. Vast
areas laced with land mines lay barren, producing no food. Mozambique
and Angola, the other Portuguese colony that also went directly from an
independence fight to a civil war, shared the title of Amputee Capital of the
World as thousands upon thousands of farmers lost arms and legs after
stepping on mines in their fields.

Mozambique ended up at the top of the Human Suffering Index compiled by the Washington, D.C.–based Population Crisis Committee. In

a comparison of living conditions in 130 countries, the Mozambicans had it the worst. The most miserable of all were the peasant farmers. One group of 178 families, fleeing the fighting in the countryside, abandoned their farms and gathered together in a makeshift settlement called Village Seventh of September, named after the day in 1974 when the Portuguese rulers agreed to work toward giving Mozambique independence. That was a joyous day, effectively ending a ten-year bush war to topple the colonialists. The Portuguese had occupied nearly every position that required a little skill. So when they left, the country fell into the hands of people who had never held anything much more sophisticated than a hoe or a gun; the new rulers reckoned that fewer than a dozen of their colleagues held university degrees. The nation's illiteracy rate was 93 percent. On their way out, resentful at leaving a country they felt was theirs, the Portuguese poured cement down the air-conditioning shafts of a new luxury hotel being built on the Indian Ocean coast outside the capital of Maputo, rendering it uninhabitable. They drove their cars into the sea. They even took the keys to the national bank. The joke around Maputo, gallows humor for sure, was that when the Portuguese pulled out, even the shoeshine boys left, so thoroughly had they controlled every aspect of the economy.

The end of colonialism didn't stop the fighting, either. After independence, those Mozambicans opposed to the new Marxist government retreated into the bush and started their own guerrilla war. These rebels were supported in various ways by the white South African government, which was eager to keep its neighbors in turmoil so antiapartheid forces couldn't gain a foothold across its borders. Mozambique's civil war laid further waste to the countryside and forced even more peasants to abandon their land and seek refuge in bigger settlements, like the one called Village Seventh of September.

Agriculture ground to a halt. Shortages of everything from meat and vegetables to lightbulbs and gasoline crippled the economy. The large town of Beira may have been the only seaside city in the world with a shortage of fish. "I don't know where they all go, but we never see any," complained the manager of a grocery store that had no groceries, except for some canned tomatoes and juice. "We get some meat for Christmas and Independence Day, but never any fish." Most of the bounty of Mozambique's seas ended up in the Soviet Union and East Germany in barter deals for military hardware.

All the weapons couldn't protect the farmers in Village Seventh of September. Farming individually away from the village was too dangerous. So every morning, the villagers left their bamboo huts and together looked for a safe piece of land that might grow something. In the afternoons they returned usually no better off than they were the day before. With nothing to do, the men sat under a circle of shade trees, drinking beer brewed from local plants. The women shuttled back and forth to the nearest safe source of drinkable water two miles away. Food aid kept them alive.

Even farmers with land safe from the fighting couldn't plant to capacity. Matias Michaque planned on harvesting a bounty of potatoes, but he ran out of seed. There was a nationwide shortage. "I received only half the seeds I needed," he said. "I grew one ton of potatoes, but I could have grown two." He was one of the few private farmers receiving special assistance from the socialist government, which was trying to reverse the disaster of its collectivized farms. Michaque's farm north of Maputo had a crude drip-irrigation system and a few rudimentary machines. While he talked to a reporter in 1986, he instructed a worker walking behind a motorized plow to steer it to the other side of the field and leave it idle. It was making too much noise for the conversation. But he didn't dare turn it off. "Once I turn it off, it's too hard to start again," Michaque said. "A part is broken, and we have no spares in this country."

Not far from his farm, a group of workers cleared some land about the size of a football field. It was a Green Belt experiment station, where the government intended one day to teach peasants how to plant rice, corn, lettuce, tomatoes, and coffee and how to raise livestock. A sleepy man in charge of the project said it represented the future of Mozambican agriculture—"once the fighting stopped," he said. At that moment, though, while Asian agriculture was mechanizing and steaming ahead with the Green Revolution, the only activity at Mozambique's farming showpiece was this: a worker, sitting on the front stoop, whittling a wooden rake.

This was the Africa Borlaug entered in 1986. With the initial backing of about $3 million a year from Sasakawa—a pittance compared with the big bucks and manpower that had flowed in support of the Asian Green

Revolution—he worked with the Carter Center to plant several million demonstration plots in fifteen countries. Borlaug believed there was nothing fundamentally wrong with Africa's farmers that would prevent them from seeing the same results that their counterparts in Asia and Mexico had experienced when presented with better seeds and fertilizer.

Buoyed with that optimism and confidence, Borlaug's team first set out for Ghana, in tropical West Africa, in 1986. They headed up to Kumasi in the Ashanti region, where chiefs reigned from gold-encrusted thrones, to prospect for the new gold: bright-yellow kernels of corn. Bouncing over a deeply rutted dirt road, Borlaug came to the small village of Fufuo.

Farmers who used only their hands and machetes to coax food from the stingy red soil enthusiastically welcomed their visitor and his promise to triple their yields. Borlaug arrived bearing seeds of a new breed of corn unusually high in protein for a population short of meat and milk. And he distributed bags of fertilizer to revitalize the soil and bottles of weed killer that would help the farmers till more land. Villagers bought these curious items with small low-interest loans provided by Sasakawa and then followed Borlaug's directions.

For the first time, they planted in straight rows, with a uniform distance between seeds. They spread the fertilizer on a regular schedule and in doses measured by the caps of Coca-Cola bottles. They sprayed the herbicide in judiciously portioned amounts; they were told it would spare them the considerable time it takes to dig up weeds and conserve the moisture lost when the soil is disturbed.

Every year their yields improved, and then, in 1989, they harvested a miracle. "The crops were so big, and there were cobs on each stalk," said farmer Emmanuel Boateng, his eyes large with amazement. "We were used to having many stalks with no cobs."

Fufuo's farmers were accustomed to gathering only five one hundred–kilogram bags of corn per acre. Now they reaped fifteen bags. The promise of their elderly white-haired visitor had come to pass. So abundant was the harvest that Borlaug pitched in with the work, and he insisted on a strict harvest protocol. For example, he gave orders that the husking needed to be done in the field, so any pests would stay there and not come into the areas where the corn would be stored. One day, farmers brought the corn into the village while the corn was still in the husks.

"Bring me a chair," Borlaug barked. For hours, into the evening, he sat with the women, pulling the husks off the corn. "You did all this work, growing the corn, and now you endanger all you have done," he scolded them. No one slept in Fufuo that night until the last ear was husked.

"He really knocked our heads together that day," Boateng recalled. "Oooh, it was a bad day for us."

But the harvest was good, very, very good—so good that even fifteen years later the villagers were still talking about it. Corn is the staple food of Ghana, but never before had the folks of Fufuo produced enough to feed themselves *and* still have something left over to sell to the world beyond their collection of mud-brick homes. In that bumper year, they made enough money to pay off their small loans from Sasakawa and to begin planning investments in schools and roads.

"Borlaug is our hero, our savior. He showed us what we were capable of doing," Boateng said. "We are so grateful for what he has done for us. Every time we pray, we pray for him: 'Lord, we know he's elderly, please extend his life and give him good health.'"

Borlaug's Africa strategy was to go from village to village, introduce his methods, show farmers the possibilities, and then move on to other villages. After the harvest of 1989, he said good-bye to Fufuo. The farmers remembered his lessons, and they tried to keep practicing what he preached.

The Sasakawa team set out to spread Borlaug's gospel across the continent. They arrived in Ethiopia in the early 1990s, when the pious pledges of "never again" from the 1984 famine had been reduced to muttering doubts. The country's food deficits were the largest in the world. Food aid from 1989 to 1993 had been running between 500,000 and nearly 1 million tons of grain a year. But hope was stirring. Communist dictator Mengistu had been driven into exile by advancing opposition forces, and the new government, which had seen food used as a weapon against its supporters during the civil war, assumed power with a determination to boost the country's agriculture.

Borlaug and his colleagues started with 160 trial plots in four of the most fertile regions of the country. As in Ghana, they showed peasant farmers how to better plant and harvest, they introduced hybrid seeds and more effective fertilizer and weed control, and they provided small credit facilities. By 1995, the Sasakawa program had spread to nearly 5,000 plots.

As harvests improved, ambitions accelerated. The government launched the National Extension Intensification Program, which helped to distribute seeds, fertilizer, and credit for 32,000 plots.

Amid this agricultural expansion, former U.S. President Jimmy Carter, whose Carter Center was a partner in Borlaug's African efforts, visited Ethiopia. The Sasakawa staff regaled Carter, who himself had farmed, with stories about impressive harvests and suggested he go to the fields and see for himself. Carter's schedule was tight, but when he saw pictures of the crops, lush and green, he decided to go. He called Prime Minister Meles Zenawi and urged him to drop whatever he was doing and join him on the tour. Upon reaching the fields, neither man could believe their eyes. Standing before them were stalks of corn as tall and strong as any in America. Meles promptly ordered that the program be multiplied tenfold, spreading the benefits to farmers across the country. In 1996, the intensification program expanded to 320,000 plots.

Meles publicly declared that his government was aiming to bring the new technology and methods to at least 2 million farmers in 1998. Ethiopia's National Seed Enterprise began widespread distribution of hybrid corn seed, and the Iowa business that Henry Wallace helped start, Pioneer Hi-Bred, introduced its hybrids. The use of fertilizer doubled. Blessed with good rains in the highlands, yields soared. National grain and cereal harvests in the second half of the 1990s averaged nearly 11 million tons annually, about 4 million tons more than in the 1980s. By 1999, 4 million farmers were participating in the program.

Despite such successes, Borlaug worried that they wouldn't be sustainable without the wider international support he enjoyed during the original Green Revolution. And he feared that structural adjustment, which demanded cutbacks of that support, was dooming the progress his program demonstrated was possible. There were too few private-sector entrepreneurs figuring out how to profit by moving crops from areas of plenty to areas of scarcity, and no government agencies to fill that void.

This had already happened in Fufuo, Ghana, after Borlaug left. Farmers there were retreating from their heights. Unlike in Asia a generation earlier, their bounty quickly faded. Ghana, caught in the demands of structural adjustment to limit aid to its farmers, couldn't follow the Green Revolution's proven formula of fertilizer subsidies, crop-price supports, or any other equivalent to the cheap financing needed to sustain an agricultural boom. The government, following orders from international lenders, was retreating from agriculture. And, as in most other African countries, Ghana's private sector wasn't sufficiently developed to fill the gap and provide the fertilizer, seed, and storage and distribution facilities. Local banks charged farmers 33 percent interest on loans. There was no investment to fix the farm-to-market roads, which became impassable in the rainy season.

"I sit here day in and day out and farmers say to me, 'International politics will make sure we don't develop.' What is the moral position of that?" asked Kwame Amezah, an official in Ghana's Agricultural Extension Services in the 1990s. Ducks and goats roamed the lawn outside his office in the capital city, Accra. "Sasakawa has brought technology to the farmers that has helped a lot. The question is, how does the farmer fund the technology? The thinking of the Western world is that the government shouldn't provide these services; the private sector should. But the private sector in Ghana isn't strong enough yet."

The consequences were devastating, and predictable. With loans hard to come by, fertilizer use plummeted, any old seeds were planted, and yields fell from their peaks. Without a well-functioning market for their crops, farmers had little incentive to produce a surplus. And even if they did, it would often rot in flimsy storage bins before it could be sold. In village after village, the departure of Borlaug's team resulted in a decline in production. In Fufuo, the temptation grew to abandon Borlaug's corn and switch to cash crops desired in the West, such as cocoa and ginger, even if it meant less food at home. A decade after the memorable bumper corn crop, the village's harvests slid back toward pre-Borlaug yields.

Fufuo's farmers felt they had badly let down their hero. One of them, Kwaku Owusu, moaned, "We have shown we can produce more, but sometimes we wonder, 'What's the use?'"

Borlaug harbored a similar sentiment. He felt he was fighting on his own, armed with merely a popgun against the world's development institutions arrayed against his way of doing things. And, he thought, the fight was growing increasingly unfair, for the rich countries that were demanding cutbacks in African agriculture continued to support their own farmers lavishly so they would have the upper hand in global trade. He feared that the backsliding in Ghana would also happen in Ethiopia and Mozambique and Mali and elsewhere he had sown the seeds of revolution. All his work would be for naught.

As the new millennium approached, and as the funding for Sasakawa Africa was thinning, Borlaug joined Benedicta Appiah-Asante, the head of Sasakawa's Ghana office, for breakfast at an Accra hotel. Borlaug, eighty-five years old, poured the tea. The pot wobbled.

"Look at me, I'm old," Borlaug told his disciple. Staring into his teacup, he confessed, "I won't live to see the breakthrough in Ghana's agriculture. But you will. I am counting on you."

Appiah-Asante couldn't speak as she choked back tears. She silently fumed at her country and the world for letting down her mentor, who had never before seemed so resigned.

After a subdued breakfast, Appiah-Asante retreated to her hotel room and cried. "When will this breakthrough come?" she asked herself over and over. "When will it come?"

CHAPTER 4

Good for the Goose,
Bad for the Gander

FANA, MALI, 2002

The dawn of a new millennium did little to lift the chances of an agricultural breakthrough in Africa. The United Nations orchestrated a flurry of pledges to put a big dent in global hunger and poverty by 2015. And then the September 11, 2001, terrorist attacks in New York City and Washington, D.C., prompted an outpouring of determination to relieve the misery, and disaffection, in the poorest precincts of the world. But those intentions were undermined by the policy actions of Western governments, which continued to elevate the interests of their own farmers above all others. Preventing state support to Africa's farmers in favor of promoting free-market virtues and private-sector investment that never materialized had been devastating enough. The twenty-first century opened with an escalation in the subsidies American and European governments paid their farmers. These were acts of supreme hypocrisy that knocked back any advances Borlaug had engineered in the African fields, and they set the table for a hunger season like no other.

The news that all Africa dreaded to hear was plucked out of the air on a muggy May day in 2002 by a crude television antenna perched precariously on a tin roof of a rickety shack in Mali's cotton fields: The United States Congress had passed a new Farm Bill, increasing the subsidies paid to American farmers. Diamba Coulibaly stared at his black-and-white TV, which was powered by a car battery. Anxiously, he cocked his ear for the next headline: American cotton farmers would be getting the biggest boost of all. The commentary suggested that these subsidized U.S. farmers would produce more cotton, which would increase the global glut of the "white gold" and put more pressure on the world price. The bottom line: The unsubsidized Malian farmers, who sell almost all of their cotton on the world market, would end up with less.

"That's not right," Coulibaly said. "For us, all farmers in America and in Mali are members of the same family. We shouldn't let one group of brothers make all the profits while the others get nothing."

The white-whiskered farmer suffered from a grotesque malady that had long ago vanished from farms in the developed world: a large goiter, the size of a baseball, bulged from his neck. "Iodine deficiency," Coulibaly said matter-of-factly.

He was fifty-nine years old, which made him ancient in a country where the life expectancy was just forty-eight years. A flock of children hovered around him outside a cluster of one- and two-room mud-brick huts. They were his nieces and nephews and grandchildren. Many of them had distended bellies, a sign of chronic malnourishment common to rural West Africa.

"What do you do if you can't pay expenses?" the old man shrugged.

Coulibaly was one of the elders of an extended family of eighty-six people in Mali, one of the poorest countries in the world. The uneven plowing fields of the global agricultural system had yielded a bitter paradox. Farming was meant to feed and nourish, but at the beginning of the twenty-first century the inequities in the world trade of agricultural goods had spread malnutrition and hunger across Africa. In West Africa, Mali's cotton growers faced the same plight as Ghana's corn and rice farmers, who were undercut by the import of cheaper subsidized corn and rice from the United States, and Senegal's tomato growers, who saw their livelihoods vanish as cheaper subsidized tomatoes rolled in from Europe.

The year before, in 2001, the Coulibalys had harvested about forty tons of cotton, one of their best yields ever, and barely broke even. Their current crop was looking good, but the wizened Diamba expected the family to lose money, as cotton prices were dropping and the costs of everything from fertilizer to ginning were rising. Once again, he said, he would have to put off doing something about that goiter and the kids' malnutrition.

Certain that the U.S. Farm Bill would widen their misery, Coulibaly had a news flash of his own that he wanted to send back to America: "We are all our brothers' keepers," he said. "If we are not in peace here, you won't be in peace there."

Nine days after the September 11, 2001, terrorist attacks on New York City and Washington, D.C., President George W. Bush spoke in the U.S. Capitol before a joint session of Congress and uttered a question he believed many Americans were asking: "Why do they hate us?" He provided some ready answers. "They hate what we see right here in this chamber—a democratically elected government," the president said. "They hate our freedoms—our freedom of religion, our freedom of speech, our freedom to vote and assemble and disagree with each other."

The farmers of the developing world, particularly the cotton growers of West Africa, would say that President Bush provided a different answer to his question eight months later when he signed the Farm Bill. With a flourish of his pen, attaching his signature on the bottom of the bill, the president increased the subsidies the U.S. government pays to American farmers, and, in turn, increased the poverty of millions of other farmers in the developing world, especially in Africa, whose governments can't afford to pay similar subsidies.

"You have to know where your freedom ends and another's begins," scoffed Mody Diallo, a cotton farmers' union official in Mali. He didn't hate America's freedoms; in fact, he greatly admired them. He wanted those freedoms for himself and his countrymen and all people of the world. But, he said, "You should enjoy your freedom up to the point of hurting someone. If I have money, I can enjoy it any way I want, but I must be concerned that I don't hurt my neighbor. The Americans know that with their subsidies they are killing so many economies in the developing world," he continued. "This is where America is heading: It wants to dominate the world, economically and militarily."

Diallo's dark interpretation reflected another irony: His view of America was exactly the opposite of what U.S. politicians were trying to project. After the shock of September 11, Americans better understood that fear and misery in poor countries could create a rich environment for resentment and terrorism. America needed to emphasize its generosity and goodwill throughout the world. Reducing poverty in the developing world became a prime pillar of U.S. foreign policy. In November 2001, the United States took the lead in launching a new round of world trade talks in Doha, Qatar, designed to bring the poorest nations more fully into the global trading system. These negotiations on a new set of international trading rules, intended to stretch over several years of meetings, were dubbed the "development round."

A few months later, in March 2002, the United States and Europe were at the front of the line at a conference in Monterrey, Mexico, called the Summit on Financing for Development. The world's richest countries pledged billions of dollars in fresh aid to spur economic development in the poorest countries. The Doha-Monterrey strategy was to deliver a one-two punch to poverty: open trade, increase aid.

President Bush arrived at Monterrey pledging a 50 percent increase in American foreign aid over three years and talking about linking greater contributions to developing nations with better democratic performance and economic freedom. "We fight against poverty because hope is an answer to terror," he told his fellow leaders. "We fight against poverty because opportunity is a fundamental right to human dignity. We fight against poverty because faith requires it and conscience demands it." He also said in Monterrey, "To be serious about fighting poverty, we must be serious about expanding trade."

Then, two months later came the Farm Bill, which put nonsubsidized African farmers at a distinct disadvantage in international trade. "Such hypocrisy!" shouted Madani Toure in the Malian capital, Bamako, a few weeks after the bill was signed. Toure was the prime minister's adviser on economic matters, and as such he wasn't shy about sharing his opinions on the impact of subsidies. In the middle of the interview, a violent thunderstorm shook his office. Hail and rain pounded the corrugated tin roof. Water seeped in through tiny cracks in the walls. The lights flickered on and off and then died. All around Bamako, as Toure ranted, the electricity went down—as if to reinforce what he was saying. "The whole world seems to agree that poverty needs to be reduced in countries like ours," he fumed. "Yet the cotton subsidies, if they continue, will lead to a crash in our economy."

A cry of hypocrisy also reverberated throughout Ghana. "America started subsidizing its farmers to help them assure their own food security, but we're not allowed to do the same!" bellowed Franklin Domkoh, the director of Ghana's extension services. "With the mere mention by us of subsidies, our development partners start howling. They want to catch us and chew us up!"

On the other side of the world, Norman Borlaug brought his fist crashing down on his desk at Texas A&M University when he considered the implications of the Farm Bill. A boost in American subsidies would impoverish the same farmers in Mali, Ghana, and elsewhere in Africa that he had been nurturing with the Sasakawa program. "I'm a biologist, not an economist," he roared, "but even I can see those policies aren't working."

At the Farm Bill signing ceremony inside the Dwight D. Eisenhower Executive Office Building, President Bush praised the legislation for assisting American growers. "The bill is generous, and will provide a safety net for farmers," he said to a large crowd of smiling agricultural leaders, their lobbyists, and farm folk listening by radio.

As he left the podium, President Bush turned to the chorus of farmers applauding behind him. The first farmer he shook hands with, and congratulated, was Kenneth Hood. Hood was the courtly chairman of the National Cotton Council, the influential trade association of the cotton industry and one of the most powerful lobbying forces in Washington, as well as a partner in a sprawling cotton and grain farm near Gunnison, Mississippi. He had successfully fought to weaken proposals to block subsidy checks to the richest farmers.

America's 25,000 cotton growers, who were already pocketing more than $3 billion in subsidy checks, were on average the wealthiest farmers in the country. The average net worth of a full-time cotton-farming household, including land and nonfarm assets, was about $800,000, according to the U.S. Department of Agriculture. Now, they were receiving the biggest subsidy boost of all, a whopping 16 percent.

In Mali, where millions of people were dependent on cotton, the farmers had just been told by their government that they would be getting about 10 percent *less* from the state cotton company. A global cotton glut, driven in part by surplus production in the world's biggest cotton exporter—the United States—had beaten down cotton prices by 66 percent since 1995. The subsidies protected American farmers from this price drop—the "safety net" President Bush mentioned—and encouraged them to grow even more, adding to the global surplus. The Malian government, hard-pressed to provide even the most basic health care and education to its citizens, couldn't afford to pay subsidies to its farmers. This was their reality: When the world price drops, the farmers lose money. And so does the entire country, which leaned on cotton to provide its major export earnings.

Mody Diallo, the farm union organizer in the southern regional center of Bougouni, was eager to talk about the impact. He left his own cotton field and sped to an interview on a battered motor scooter. He wore green pants with holes in both knees and a ragged purple T-shirt. As a cotton farmer himself, he didn't begrudge the American farmers their subsidies; he wished the Mali farmers could receive equal amounts. What he resented, he said, was that America's domestic politics could so blithely reach all the way to Mali and smite him and his neighbors. With farming being the world's biggest occupation, the U.S. Farm Bill, which set new subsidy levels every five years, impacted more people across the world than most economic acts of the American government. But despite its global consequences, the Farm Bill was shaped for the most part by narrow domestic political considerations: which congressmen could get the most money for the farmers of their districts. "What's too bad is subsidizing so much that it hurts the poor elsewhere," Diallo fumed. "The Americans can have their subsidies, but they must be at a level where others can survive. The subsidies should be regulated, so the farmers can keep producing and the Third World countries can keep producing and survive."

Diallo, forty-two, sat on a metal chair on the veranda of the Cyrano Restaurant. It was early in the afternoon of a sweltering day. Two big yellow soccer ball balloons—a promotion to attract customers during that summer's World Cup tournament—hung from the restaurant's awning, which provided a welcome slice of shade.

A wiry, determined man, Diallo had helped organize a cotton-planting boycott among local farmers a few years earlier to protest falling prices. Production plummeted, and the shock staggered the entire economy, cutting the gross domestic product by 3 percent. Midway through the growing season, the government, fearing social instability, raised the price back to the previous year's level, but it was too late for those who didn't plant. It was a huge sacrifice for some of the poorest farmers on earth, who mainly tilled their fields walking behind a plow pulled by oxen. Of the 37,236 cotton farmers in his region, Diallo said, only 5 had tractors. A single American cotton farmer, working vast fields, might have several himself.

Since cotton is the main cash crop for most Malian farmers, when the cotton crop fails, or the price drops, schools don't get built, clinics don't get stocked with medicine, food doesn't get bought. In Mali, nearly half of the children under age five were underweight.

"The point I want to make is this," Diallo said, hopping back on his scooter to return to his ten-acre farm. "The U.S. talks about reducing poverty in the developed world, but in its own policies it adds to poverty."

U.S. agricultural subsidies give American farmers a huge competitive advantage in the global marketplace. When commodity prices fall, their government checks swell so that they can continue to operate at full speed while farmers elsewhere must retreat. This was a big reason U.S. cotton farmers, for example, had been able to export as much as 74 percent of their crop and control about 40 percent of world trade in 2002, an astounding record given the decline of the cotton farmers' traditional customer—the U.S. textile industry—and the fact that other countries could grow cotton more cheaply. For unsubsidized African farmers, going up against subsidized American farmers was like a clean athlete competing against one on steroids.

While the subsidies protected the incomes and livelihoods of American farmers, they also negated so much of America's big-hearted capacity for doing good abroad. As Mody Diallo could see from half a world away when the Farm Bill was enacted, petty domestic political considerations festering in a year of congressional elections trumped international policy.

The boost in U.S. farm subsidies—along with the egregious subsidies European governments paid to their farmers—would eventually torpedo the world trade negotiations that began in Doha, Qatar, in November 2001. The West African cotton countries refused to go along with any trade deal unless American cotton subsidies were greatly reduced. The Americans wouldn't budge on their subsidy regime as long as the Europeans held tight to theirs. The West African position was simple: If the so-called development round of negotiations couldn't deliver the one change that would benefit millions of people in the world's least-developed corner, what good was it? By sticking to their guns, the West Africans shot down any new global trade deal, for under World Trade Organization rules, any agreement must be a consensus of all member nations. "What interest do we have in joining in an international agreement if the only commodity we have to participate in international trade—cotton—isn't treated justly?" Mali's minister of industry and commerce, Choguel Kokalla Maiga, later asked.

The lack of progress on the trade front, in turn, undermined much of the rich world's development aid. For instance, in 2001, U.S. assistance to Mali totaled about $40 million. The country's loss on the cotton crop that year was about $30 million. So the United States gave with one hand and took with the other.

America wasn't alone in this give-and-take. Overall that year, the thirty members of the Organization of Economic Cooperation and Development (OECD), a club of the world's most developed countries, gave a total of $52 billion in development aid to the world's poorest countries. But they aided their own farmers nearly six times as much with overall agricultural support totaling $311 billion. The impact of those rich-world subsidies on global trade, the United Nations noted in a report, cost the poorest countries an estimated $50 billion in export revenues. The bottom line: The loss on trade negated the aid.

The front line in any post-9/11 war on poverty would run through Mali and West Africa. If you laid a map highlighting the poorest nations in the world over a map highlighting predominantly Muslim countries, West Africa stood out like no other place on earth. The poverty drove many citizens of West and Central Africa into the crowded cities of Europe, increasing social tensions as they competed for housing and jobs and for cultural and religious recognition. At the same time, Western diplomats nervously watched reports of another migration wave: the movement of people northward through the Sahara, across the Algerian border, for religious training abroad. Although the secular governments of West Africa vowed they wouldn't allow their countries to become recruitment camps for terrorist organizations seeking to enlist the world's disaffected, they warned that frustrations were rising along with the poverty.

At the office of the U.S. Agency for International Development in Bamako, an official said that America's aid to Mali, intended to counter the poverty and the disaffection, was mainly spent on health and educational projects and programs to spread the word about democracy. But, he was asked, if America really wanted to reduce poverty in Mali, wouldn't it concentrate its aid on improving the efficiency and profitability of the cotton industry, the region's biggest employer and largest export earner?

"Can't," said the USAID official.

Why not?

"Bumpers," he said.

Dale Bumpers was a senator from Arkansas who authored an amendment to legislation in 1986 stipulating that no foreign assistance funds be used for "any testing or breeding, feasibility study, variety improvement or introduction, consultancy, publication, or training in connection with the growth or production in a foreign country for export if such export would compete in world markets with a similar commodity grown or produced in the United States." In other words, the U.S. government couldn't help foreign countries develop crops that could compete with those of American farmers. The Bumpers amendment was a response to a protest by the American Soybean Association over a USAID research project that developed soybean varieties for cultivation in countries such as Brazil and Argentina. Both those countries became huge soybean exporters and stiff competition for American soybean growers.

Bumpers, who retired from the Senate in 1999, said in a 2007 interview that he had only a vague recollection of the issue and mainly remembered the raging "brouhaha" over subsidies between the Americans and Europeans. Speaking in his office at a Washington law firm, he said, "The Europeans were ticked off thinking we were subsidizing our farmers much higher than we should be, and our farmers thought they were subsidized too much. It was a catfight between the two blocs." The Africans have a saying for this: "When elephants fight, the grass gets trampled." In the protectionist wars of the 1980s between the United States and Europe, Africa got trampled. Bumpers said it must have been a misstep. "We wanted to help the Africans," he said, noting that he and others in the Senate eagerly supported the efforts of Senator George McGovern to feed hungry children. "Isn't it amazing how man can screw up things so badly for reasons they can't even explain?" he mused.

At the same time that the United States was restricting official government assistance to foreign farmers, the World Bank, International Monetary Fund (IMF), and other development agencies were ordering African governments to stop aiding their own farmers. Subsidies, derided as wasteful and anathema to free trade, were a prime target of structural adjustment. Of course, all along the way, the United States and Europe—the powers behind the World Bank and IMF—couldn't stop themselves from bingeing on subsidies, generously fattening their own farmers, be they Alpine dairy herders, Scandinavian sugar beet growers, Rhineland vintners, or Great Plains wheat harvesters. This duplicity—what's good for us in the rich world isn't good for you in the poor world—created one of the most glaring and enduring injustices in geopolitics and world trade. In a 2002 study of the European Union's subsidy regime, the Catholic Agency for Overseas Development of the Catholic communities of England and Wales calculated that under the EU's dairy subsidies, the average European cow received support amounting to $2.20 a day, or $800 a year, which was more than the income of half the world's population.

Irony piled on insult. The West African countries, after all, had been encouraged by the World Bank and other development organizations to embrace cotton as the engine that would lift the region out of poverty. West African cotton, virtually all of it handpicked, was considered to be of the highest quality, and the lower production costs would give the Africans a leg up on international competitors. But the $5 billion in subsidies reaped by cotton farmers in the United States, Europe, and, to a lesser extent, China, torpedoed that development strategy. A joint report by the World Bank and the IMF estimated that the removal of U.S. subsidies would produce a drop in American production that would lead to a short-term rise in the world price of cotton. In turn, that would increase revenue to the African countries by about $250 million annually—a princely sum in a region where vast numbers of people live on less than $1 a day.

"How much?" Diamba Coulibaly, the old Mali farmer with the goiter, asked when he heard those numbers. Over the years, a parade of experts had come and gone, experimenting with his soil, seeds, and farming techniques to boost farm productivity and rural incomes. Still, his goiter grew, as did the misshapen bellies of the children. Why, the old man wondered, had no one experimented with taking away subsidies?

But Americans and Europeans—farmers and politicians alike—were addicted to their farm subsidies. After the 2002 U.S. Farm Bill was enacted, Ronnie Shows, a Mississippi Democrat on the House Agriculture Committee, scoffed at suggestions that U.S. cotton subsidies should be reduced to help Africa. "What good does it do to make our own people poor?" he asked.

While the subsidy schemes on both sides of the Atlantic had been initiated with good intentions during times of much poverty and desperation, over the years they became entrenched. The political will to scale them back grew ever dimmer as farmers became wealthier relative to the rest of society and better able to finance powerful lobbies in Washington. In fact, although America and Europe were tight allies in the arms race with the Soviet Union, they furiously battled each other in an escalating farms race by subsidizing the prices that foreign customers paid for commodities such as wheat.

The U.S. government created its subsidies during the Great Depression to fight rural poverty. During the Dust Bowl of the 1930s, dirt blowing from the Plains was deposited on the roof of the White House. At the time, 25 percent of the U.S. population lived on farms, and, in general, they were the poorest segment of America. Washington decided then that it was too risky for the economy and the country's food supply for them to go it alone. Under the new plan, farmers could get federal money for producing commodities—including corn, cotton, and wheat—when market prices fell below certain levels. Production could stay high even when commodity prices were low.

Policy makers intervened on behalf of farmers in ways they hadn't for other occupations. Washington had long viewed farmers as central to the country's economic and political development. From the early years of America's life as an independent nation, farming had been the necessary engine for settling the U.S. frontier and replacing the indigenous culture. Fostering a class of family farmers was also more democratic than letting the wealthy get control of the land. That philosophy drove the Homestead Act of 1862, which made it possible for a U.S. citizen to own 160 acres of public land for free, excluding a small filing fee. About 270 million acres, or 10 percent of U.S. land, was eventually given to homesteaders this way.

Washington's involvement in agriculture deepened after World War I when it came to believe that the nature of agriculture made farmers uniquely weak players in the economy. In addition to living at the mercy of Mother Nature, farmers worked in the shadow of boom-and-bust commodity cycles over which they had little control. Perversely, farming success often led to hard times because big crops tended to depress prices. And when gluts did materialize, farmers had a hard time getting out of the way. Most farmers planted just once a year, and their equipment, experience, and the climate limited their alternatives.

In Western Europe, lying in ruins after World War II, governments were determined that their citizens should never again suffer the hunger and food rationing endured during the war. The Common Agricultural Policy, or CAP, hastened the recovery in the countryside by encouraging farmers to grow almost everything Europe needed. The goal was self-sufficiency in basic foodstuffs, and the way to achieve that would be a rigid, production-oriented subsidy policy. CAP would become one of the cornerstones of the European Union.

When West Germany and France moved to create the Common Market in the 1960s, France insisted on protection for its heartland farmers in exchange for allowing in German manufactured goods. By the end of that decade, European farmers were locked into a policy of guaranteed high prices for crops buttressed by massive production subsidies to encourage higher output and lofty tariff barriers to hold back competition from food grown outside Europe. CAP worked as Western Europe moved toward food self-sufficiency. But it did its job too well; by the 1980s, the EU was contending with almost permanent surpluses of major farm commodities, some of which were exported with the help of a new set of subsidies, which in turn wreaked havoc on world commodity prices and depressed farm-based economies in the developing world. The surpluses that weren't exported had to be stored within the EU, leading to the fabled "wine lakes" and "cereal mountains," as the European press described them. CAP spending ate up two-thirds of the total EU budget. Taxpayer objections led to a ceiling on CAP, but the essential subsidy payments to farmers were undiminished. By the turn of the twenty-first century, this support was still hovering around $100 billion a year.

Some of that money was going to support sugar farmers wearing boots and rain slickers in Ireland and Britain and parkas and long johns in Sweden and Finland. Growing sugar had mainly been an economic pillar of countries with hot, sunny climates near the equator. Sugar cane, which thrived in many of the world's poorest countries, was a classic crop of developing economies. Once planted, it grew like grass, requiring little investment or sophisticated maintenance.

Up to the 1970s, the EU was a net importer of sugar, supporting the economies of many of its former colonies in Africa and the Caribbean with its purchases. Then CAP subsidies to sugar beet growers in Europe kicked in, and a sugar industry flourished in the most unlikely places—much nearer the Arctic Circle than the equator—even though the cost of producing sugar was two to three times higher in Europe than in some developing countries. By the dawn of the new millennium, the EU had become the world's second-biggest exporter, after Brazil, of all forms of sugar and the biggest exporter of refined white sugar.

The sweet deal for European sugar beet growers resulted in surplus production of up to 6 million tons annually, which was dumped on the world market. Farmers sold their surplus cheaply just to get rid of it, having already pocketed a profit from the subsidies. The EU's excess sugar, which at one point represented about 20 percent of annual exports from all countries, thus drove down the world price. (The United States also protected its sugar growers with tariff and quota barriers, but it exported very little.)

In its defense, the EU pointed to a Byzantine system of preferential access that member states extended to imports from some former colonies, such as Mauritius and Fiji. But EU sugar producers wouldn't simply allow that sugar into their market because it might undermine the high local price. Instead, the EU imported the raw sugar at the high price, refined it, and shipped an equivalent amount of white sugar back to world markets. This cost EU taxpayers $800 million a year in extra subsidies and expanded the world glut.

The developing world's resentment of the EU's sugar subsidies crystallized at the World Summit on Sustainable Development in Johannesburg,
South Africa, in 2002. European leaders took to the podium to thump
their chests about all the good work the EU was doing to reduce poverty
around the world, particularly by coming to the aid of downtrodden farmers. But when it came to the summit's contentious negotiations on reducing the agricultural subsidies of rich countries, the EU rallied to the defense
of its own farmers.

When negotiators from the developing world wanted a summit decla-
ration calling for the rapid elimination of farm subsidies, EU delegates
twice walked out of the closed-door meetings. The developing world was
outraged. In protest, the international aid organization Oxfam dumped
heaps of European sugar, packaged in little sachets, near the cafés where the
delegates dined. "Less sweet than it tastes! 100% Pure EU Sugar," advertised the sugar sachets. "Made in Europe, Dumped in Africa. Contains:
Hidden subsidies (70%), artificial prices (30%). Brought to you by EU
consumers and taxpayers for $1.6 billion a year. WARNING: Devastating to
African farmers."

Several hours' drive to the southeast from the summit in Johannesburg,
in the sugar cane fields north of Durban, the impact on African farmers
was on full display. Monica Shandu, freshly crowned national Cane
Grower of the Year, was on her way home from church, walking the three
miles up and down hills because she couldn't afford a car or tractor. She
and her extended family lived without electricity or indoor plumbing in a
cluster of several mud huts and a small, half-finished cinder-block house.
The mother of four and grandmother of two harvested her award-winning
crop spread over four acres by hand, swinging a machete day and night.
After expenses, she pocketed just $200 a year. "Prices are really so low,"
Shandu said, clutching her Bible and keeping up her steady pace.

Unlike the European sugar beet farmers, Shandu and the rest of South
Africa's cane growers were at the mercy of the world price. Of the country's
2.6 million tons of sugar production in 2002, more than half was exported,
where it collided with the sugar being dumped by Europe. Agricultural
economists calculated that if the EU cut its production and stopped selling
on the world market, the sugar price would improve by about 20 percent,
and South Africa would reap about $40 million more from its exports. It

also would make expansion of cane farming more economically viable and generate a further $60 million. This loss of $100 million in potential earnings nearly erased the $120 million in development aid the EU extended to South Africa.

Monica Shandu's loss was Dominique Fievez's gain. Fievez was a prominent sugar beet grower in the fertile Somme region of France, about a hundred miles north of Paris. He lived in a gabled chateau set amid a park of oaks, lilacs, and manicured lawns. Like his father before him, he cultivated 60 acres of sugar beets under a lucrative EU production quota that brought in a government-guaranteed price nearly triple the world price that Shandu received. The OECD estimated that a French farmer with an average sugar beet plot of 33 acres received subsidies of about $23,000. Fievez's plot—and take—was double that. He said he would like to turn the whole 420-acre farm over to sugar beets, since it was on average about 50 percent more profitable than his other crops of wheat and corn. But anything over his quota he would have to sell at the depressed world price, like Shandu did. So he stuck with corn and wheat.

Fievez was the president of the regional branch of the General Confederation of Sugar Beet Growers, a powerful farm lobby. Just before the European Commission was due to make a new set of proposals for CAP reform in the months before the Johannesburg development summit, he joined 10,000 fellow farmers in a protest outside the European Parliament in Strasbourg, France. When the reform proposals were released a month after the farmers' protest, the sugar regime wasn't touched. "We must have prices guaranteed in line with our cost of living," Fievez told our *Wall Street Journal* colleague Geoff Winestock. The farmer worried that killing subsidies could devastate the French countryside and stir turmoil in France. "I must have something to hand down to my children," he said.

The contrast between rich and poor in the world's cotton fields was never more apparent than one day in early June 2002 when the ink was still drying on the Farm Bill. Rain had just fallen in Korokoro, Mali, a flyspeck of a village in the Niger River basin, and the Sangare family rushed to prepare its fifteen acres for cotton planting to catch as much of the early rains as possible. One of the brothers hitched a one-blade plow to two lanky oxen. He walked barefoot behind the plow while a young nephew walked in front of the oxen, guiding them in a reasonably straight line over weeds and rocks and hard lumps of soil.

Drenched in sweat, they wondered whether it was all wasted effort. After the previous harvest, once the farming costs were paid, the Sangare family was left with less than $2,000 for the year to support two dozen family members and relatives. Now, with world cotton prices at their lowest in three decades, they were told by the government they would be getting a few cents less per pound of cotton while fertilizer and pesticide costs were rising. Would they earn enough to replenish their cattle stock? To send the younger children to school? To feed everyone for the entire year?

"We'll have to reduce what we can buy," said one of the Sangares as several family members sat under a tree and pondered the future. "These prices are really going to ruin us."

On the same June day that the rain came to Korokoro, cotton seedlings pushed up through the thick black soil of Perthshire Farms, a 10,000-acre cotton plantation half a world away in America's Mississippi Delta. Kenneth Hood, the eldest of four brothers running the farm and chairman of the National Cotton Council—the man first in line to shake the president's hand after the signing of the 2002 Farm Bill—climbed into the air-conditioned cab of a $125,000 Case tractor and prepared to give the seedlings a dousing of fertilizer. The enormous tractor, one of twelve on the farm, was equipped with digital displays, four-wheel drive, and an air-cushioned seat. The sixty-one-year-old Hood, wearing a button-down Oxford shirt, fiddled with a global positioning satellite system that indicated how much fertilizer to squirt onto the plants.

There was no obvious sign in Gunnison, Mississippi, that world cotton prices were at rock bottom. The Hood family was continuing to buy parcels of land. The next day Hood would be traveling to New Orleans to chair a meeting of the National Cotton Council at the Ritz-Carlton Hotel. "There are lots of reasons to be optimistic," he declared.

The Hoods had collected roughly $750,000 in subsidies the year before, and now the new Farm Bill offered them the prospect of even more. Across Mississippi, the 1,700 or so cotton farmers could count on receiving hundreds of millions of federal dollars, which were cherished as vital to keeping the cotton industry alive. As in rural Mali, cotton was the single biggest part of Mississippi's Delta economy. Cotton and the various businesses that depended on it generated more than $3 billion in revenue for the region. About half the jobs in some Delta counties were tied to supplying goods or services to cotton farmers or working for them.

The Mississippi Delta farmers were so dependent on subsidies because they were among the highest-cost cotton producers in the world: It could take $600 to produce an acre of Delta cotton. One mechanical cotton picker, capable of reaping enough cotton in a day to make 150 bales, each weighing 480 pounds, could cost $300,000. Much of the cotton land was irrigated. The seed was premium priced because it was genetically modified to resist bugs. Expensive fertilizers spurred growth in the spring, and defoliants exposed the boll for harvest in the fall.

Delta cotton farmers could grow corn, soybeans, and wheat much more cheaply, but switching crops would render much of their investment worthless. "I can only run cotton through my cotton picker," said Ed Hester while leaning on the hood of his Chevy pickup as a crop duster circled on the horizon. And why should he change? His 4,200-acre farm in Benoit, Mississippi, a stretch down the road from the Hood farm, received about $400,000 in subsidies even before the new Farm Bill increase. "Cotton is still king in my book," Hester said.

"The Delta needs cotton farmers, and they can't exist without subsidies," Hood insisted. As for the ragged farmers in Mali? Well, there wasn't much sympathy for them in Mississippi. If they can't keep up, Hood suggested, "Maybe the farmers in Africa should be the ones not raising cotton."

That would leave more than 2 million households in West and Central Africa who relied on cotton utterly destitute. And several national economies would be without an export crop. Bakary Traore, president of Mali's state cotton company, had a better idea. He didn't want to deprive the American cotton farmers of their income. Not at all, for he, and all Malians, knew what it was like to have nothing. "It would be better [for the United States] to pay their farmers *not* to plant cotton," he said. That way, the cheap handpicked Mali cotton would be better able to compete on the world market. And the Sangare family could fulfill one of its dreams. Madou, the eldest brother, said their plan was to earn enough money from cotton to send youngest brother Bala to high school and then to college in

France, or even the United States—somewhere with better jobs and prospects than Mali. Then Bala would send money from his job back to the brothers in Korokoro, alleviating their dependence on the cotton price. But with cotton revenues dwindling, the dream was fading. "We want Bala and all our children to have better lives than us," Madou said. "We want them to eat better, have better health, be better educated." Beyond the cotton, this aspiration—a better life for the children—was the one thing the Sangares had in common with U.S. farmers. "Isn't that what everyone wants?" Madou asked.

It was certainly what farmers across Africa wanted. But international development practice had left them to fend for themselves in a global trading system increasingly tilted against them. As the U.S. Farm Bill went into force, hunger spread across Africa, dashing dreams and stealing lives.

In Ethiopia, two decades of neglect and hypocrisy were about to erupt into another epic famine.

CHAPTER 5

Glut and Punishment

ADAMI TULU, ETHIOPIA, 2003

By the time the rains failed and drought crept across the land, Ethiopia's descent into famine had already begun. Not even the best seeds, the most abundant fertilizer, or the smartest science could hold back disaster. In fact, the advances Norman Borlaug and his disciples had introduced had inadvertently precipitated the famine. They had helped Ethiopia's farmers produce one good harvest after another through early 2002. But without international investments to modernize agricultural markets and improve rural infrastructure to better move and absorb the bumper yields, and without a government-supported safety net to encourage farmers to keep planting even when their surplus production pushed down prices a catastrophic 80 percent, the bounty led to a bust. While American farmers raked in ever-higher subsidies to protect them from market volatility, Ethiopia's farmers crashed along with the prices. Production costs were suddenly higher than what they could fetch for their crops, so many of them simply stopped trying to grow as much food. In one of the cruelest ironies of the structural adjustment period, Ethiopia's farmers failed even as they succeeded.

Up on the Boricha plateau, failure meant starvation and a mournful procession of peasant farmers, like Tesfaye Ketema, carrying their dying

children to the therapeutic feeding tents. Down below on the floodplains
of the Rift Valley lakes, where larger commercial farmers had sown acre
upon acre of wheat and corn, failure meant financial ruin.

Chombe Seyoum, one of Ethiopia's model farmers, a young man who
had a decade earlier enthusiastically enlisted in his country's efforts to ig-
nite a Green Revolution, choked back tears as he kicked at a clump of hard
soil in his parched fields in May 2003. With starvation all around him, he
had, incredibly, turned off his irrigation system, and a 200-acre plot that a
year earlier had yielded a cornucopia of corn, cabbage, tomatoes, beans,
bananas, and papayas turned to dust. It was crazy behavior, he acknowledged, but he could no longer afford the cost of diesel fuel to run the water
pump. "I hate this," he muttered as he trudged across his barren land. "It
didn't have to be this way."

Throughout the 1990s, Chombe's family had steadily expanded its
farming operations in several parts of the country and invested in ma-
chinery and modest irrigation systems. By 2002, he was farming more than
4,000 acres in total, including fields of corn and wheat that rippled to the
horizon just like the amber waves in Illinois and Iowa. In the farming seasons of 2000–2001 and 2001–2002, he reaped his best harvests ever. And
he lost $250,000.

Any similarities between Chombe and farmers in the American Midwest ended at mere appearances. Chombe didn't have futures contracts to
lock in a price for his grain or crop insurance or government price supports to help him hedge his risk or federal subsidies to encourage him to
grow as much as he could—all the benefits available to American farmers.
All that the irrigation system and tractors and good seeds and large fields
meant was that Chombe had more to lose. And he pretty much lost it all.

Sasakawa Africa and the Ethiopian government had put the country on
a mad push to produce, produce, produce. Harvests multiplied through
the late 1990s, and then came the bumper year of 2000–2001, when fields
burst with about 13 million tons of grains and cereals. The next season,
with good rains watering the country, Ethiopia's farmers again harvested
nearly 13 million tons. Suddenly, Ethiopia rivaled South Africa as sub-
Saharan Africa's largest grain and cereal producer. It was an astonishing
development in this land of epic hunger, a miracle unimaginable during
the famine of 1984.

But in the drive to increase production, few people in Ethiopia or internationally had thought about what to do with the bumper harvests when they finally arrived. It was only in March 2002 when the government summoned a crisis meeting of economists and development theorists that Ethiopia's market situation was assessed. The participants looked at how to move the surplus production of corn and wheat to the food-deficit areas within the country (which were being supplied by international food aid), only to find that the country's transportation network still relied heavily on donkeys and that the local markets were woefully undercapitalized to buy and store the harvest. They explored export possibilities, only to find that the roads to the port were wretched and that few ties existed with foreign buyers.

They discovered that structural adjustment and the neglect of agriculture beyond the growing of crops had taken a frightening toll. The government had pulled the state out of agriculture in 1990 in favor of the private sector, but the private sector hadn't filled the void. At the same time, international donors had put agriculture on the back burner, so there was little investment funding to be had. The United States was providing an average of about $250 million of food aid a year to Ethiopia, which was almost one hundred times more than its agricultural development aid to the country. Ethiopia itself was squandering $1 million a day on a war with neighboring Eritrea, money it could have spent on rural development.

And so Ethiopia's record harvest turned into disaster. With a dearth of storage facilities, all of the crops came on the market at the same time. And with the country's internal markets horribly underdeveloped and export markets nonexistent, the nationwide glut of corn and wheat triggered a free fall in grain prices, a plunge from $10 to $2 per 100 kilograms (about 220 pounds). The price farmers reaped was far below their costs to sow.

In the 2002–2003 planting season, fertilizer use in Ethiopia plummeted 27 percent. Hybrid-seed sales tumbled 70 percent. To further cut down on expenses, the larger commercial farmers, like Chombe, took land out of production and turned off irrigation systems. Ethiopia's Green Revolution not only came to a screeching halt but slammed into reverse. Corn plantings for 2002–2003 were expected to fall by at least a quarter. And then drought hit, slashing even further into the harvest.

One year after its crisis meeting to deal with the bumper crops, the government in early 2003 made another emergency call on the international community: Please send food aid.

Absurdity compounded tragedy. While the country begged for food, great stretches of fertile land in the more drought-resistant Wheat and Corn Belts lay fallow or were being underworked. And while food aid poured in from abroad, an estimated 300,000 tons of surplus Ethiopian grain rotted in the countryside because it wasn't profitable to harvest and bring to market.

Drought widened the misery, but it was only a supporting villain in this tragedy. As Emmanuel Otoro concluded while walking through the emergency feeding tents in Boricha and speaking with the parents of the starving children, the markets failed before the weather did.

Feast begot famine. Incredibly, in a country of chronic hunger and in the midst of famine, grain farming became a highly unprofitable business.

Chombe, a quarter-million dollars in the hole, never thought he would see the day. But by 2003, after two bumper crops, "I was on the verge of bankruptcy," he said. As the prices plummeted and bankers called his loans, he explained, "I had to sell at harvest time when the price is the lowest. Everybody was bringing their crops to market. I had to take whatever price I could get." Even though the price was below his costs for seed, fertilizer, fuel, and labor, he had bills to pay, particularly the interest payments on the loans he had negotiated to finance the irrigation system and to expand his farming.

Now he was retreating. In the 2001–2002 season, he had planted 2,700 acres of corn, sorghum, and soybeans on his farm in Wolega, to the west of Addis Ababa. The next year, he planted just 500 acres. "I was so scared the same thing would happen again," he said, his round face flashing a hint of panic. "I could see in my books that growing so much wasn't profitable. My expenses were higher than the price at harvest."

A friend and neighbor in Wolega, Bulbula Tulle, found himself in the same scary position. Bulbula had also reaped his best harvest ever in 2002, and he promptly lost nearly $200,000. The next year, he, too, cut back his planting from 2,700 acres to 500. In May 2003, grass and weeds grew on his idle land, feeding grazing cows rather than hungry people. "I knew that when I cut the size of my farm, I'm contributing to the food shortage," Bulbula said. "It's horrible. But at least I'm not losing money."

Chombe's roller-coaster farming journey had mirrored his country's. His father had been a farmer in the southern region of Bale, the country's Wheat Belt. He was the first in the area to have a John Deere tractor—he was among the first to have a tractor of any kind—along with a couple of harvesting combines. Chombe loved the machines and the work in the fields and wanted nothing more than to grow things. But it all came to an abrupt halt in the mid-1970s when the communist regime that had deposed Haile Selassie nationalized the country's agriculture and confiscated the family farm. Chombe's father, pushed out of farming, took up pressing flaxseed into cooking oil. And, Chombe remembered, he made a vow to his family: "What we have has been taken away. I will invest in education. That can't be taken away."

As a college student in Addis Ababa, Chombe watched helplessly when the famine of 1984 killed so many countrymen. His family should have been growing as much food as possible. Instead, all he could do was pitch in with the construction of shelter for the hungry refugees. After he graduated from college in Ethiopia—the first in his family to do so—he traveled way up north, to Edinburgh, Scotland, in the mid-1980s to study civil engineering. Now he would build things, urban structures, but his heart was still on the farm.

Once the communists were toppled and the new government of Meles Zenawi embraced the efforts of Sasakawa Africa to boost farm production, Chombe returned to Ethiopia in 1993. His family was back farming, and Chombe chucked his engineering degree and eagerly enlisted in the nascent agricultural revolution. Finally, he was growing things again.

Commercial farming in a country of chronic hunger would be a noble pursuit, Chombe reckoned, and a no-fail proposition. "I want to help the country, grow food, employ people," he would tell whoever asked. He was so proud of his harvests that he took pictures of the green carpets of corn and amber waves of wheat and hung them on his office walls.

Now, in 2003, standing in his barren two hundred–acre field in Adami Tulu near Lake Ziway, he was hanging his head in shame. "I turned off the irrigation," Chombe said, still incredulous at his action. He managed a wan gap-toothed smile. "We're in a famine, and my irrigation is off."

He really had no other choice. He had been growing corn for hybrid-seed production under contract with a seed company. But the company had canceled its order when the demand for hybrid seed collapsed along with the harvest prices. "They told me that farmers were in too bad of a financial position to buy my seeds," Chombe said. But he already knew that. Even he was using the cheapest seed on his own farms. "I couldn't afford the hybrids myself," he said.

Without the contract, he had no money to pay one hundred dollars a day for the diesel gas that fueled the irrigation system. So he shut it down. He didn't plant; the land was left barren. No seed corn, no vegetables. When the rains failed, the banana and papaya trees withered and died.

Chombe hurried across the desolate landscape toward the shade of a big fig tree beside a narrow creek. It had always been one of his favorite spots, a cool escape from the broiling sun and a refuge from the work in his fields. His presence startled a pair of monkeys, who scampered up the tree, knocking loose leaves and figs. The farmer made a playful noise, and the monkeys chattered back.

Under the tree, Chombe parted a stand of tall grass and showed off a little motor and pump connected to a tangle of pipes. The irrigation system pulled water from the creek, which meandered from Lake Ziway, and then fed it to the field. The chug-chug-chug rhythm of the pump had been the metronome of Chombe's work here. Now there was only uncomfortable silence. "I loved coming here when the stream was full. I would sit and have my coffee," Chombe said. He closed his eyes and sighed. "This *was* a paradise." He spat out the word *was*. His paradise had gone to hell. Everything was a burnt brown. Dirt devils and tumbleweeds skittered across the field.

Chombe squinted in the bright sun as he trudged dejectedly along the irrigation line. The earthen works that held the pipes and formed the canals were beginning to crumble. In the field where crops once grew, Chombe kicked loose a clump of parched dirt and bent down to scoop up a handful of soil. "What a waste," he said. "This could have been avoided. *If* the government could have bought grain, the prices wouldn't have fallen so much. *If* someone could have provided finance and credits, we would have continued producing. *If* the private sector worked. *If* there were markets." Chombe let the dirt fall through his fingers. So had the world let the Green Revolution slip from Ethiopia's grasp.

Chombe watched the wind lift up his topsoil and carry it away. "It's all very sad," he said. "Even during the big harvests, we cried out that something wasn't right. But it was too late."

Eleni Gabre-Madhin had been crying out for two decades.

She was an economics student at Cornell University in the United States when famine ravaged her country in 1984. One night, at dinner, a food fight erupted in the campus cafeteria, with all manner of nourishment being hurled through the air and then consigned to the garbage can. Eleni jumped up from her table, climbed on a chair, and shouted, "Stop!" She scolded her fellow students for wasting food when so many people in her country were starving.

It was a galvanizing moment for her, "a turning point in my life," she would later say. Her cafeteria outburst led her to ponder more deeply what was happening in her country. She focused her studies on the failure of agricultural markets, how so many people could starve in the northern stretches of her country while a surplus of food languished in the fertile southern regions.

Eleni wrote her doctoral thesis on Ethiopia's antiquated grain markets and continued her investigations at the International Food Policy Research Institute in Washington, D.C., and the World Bank, where she got a close-up look at the debilitating schizophrenia in development theory that was wracking Africa. At the same time farmers were trying to catch up to Asia's Green Revolution, their governments, under the thumb of structural adjustment, were beating a hasty retreat from agricultural markets. When production increased, as it did in Ethiopia in the late 1990s, it only served to expose the market vacuum left in the wake of the Western demands. The reforms, Eleni noted in a 2001 study, "seem to have thrown the baby out with the bathwater."

By failing to follow up the market reforms with private-sector market development, the practitioners of structural adjustment, she believed, also threw out the lessons of history. The key elements that transformed agricultural markets in the developed world were never applied to Africa.

The fortunes of farmers in the American Midwest, for example, greatly improved with the establishment of the Chicago Board of Trade in 1848. Before, farmers would haul their grain to the market with little prior knowledge of price, and usually they brought it shortly after harvest when prices were at their lowest. Nor was there much warehouse space to store the grain, nor any standard grading to certify the quality. The farmers mainly had to take what the traders offered. Sometimes, if they arrived at the market amid a surplus and they couldn't find a buyer or if the price was below their transportation costs, farmers would dump their grain in Lake Michigan rather than haul it back home.

The Board of Trade set standards of quality, product uniformity, and routine inspections of grain. And it developed "futures contracts," which allowed farmers to sell their harvest in the future at a preset price. No longer did they have to sell their produce at harvest time and settle for low prices. Over time, farmers were also able to use these contracts as collateral to obtain bank loans. And no longer did they physically have to haul their grain to the Chicago market for sale; they could ship it directly to the contract buyer.

The incentive-sapping conditions that were eliminated by these Board of Trade innovations were still afflicting farmers in Ethiopia 155 years later. It is why Chombe turned off his irrigation, and why Tesfaye carried his starving son to the emergency feeding tent, and why so many other farmers left their harvests in the field to rot, behaving just like the American farmers who dumped their grain into Lake Michigan.

In the previous two decades, dozens of commodities exchanges had popped up in the developing world, most of them in Latin America and Asia. In emerging food-producing powers like Brazil, India, and China, the exchanges would fuel the agricultural revolutions. Yet in Africa no one bothered with the markets. The United States had spent considerable money, time, and effort promoting its model of democracy in Africa. But no evangelist of American capitalism had invested the same energy to promote its model of grain trading.

And so, in Ethiopia, while agricultural production increased at the dawn of the twenty-first century, the grain market was stuck in the Dark Ages. A farmer sold his surplus crop to a trader who showed up at his mud-and-sticks house with a take-it-or-leave-it price. That trader loaded the produce on donkeys or broken-down trucks and hauled it to the central market in Addis. There, he upped the price, taking into account the transportation cost, and sold the grain to another level of traders, who repacked each bag, checking the quality along the way. These traders, too, set a new higher price to account for their handling, and sold the grain to another set of traders who again checked the quality and then reloaded the grain on donkeys and trucks and dispatched it to various parts of the country, where it was sold for a still higher price, accounting for the last leg of transport.

All along this torturous route, road and telecommunication networks were remedial at best and utterly absent in many places. And there were no institutions to establish prices, swap information, grade the quality of product, or legally enforce contracts. As Eleni noted in her studies, there was no reliable way to connect buyers and sellers or farmers and consumers. She found that only one-quarter of the country's total cereal production reached the market, and that Ethiopian farmers sometimes received merely one-third of the final price paid by the ultimate consumer. "The market side hasn't been thought about at all," she fumed after the crisis summit that the government convened in 2002. "It was considered a second-generation problem. The emphasis was on, 'Let's just produce.'"

Market solutions, she insisted, were the way out of the crisis. Later that year, in December, Eleni first met Norman Borlaug at a seminar in Washington. She approached him with an urgent question: How did he and the other engineers of the Green Revolution in Asia handle the markets when grain production suddenly boomed? "He just looked at me," Eleni recalled, "and he said, 'Well, we just didn't have to worry about the market in Asia. All we had to worry about was the science.'" Asia, he told her, already had fairly well-established agricultural markets.

Eleni thought back to that encounter as she walked through the sprawling, unruly outdoor grain market in central Addis in May 2003. The shock of feast begetting famine convinced her that Ethiopia could never hope to feed itself without modern markets, in particular a commodities exchange that could lift some of the risk from the farmers. "Those traders and marketers who should be taking the risk have no ability to do so," Eleni explained as she navigated her way around the donkeys and heaving crowds of traders who were haggling prices among themselves. "So the farmers have to bear all the risk. They won't advance new technology use and fertilizer use as long as they also bear the volatility of the market. Before the market reforms, the government was the risk absorber. Now, it's all on the farmer."

Amid the clamor and chaos of the market, Eleni found Yoseph Yilak, the general manager of the Grain Traders Association. Yoseph's office was a shack just a little bigger than an outhouse. His desk hogged nearly all the space. His phone, shaped like a fish, rang constantly. Pictures and icons of Jesus and the Virgin Mary hung on every wall. Bags of grain that were stacked up outside his window allowed only a few beams of light to pass into the office. The air was filled with the toxic odor of exhaust fumes from a phalanx of trucks idling while bags of grain were loaded. Traders shouted to be heard over a mad chorus of honking horns and braying donkeys.

Yoseph explained how the bumper crops between 2000 and 2002 hit the woefully underdeveloped private sector like a tsunami. When prices collapsed, Yoseph and his fellow traders didn't have the financing to buy and store large quantities of grain until the prices rose again. Rather than market entrepreneurs like him sweeping up the surplus and assuming the risk of price fluctuations, the farmers themselves got stuck with it.

He insisted that Ethiopia's farmers were simply making rational decisions when they cut back on planting. "The farmers have so many problems," he said. "We could help. We could build warehouses to store their grain. We need trucks to move it. But we don't have any money, either. I go to the bank to get money to build a warehouse. The bank says I need collateral. I have no collateral, so I get no money. I'd like to have a truck to take the grain to the places of the country that need food. But I need collateral to buy a truck, too."

Yoseph leaned back in his chair under a picture of Jesus. He opened his arms to take in his tiny domain. "Does it look like I have any collateral?" he asked, sarcasm dripping from his words.

If he had a truck, he said, he could buy directly from the farmers and then deliver to customers. "I'm a trader," he said, "but I don't talk to farmers. How strange is that?" Instead, Yoseph and most of the other Addis traders relied on a series of middlemen in a Rube Goldberg–like scheme of commerce that jacked up prices and overly complicated distribution from those with surplus to those who starve.

Eleni relayed the frustrations of Abdu Awol, a trader in the western region of Wolega, who embarked on a rare effort to complete a long-distance sale himself. He set off to take a truckload of grain nine hundred kilometers to northern Ethiopia, where he heard that demand and prices were higher. For two and a half weeks he bounced over potholed roads and dirt trails. Some of his sacks burst along the way; he had to pay bribes to pass through numerous checkpoints. Once he arrived at his destination he couldn't find a buyer offering the prices he had heard were available. "In the end," Eleni said, "he sold at a loss and never tried again."

Yoseph, who had heard many such tales around the market, rolled his eyes. "We must modernize our system," he said wearily. "I have written so many papers to the government, but I hear no answers."

There were many cries in the wilderness before the 2003 famine. Some of the most persistent came from the Famine Early Warning System Network (FEWS NET) and the Ethiopia Network on Food Security that had been set up by the international development agencies of the United States and the European Union after the 1984 disaster. Everyone was on high alert for the looming drought, of course, keeping a close watch on the satellite imagery provided by the U.S. National Oceanic and Atmospheric Administration and the U.S. Geological Survey. But the low-tech market warnings of a battalion of researchers, called "ground-truthers," were largely ignored. These ground-truthers, bearing pens and notebooks, regularly patrolled markets, farms, and households to chart supply and demand and the impact on prices. They peered into the dark recesses of mud-walled huts and climbed into ramshackle storage bins to gauge family food reserves. They interviewed farmers about their intended use of fertilizer and hybrid seeds.

In the years leading up to the 2003 famine, though, nobody could handle the truth about their market warnings: that surplus production building up in the markets was leading to falling prices and declining farmer incentive. "A glut is not a problem in the eyes of many," said Alemu Asfaw, the Ethiopian country representative of the early warning network at the time. A tall, thin, normally soft-spoken man, Alemu had been shouting from the ramparts. "They thought we were crying wolf," he said. "Nobody was listening."

In a series of monthly reports of the Ethiopia Network on Food Security, the ground-truthers authored the writing on the wall for the coming famine and, it turned out, for the global food crisis beyond that. It was there for all to see:

February 2001—"The wholesale prices for staple cereals continue to fall, creating a possible disincentive to surplus production. . . . Market supply is driving prices below farmers' expectations and may discourage farmers for the next production season."

January 2002—"Prices of major cereals continue to be very low. . . . Protection of smallholder agriculture from the adverse effects of declining cereal prices remains both a marketing policy and social policy challenge. Reversing the current trend of low prices cannot be entirely left to supply and demand alone. Some price support efforts are still required in order to maintain farmers' production incentives."

February 2002—"The persistent decline in cereal prices throughout 2001 . . . could result in severe financial difficulties for farmers. For maize [corn] whose price declined more sharply than for other cereals, a possible reduction in area planted is anticipated next season. . . . Maize production is expected to be about 24% lower."

April 2002—"Current price trends are very worrying, particularly for maize, because producer prices often fall below cost of production in many areas. A significant decline in the use of purchased inputs (improved seeds and fertilizer) was previously documented and reported during the 2001–2002 production season. Further decline in input use and consequent decrease in production can be expected during the 2002–2003 production season unless the current downward price trend is reversed. . . .

"In order to maintain the production incentives of farmers in surplus areas, long-term strategies are required in addition to short-term measures such as purchase of food aid on the domestic market and the use of cash-based public works programs for relief assistance. These may include: incorporating marketing advice to farmers in agricultural extension, revitalizing and expanding a public grain market information system, expanding rural road infrastructure and promoting cross-border trade."

September 2002—"The failure of the rains will require assistance in 2003 for about 10.2 million people in a likely scenario requiring more than 1.5 million metric tons of food aid, and 11–14 million beneficiaries under a worst-case scenario requiring 2.2 million metric tons of food aid for 2003. The hunger gap is expected to peak between March and June 2003, when the poor 2002 harvest has begun to run out and before any harvest from 2003 is available.

"FEWS NET has made a preliminary estimate of the 2002–2003 production to be between 9.56 and 10.33 million metric tons, representing a 15% and 8% decrease, respectively, from the previous four year average. . . . While poor rainfall and lower usage of inputs triggered this decline, it is underpinned by a long-term deterioration of income and possession of productive assets."

December 2002—"The government of Ethiopia and the United Nations launched a joint appeal for over 1.44 million metric tons of food aid to feed 11.3 million people in 2003 due to rainfall shocks that worsened previously desperate conditions. A further three million people required close monitoring."

February 2003—"Food aid to supply supplementary feeding programs is critically low, meeting only 32% of requirements at the same time that critical levels of malnutrition are being reported in many areas of the country."

April 2003—"Ethiopia is in the throes of a critical humanitarian crisis."

The ground-truthers were right. The worst of their worst-case scenario came to pass. Within the next few months, 14 million people were receiving food aid.

Some of the hungry were Chombe's neighbors who had worked for him until he took land out of production and shut down the irrigation. A decade earlier he had become a farmer to grow food and employ people. Now, on his land in Adami Tulu and Wolega, he wasn't doing much of either. Thank God, he said, he had still planted wheat and barley on the full 1,500 acres he worked in the southern Bale region, near his family home. He didn't even bother taking that harvest to the markets because the price was so low. Instead, it became food aid for his workers and their families. "Better to be producing and feeding ourselves," Chombe reckoned, "than to be begging."

But many of his countrymen preferred to beg. The world, it seemed to him, had gone completely mad in 2003. In past years, he had used his combines to harvest his neighbors' wheat. In 2003, though, many of them said they didn't want him to cut their crop. They feared that if government agricultural officials saw them harvesting, they wouldn't get any food aid. "Isn't that crazy?" Chombe cackled on the drive back to Addis Ababa from Adami Tulu. "Their main worry is food aid, not feeding themselves. That's what's become of us."

Chombe headed to the Addis Hilton for a drink at his favorite watering hole. The lobby was packed with famine relief workers from humanitarian agencies around the world.

Takele Gebre, slumped in a chair near the lobby bar, laughed ruefully at the scene. He was the head of Sasakawa's Ethiopian operations, and he was consumed with a feeling of betrayal. "*Now* they come to help us," Takele said derisively, sweeping his arm in the direction of the scrums of foreigners crowding the check-in counter. "They send us their so-called experts and their grain when we are starving, but when it comes to helping agriculture develop into a business, where were they? What we had been trying to do was to help farmers produce more. But there was no help with the other things—credit systems, input systems, markets—and that led to the collapse. Where were these people then? We should have advanced simultaneously on all of this." He shook his head, contemplating the missed opportunities. "Increasing production is the easiest part," he added. "But to keep agriculture moving, to inspire the farmers, you need to do all these other things as well. We have to make agriculture market oriented. If we don't, we'll keep having these terrible shocks."

He stared into his cup of coffee, stirring idly. "It's not in the interest of others to help us become self-sufficient," he finally said. "They would rather send us food aid. You don't believe me? Go to the town of Nazareth. It's close by, just east of here. You'll see what I mean."

"Yes," echoed Chombe. "Go to Nazareth. You won't believe your eyes."

CHAPTER 6

Who's Aiding Whom?

NAZARETH, ETHIOPIA, 2003

The main road to Nazareth is paved with good intentions. It begins at the port of Djibouti on the Gulf of Aden and runs west through the Afar Desert, past the ancient sands where the bones of our hominid ancestor "Lucy" were found, and finally along the Awash River basin up to the Rift Valley highlands and on to Addis Ababa. In times of great hunger, this is the road that brings relief to Ethiopia. Over the years, millions of tons of grain grown by American farmers, and the good intentions that travel with them—to feed starving Ethiopians while helping U.S. agriculture—have made this journey.

There is a second, less-traveled, road to Nazareth. This one shoots up from the south, from the Arsi and Bale regions where Chombe Seyoum's family has long farmed. In good years, when the rains generously sprinkle the highlands, caravans of trucks make the trek north laden with the bounty of Ethiopia's wheat and corn farmers.

The two roads meet in the center of Nazareth, in a cacophonous cluster of unbridled commerce: market stalls, bus stops, outdoor restaurants, transit hotels, and chicken and goat auctions. During 2003, as trucks piled high with food came speeding into that intersection from both directions, there was a spectacular collision: The mythology of American food aid ran smack into the reality of African agriculture, where hunger and plenty, shortage and surplus, sometimes exist side by side in the same country in the same year.

Jerman Amente, a thirty-nine-year-old Ethiopian farmer and grain trader, had a roadside view of the collision. Standing in the dirt parking lot outside his grain warehouse, he could feel the trucks rumbling in from Djibouti, massive double-load wagons stacked to the top with 220-pound white woven-plastic bags bearing the characteristic red, white, and blue markings of American food intended for starving foreigners. The trucks came in waves, carrying in all more than 1 million tons of wheat, corn, beans, peas, and lentils from the United States. The ground shook as they rolled over the potholes.

Jerman shook with anger whenever he saw those trucks, for inside his warehouse, a vast concrete cavern, was an astonishing sight in a country then suffering from epic hunger: bag upon bag of *Ethiopian* wheat, corn, beans, peas, and lentils stacked in towering columns stretching toward the ceiling. This was what Chombe and Sasakawa's Takele Gebre wanted everyone to see. It was the bounty from the two seasons before, the bumper crop from Jerman's farm and from the fields of his neighbors in Arsi and Bale and the grain-growing regions out west. This was the fruit of Sasakawa and Borlaug's effort to introduce farming methods that would boost production. These crops were also preserved in white sacks, though they bore the green, yellow, and red stripes of Ethiopia. While American-grown food poured into the country, this homegrown Ethiopian surplus languished untouched.

Jerman, a short, wiry, energetic man, scrambled to the summit of one of his mountains of grain and comically posed for pictures. "I should hold a sign saying, 'Please send food. In Ethiopia we have no food!'" He howled wickedly. "I don't think Americans can imagine this."

No, in 2003, Americans imagined their food aid arriving to save the day amid blighted landscapes of misery where everything was brown, dying, and grim. Their perceptions of the situation—and of their own best intentions—were perhaps most clearly expressed on one of the trucks that rolled up to the Ethiopian government's strategic grain storehouse in Nazareth, groaning under the weight of American wheat and corn to be unloaded there. The truck's passenger-side window had been converted into a stained-glass painting of Jesus. It was perfect imagery: Jesus, in Nazareth, bringing salvation to the Ethiopians.

Americans certainly didn't imagine their food aid arriving in green fields, rolling past warehouses full of local food. They didn't imagine African countries producing grain surpluses, certainly not those countries with all those starving people. And they certainly didn't imagine their aid being welcomed by bitter sarcasm from the local farmers.

"American farmers have a market in Ethiopia, but *we* don't have a market in Ethiopia," huffed Kedir Geleto, who managed a grain-trading operation in Nazareth. Kedir, with Jerman, led a tour of their warehouses in Nazareth, just off the main road from Djibouti to Addis Ababa. Doing a quick inventory in their heads, they estimated that at least 100,000 metric tons of Ethiopian-grown grain, beans, and peas were idling here. And, they believed, there were another 50,000 tons stored elsewhere in the country. It was surplus food they hadn't sold the previous year, when prices had collapsed. They had held it in their warehouses to prevent prices and farmer incentive from plummeting even lower. And now, with nearly 2 million tons of international food aid rushing into the country, the market was further undermined.

The two traders knew that their grain wasn't nearly enough to feed all of their countrymen, and, as Ethiopians, they were grateful for the international food aid. "We really appreciate it," said Jerman. Yet as farmers and businessmen, he and many of his colleagues were also disgusted and discouraged.

Jerman reported that some farmers hauling their own grain up from the south, hoping to sell it on the markets, had pulled a U-turn in Nazareth when they met the food-aid trucks coming in from the east. They returned to their farms and stashed the grain in flimsy storage facilities, breezy bins open to the elements, where insects and pests and the heat would ruin it in a matter of months. What kind of incentive was this for farmers to improve their harvests? With food aid flooding into the country, what was the use of producing a surplus?

"We don't oppose food aid. When there's a deficit in the country, of course we need it. But when there's plenty of food in some part of the country, then it's unbelievable," said Bulbula Tulle, Chombe's neighbor who had his own storehouse in Nazareth.

Why, the men wondered, didn't America provide cash aid to buy up the local surplus, and *then* send food to cover the rest of the shortage? "If the Americans really want to help us, to feed our hungry and to help our farmers," Kedir said, "first of all they must buy what is available from the farmers and merchants in the country."

But the Americans couldn't buy from the local farmers. Since the 1940s, the U.S. Congress followed the principle that American food aid must be grown in America. As the years went by, U.S. business and political interests had come to wield ever more influence over food-aid policy, keeping the focus on what was best for American agribusiness and for the politicians it supported rather than on what was best for the world's hungry. Even as American generosity grew—half of all international food aid is provided by the United States—so did its self-interest.

"If we take the perspective of the American farmer, it is logical to supply food aid to the world. This is the right policy for America," said Jerman. "But if the main aim of aid is not only to support American farmers but to support the poor country, then the donors must do what is best for the Ethiopian farmers and the Ethiopian people. If this is the aim, to solve the hunger problem, then the U.S. must change. Don't only send your food."

Following the 1984 famine, Ethiopia routinely had been the largest annual recipient of emergency food aid in sub-Saharan Africa. U.S. food aid alone was running at more than $250 million a year leading up to 2003. As the volume of this emergency food aid expanded, the amount of longer-term aid to help develop Ethiopian agriculture and avert future famines contracted. In 2003, U.S. emergency food aid jumped to more than $500 million, compared to less than $5 million spent on agricultural development projects. And when that food aid came streaming in while Ethiopian farmers couldn't sell their surplus from the year earlier, a dark cynicism spread across the land: Maybe food aid was meant not to solve the hunger problem but to perpetuate it. "American farmers need Ethiopian famine," said Bulbula bluntly. "If American farmers aren't putting their crops in here, then where would they go?"

The dependency ran two ways. The regular deluge of food aid had turned Ethiopia into a global welfare state. And its reliance on the huge volumes from the United States bred a bizarre dependency on weather and grow-ing conditions in the American Midwest. "You hear people say they don't care whether it rains in Ethiopia as long as it rains in Iowa," said Mesfin Abebe, an adviser to the deputy prime minister and minister of rural de-velopment during the famine. He sat on a brown sofa in a government of-fice building atop a hill in Addis Ababa, stirring a cup of tea. A photo of a donkey running across the desert rested on a wooden cabinet; a lonely red tie hung on a metal hat stand. The city and all its poverty sprawled be-yond his concrete balcony.

"Food aid in Ethiopia has really perpetuated a dependency syndrome. The government is painfully aware of this," lamented Professor Mesfin, stroking his goatee as he gazed out the window. It was shameful, he said, that many Ethiopians had become so food-aid dependent, waiting in line for hours once a month to get their white bags emblazoned with the Amer-ican logos rather than working to try to feed their families themselves. "They consider it their right to get food aid," he said, "whether they are starving or not."

A day's drive south of Mesfin's office, the 120 families of Boditi, in the highlands near Boricha, were starving. They were so desperate for food that they rushed forward the minute relief-aid workers began haul-ing bags of American wheat out of a small storage shed. Village elders, wielding long, thin whiplike sticks, chased back the most aggressive, par-ticularly those scrambling about with reed baskets to capture any spillage from the bags.

Laa Lakamo, a father of ten, patiently waited his turn on his little plot of land beside the distribution site. "I don't have enough to feed any of them," he said of his children, some of whom stood at his side, holding tight to his legs. The drought had wiped out his corn and beans the year before. The area inside his one-room hut where he would normally store food was barren. He actually had less than nothing, he said, for he was in debt to creditors for two years' worth of fertilizer and seed. His clothes were in tatters. He balanced a square piece of black and green carpet on his head to ward off the blazing sun.

But at his feet, as he waited for his food-aid ration, green stalks of corn shot up from the ground, nearly to his knees. The early rains had been good, but he worried that the late rain essential to keep the corn growing to maturity would fail, extending his dependence on food aid for another year. As he watched his neighbors at the distribution site carry away bag after bag festooned with the red, white, and, blue stripes of the donor country, Laa observed, "At least the rains have been good in America."

In Nazareth, 150 miles north of Boditi, a morning rainstorm flooded the streets. It was heavy but brief, ending as suddenly as it started. The skies brightened. Roosters crowed. But the mood in the warehouses remained dark. "If we keep getting good rains all over the country, the harvest will be good," Jerman said. "But still, the food from America will come."

Jerman carried a slim, hollow silver poker as he inspected his columns of grain. Randomly, he would thrust it into a bag of wheat or corn or beans, and retrieve a sample. "Look," he said, clutching a handful of corn. "It's suitable for human consumption. It's high quality."

Tamirat Haile Mariam, a driver from the big city of Addis, leaned in for a look and gasped in astonishment. "I've never seen anything like this," he said. "We hear that we don't have any food in this country, that we must be fed by the rest of the world. But here is Ethiopian maize!"

A little moth fluttered past Jerman's face. He missed with a swat, then told his foreman, "You must fumigate." The last thing he needed was an infestation.

Jerman hurried to his wheat warehouse. No bugs there. "Come, come," he urged, approaching a tower of sacks. He inserted the poker and pulled out a handful of wheat. "This is better for us than U.S. wheat. This is hard brown wheat, good for pasta."

"This is unbelievable," said Tamirat, his eyes widening.

In Bulbula's warehouse, Tamirat grabbed some corn himself from an open bag. "Look!" he shouted. "Good for porridge!"

That gave Jerman an idea. "Lunch!" he said. "You'll see we have plenty of food, all from Ethiopia." Jerman led the way to the Rift Valley Hotel on the Djibouti-Addis road. While the food-aid trucks trundled past, the group ordered stir-fried fish and pork, Wiener schnitzel, beef kebabs, spaghetti made from that brown Ethiopian wheat, and lentil soup with the orange tinge of Ethiopian lentils.

"And in America they believe we have no food," Kedir scoffed as the feast arrived at the table.

Over lunch, Kedir and Jerman wondered if Ethiopian farmers would ever be as politically powerful as they believed American farmers to be. The two men were part of a group of grain traders and large farmers who had recently sent a petition to the prime minister's office, urging the government to seek money from donor nations to buy local grain for food-aid distribution before bringing in more from the outside. In the petition, they warned that if warehouses weren't cleared out soon, they wouldn't have money to buy up the coming harvest or space to store it. Peasant incomes would again collapse. Loans would go unpaid. Food would rot on the farms. Farmers would plant less the next year. The cycle of famine would keep on spinning. "And we'll never develop," Jerman concluded.

A waiter approached the table with a check for the lunch—less than twenty dollars for six people. Jerman moved quickly to snatch it away from the American in the group. His triumphant laugh filled the restaurant. "We have had enough free lunch from America!" he said.

On the other side of the world, in America, at the very same time, a coalition of U.S. farming groups was drafting another petition with a diametrically opposite plea. They were appealing to the White House for *more* food-aid exports. They wanted Washington to begin buying from U.S. farmers a minimum of 3 million metric tons of wheat a year to donate in food aid around the world, up from the 2.2 million tons of the previous year. American farmers were producing twice as much wheat as the country needed. That surplus needed to be moved somehow, somewhere, before prices fell. "We believe the U.S. government should 'Keep the Food in Food Aid,'" the letter said. It confirmed what the Ethiopian traders suspected: American farmers needed hungry Africans.

"We need food aid to get rid of our excess commodities," explained Jim Evans from his cab atop a wheat combine near the Idaho-Washington border. During the wheat harvest in America's fertile Pacific Northwest, Evans spent day and night piloting his John Deere combine, a twelve-ton behemoth that inhaled 1,000 bushels an hour, or about twenty-seven tons, over his 1,000-acre farm. He figured that about one-third of the roughly $200,000 he generated annually from wheat, lentils, and peas came from doing business with food-aid programs. "Food aid has a huge impact on farms here," Evans said. "Without the business, I might have to get a job at Wal-Mart."

This region was known as the Palouse, a moniker taken from the French word for "green lawn." Probably no other place in America relied so heavily on supplying food aid to feed its own local economy. The climate made the hilly region uniquely suited for growing a few minor crops, such as lentils, peas, and the soft white variety of wheat. But the thing was, Palouse farmers grew a lot more of these crops than Americans could eat. Most of the wheat grown there was consumed overseas. What they couldn't sell abroad was snapped up by the U.S. government to use as food aid, which had been consuming about 10 percent of the crop. Without those food-aid orders, wheat prices would fall, and so would land prices, wheat industry officials argued.

In 2003, farmers on the Palouse and on the Ethiopian highlands found themselves in the same leaky boat riding out the turbulent waters of bumper harvests and lower prices. But the Palouse farmers had the food-aid market as a life preserver. "We feel it would be a disaster for U.S. agriculture if the system changes," said Thomas B. Mick, chief executive officer of the Washington Wheat Commission, a farmer-funded group. The Ethiopian farmers were left to sink.

The Palouse-grown peas that were cleaned and processed at Spokane Seed Company in Spokane, Washington, were used in everything from Campbell's Soup to Gerber's Baby Food. But still, there were plenty left over, so the family-owned firm relied on food-aid orders for 40 percent of its sales. "People here know their jobs depend in part on food aid," said Jim Groth, plant superintendent, as he grabbed a handful of dried yellow peas from a giant rotating cylinder. Those peas were making their way into bags embossed with the U.S. Agency for International Development logo, part of a 420-ton food-aid order for Kenya. Kenya bordered Ethiopia to the south, but none of the Ethiopian surplus had moved there. U.S. food aid had cornered that market.

Down the street in Spokane, at Northwest Pea and Bean Company, Gary Heaton toiled in the shadows of metal silos full of lentils. His most important job as manager was scanning the government's twice-monthly order list for food aid. One line caught his eye: The government was requesting two and a half railcars of lentils for shipment to Djibouti. By the end of the year, they would be steaming in on the road past Jerman's warehouses in Nazareth. "Ethiopia has been good for us," Heaton said.

The hunger business was keeping the U.S. lentil industry afloat. When swelling Canadian production sharply depressed U.S. prices in 2001, the U.S. government nearly doubled its food-aid purchases from American farmers to 83,000 tons, which was more than half of the Palouse's entire harvest. In 2002, Northwest Pea and Bean, part of a farmer-owned cooperative, sold one-third of its lentils and peas to food-aid programs, a business valued at $2.8 million.

The plight of Ethiopia's farmers and commodity traders—and their plea that donors like the U.S. government should contribute money to buy Ethiopian crops for food aid—didn't get much sympathy on the Palouse. "The idea makes my hair stand up on end," said Jim Thompson, who raised 1,400 acres of wheat and lentils near Farmington, Washington. In August 2003, he sold $20,000 worth of lentils to the government for food aid. "I don't feel like I'm to blame for the problems in the developing world," he said, standing in the middle of one of his fields at dusk. His face was haggard from a long day in his harvesting combine. "I just try to produce as much as I can so I can make ends meet."

America's food-aid program, run by the federal government, began with good intentions in World War I, when mining engineer and future President Herbert Hoover led private efforts to feed and clothe millions of war victims in Europe. But when federal money got involved, so did politics and politicians friendly to powerful agricultural interests. In 1949, Congress passed its first food-aid law, designed to dispose of surplus crops being turned over to the government by subsidized farmers. The mandate went forth: American food aid must be in the form of U.S. crops, not money.

With price-depressing American surpluses continuing to grow, farm-state legislators such as Senator Hubert H. Humphrey of Minnesota championed a permanent food-aid policy. A law passed in 1954, called PL-480, or more popularly, "Food for Peace," gave nations easy credit for buying American crops and gave the White House a big budget for donating U.S. agricultural products around the world. In its early years, food aid was responsible for more than half of America's wheat exports.

In the 1980s, Washington cooked up novel new outlets for agricultural surplus. Rather than dispatching cash grants to U.S. humanitarian aid groups for development projects such as digging wells and vaccinating children, the government gave them food crops. The aid groups then sold these donations in the foreign countries where they worked, turning the food into cash. This circuitous system of foreign aid was given the Orwellian moniker *monetization*. Sometimes, these sales of U.S. food squeezed local products out of the market; in Ethiopia, several cooking-oil companies had gone out of business when a big shipment of American vegetable oil hit the market.

Over the years, a cozy economic equation evolved: When U.S. farm prices were depressed by production gluts, the volume of food aid rose. The size of American generosity seemed tied to conditions on the American farm. In 1999, the Clinton administration tripled the amount of wheat bought for food aid, buying millions of metric tons in the hope of lifting prices from their lowest levels in two decades. That effort included one of the biggest aid deals in U.S. history up to that time, as Washington spent about $250 million to donate wheat to Russia, countering the efforts of the Europeans and others to sell wheat there. Two years later, when food-aid orders for rice slowed in 2001, lawmakers from rice states wrote the White House, complaining that mills were closing. The next year, federal purchases of rice for food-aid programs jumped 53 percent to $81.2 million.

European food-aid policy had also originally begun as a way to get rid of surplus crops. Spurred on by subsidies tied to production, European farmers became famous for producing towering mounds of excess food. The additional costs related to these surpluses—separate export subsidies to move the commodities and payments to store or dispose of any crops that couldn't be consumed within Europe or exported—became a huge drain on the European Union's budget. Mounting taxpayer protests over these costs prompted the EU to change its farm-subsidy regime; most subsidies linked to production were scrapped, and the support was instead doled out as direct income payments to farmers to maintain income stability regardless of the amount of crop production. Within a few years, the overwhelming surpluses disappeared. And so did the rationale for moving crops through food aid. In 1996, the EU food-aid policy switched to donating cash to buy food as close to the recipients as possible rather than always sending food from Europe.

As Ethiopia descended into famine in 2003, the EU was thus able to provide cash to first purchase food available locally. In his warehouse, Jerman Amente showed off 7,000 tons of grain packed in bags stamped with the Swedish flag; Sweden had donated cash to Ethiopia's disaster-relief organization, some of which was used to buy a portion of Jerman's surplus for distribution to the hungry.

Andrew Natsios, the administrator of the U.S. Agency for International Development, wanted to do the same. He felt handcuffed by the U.S. food-aid legislation in addressing the Ethiopian famine. Buying locally would speed up the journey of food to the hungry, he argued; gathering up and then hauling U.S. commodities halfway around the world could consume more than four months. Local purchases, he said, would also encourage Ethiopia's farmers by giving them a market. And, he insisted, it would be cheaper. U.S. legislation required that 75 percent of food aid must leave the country on vessels owned by American companies (shipping companies having borrowed a page from agribusiness's political playbook), which tended to charge some of the steepest rates on the high seas. Overall, U.S. officials calculated, roughly half the cost of getting American food aid to the hungry was being consumed by transportation, storage, and handling. World Food Program logistics experts in Addis Ababa figured that transportation and handling from the United States to Ethiopia in 2003 added nearly $200 to the cost of each ton of grain.

Natsios, who grew up listening to stories of his family's experience with hunger in Greece during World War II, told *The Wall Street Journal* in 2003 that he would like to spend 10 percent of his food-aid budget on local food. But at that time he didn't dare approach Congress with that request. "It would cause a huge controversy" in the farm lobby, he said. "But we need more flexibility in the way the law is written."

He knew food aid was captive to the entrenched interests known as the Iron Triangle. The three sides of the triangle consisted of farmers and other agricultural interests, the shippers, and the humanitarian aid groups that distributed the food to the hungry. The farmers and shippers would vehemently fight any change to the requirement that all food aid be home-grown crops. And the relief agencies warned that buying food abroad and thereby slashing funds spent on U.S. commodities would erode the farm and shipping sectors' support for food aid. Without that political lobbying clout, the aid workers doubted they could win as much congressional funding for food aid solely on the principle that fighting famine and hunger was the morally right thing for America to do. Only narrow economic self-interest, they believed, could win the day.

When the petition from American farm groups asking for more food-aid exports reached the White House, there was no one with any political influence strong enough to oppose it.

Not only did the Iron Triangle not yield to the needs of Ethiopian farmers in the 2003 famine, but its representatives boldly followed the trail of hunger looking for *more* business.

In the lobby of the luxurious Addis Ababa Sheraton, where classical music wafted around a water fountain and tearoom, a sign pointed to a reception on the second floor. The host was the U.S. National Dry Bean Council, which had come to Ethiopia in the middle of the 2003 famine seeking to get its members' beans into the food-aid mix. Although about 5 percent of U.S. production of dry beans—such as pinto beans and navy beans—went abroad in food aid, none was heading to Ethiopia. The Dry Bean Council was hoping to change that. At the reception, amid cocktails and petits fours, council representatives talked up the nutritious benefit of their beans with workers from international and local organizations that distributed the food aid. "We're always looking for the perfect fit, where we can benefit our own industry and where we can relieve hunger in the world," explained one of the council's representatives in an opening presentation.

Werqu Mekasha had put on his best suit and arrived early. A short, gregarious man, he was the local director of an American-funded group that helped organize small Ethiopian farmers into cooperatives. Some of his farmers grew beans. He thought this bean council from the other side of the world might be a new customer.

When Bob Green, the executive director of the Michigan Bean Commission, wandered by and introduced himself, Werqu enthusiastically grabbed the visitor's hand. "Can you help our farmers sell their beans in America?" he asked hopefully.

"Actually," Green said, "we represent American bean growers."

"Oh," said a crestfallen Werqu, dropping the American's hand. "Then you're our competitor."

The next day, just outside Nazareth on the road to Djibouti, two Ethiopian lentil farmers were also surprised to be staring down their competition. They were barefoot, and wearing pants and shirts that were an assemblage of rags stitched together in a riotous patchwork of colors and materials. Their fields, which they worked with their hands, were behind them as they paused to watch a caravan of food-aid trucks rumble past. From one of the trucks dripped a light trail of cargo. The farmers scurried to the road and scooped up some of the spillage: lentils, most likely from the Palouse, perhaps from Gary Heaton's silos in Spokane.

"Why would America send lentils?" asked a third farmer, Bashada Iffa, who left his field to join the group. "We grow lentils in Ethiopia."

During the previous four years, Ethiopia had produced an average of about 35,000 tons of lentils, and had even exported about 1,200 tons. Bashada, a young man in his twenties, was tending his own lentils on ten acres of land stretching along the Djibouti road when he spied the food-aid caravan. He had once welcomed American grain and beans and peas. The previous year, his family received about 65 pounds of wheat and other food aid to make it through the drought. But this season, the rains returned, and his corn, beans, and lentils looked good. He believed he might reap a surplus, especially in lentils. Now, he saw American food aid as a threat. "If we have a good harvest, I think these American lentils will only hurt our price," Bashada said. He scratched his head, reaching under the bill of a blue baseball cap that had also come from the United States. "I think America should buy *our* lentils," he concluded. He readjusted his cap. Stitched into the crown were the words *Good Luck*.

CHAPTER 7

Water, Water Everywhere

Bahir Dar, Ethiopia, 2003

Tesfahun Belachew was finding it difficult to live up to his name. *Tesfahun* means "be hope" in the Amharic language, yet he was the very definition of despair. He was draped in rags and had twirled a woolly scarf into a turban on his head—the makeshift outfit of a man without a penny in his pockets. The drought had turned his field to dust, choking any chance to grow corn or millet or rice. For nine months, since the beginning of the year, his family had survived on food aid from abroad.

Any hope ran swiftly away, right past his feet. The Ribb River, a tributary of Ethiopia's mighty Blue Nile River, flowed directly beside his one-acre patch. As he paced the muddy banks of the Ribb, Tesfahun uttered one of the most confounding and pitiful laments ever heard in Africa: "The water is right here," he said. "But we can't get it out." Why not? Why not siphon out some water for irrigation? "We would like to, of course," Tesfahun explained. "We have no money for pipes or pumps, and no one will build dams or canals for us. We are told the water isn't for us. It is for Egypt."

Throughout the famine, the Blue Nile and its tributaries flowed strong and steady. The Blue Nile begins at Ethiopia's Lake Tana, which is fed by a number of smaller rivers such as the Ribb originating in the country's northern and central highlands, where rainfall is often plentiful. From Lake Tana, the Blue Nile becomes one of Africa's great waterways, cascading down a series of dramatic, untamed gorges as it carves a 560-mile arc through central Ethiopia. It rushes boldly into Sudan, and in Khartoum it meets up with the White Nile coming from the south to form the great Nile, which surges northward into Egypt.

The Blue Nile provides about two-thirds of the Nile water flowing through Egypt; in all, rivers originating in Ethiopia contribute 85 percent of the Nile water. In Egypt, that water, coursing through a vast web of dams and irrigation canals first commissioned by the pharaohs, turns millions of desert acres into fertile fields. A cornucopia of Egyptian fruits and vegetables and grains gives life to millions of people. Yet on the banks of Ethiopia's Blue Nile and its tributaries, countless farmers and their families desperately hold out their hands for food aid to stave off starvation.

The famine of 2003 exposed one of Africa's bitterest ironies: The land that feeds the Nile is unable to feed itself. Tesfahun and others had come to a brutal conclusion: The world's powers had decided that Egypt should prosper and Ethiopia should beg. "The U.S. gives us $500 million in food aid this year, and it's gone, it's eaten up. But it never brings additional value to the country," fumed Shiferaw Jarso Tedecha, Ethiopia's minister of water resources, as the famine raged. A big billboard outside the ministry proclaimed "Water Is Life"; inside, walls were plastered with posters blaring slogans like, "No Water, No Life." Shiferaw was embarrassed that so many of his countrymen were starving, and angry that his ministry was powerless to help. "Now, if that money would go to irrigation projects or power projects," he said, punching the air with a finger, "it can keep on helping every year. Every day it would make money."

But for centuries, treaties and threats and geopolitics had prevented that from happening. From the time the pharaohs built the pyramids along the Nile and first harnessed the rhythm of the river for irrigation, Egyptians had looked upon the Nile waters as their own. In the colonial era, European rulers engineered treaties that divvied up use of the lower Nile between Egypt and Sudan (where the British grew cotton), to the exclusion of Ethiopia, the rare African country never to be colonized and thus without representation at the great councils of Europe. Ethiopia's rulers feared that if they built any dams to divert water away, the country would be invaded by the more powerful countries downstream.

During the 1960s, at the height of the Cold War, the Nile waters became a bargaining chit in the high-stakes poker match between the superpowers. The Soviet Union helped its client state Egypt construct the vast Aswan High Dam to better manage the flow of the Nile. The United States countered by drawing up plans to build a series of dams on the Blue Nile in Ethiopia, an American ally at the time. A young boy named Takele Tarekegn was leading his family's cattle to drink in the Koga River, a Blue Nile tributary, one day when he encountered a group of strangers surveying the landscape. He later overheard village elders talking excitedly about "Americans" and the dams they planned to build and the bountiful harvests that would follow. From that day on, Takele kept one eye on his cows and another on the distant horizon, waiting for the Americans to return.

But the geopolitics in the Horn of Africa took a sharp turn. Egypt shifted to the Western camp and was showered with hundreds of millions of dollars from the United States and other allied countries to rehabilitate and expand its Nile canal network. In Ethiopia, the U.S. plans for dams on the Blue Nile were shelved; it was no time to upset Egypt. Those blueprints were then relegated to the dark recesses of the archives after Ethiopia's emperor Haile Selassie was toppled by a Marxist dictator in 1974 and Ethiopia became a Soviet client state. All the country got after that was military equipment from the Eastern bloc and food aid from the West. Takele never saw those Americans again.

Modern Nile politics, following the Camp David peace accords between Egypt and Israel in 1978, have continued to favor Egypt because of its strategic position in the Middle East. Even after Ethiopia's communist regime was ousted in 1991, major international lenders and development agencies were loath to support anything upstream on the Nile—be it irrigation schemes or hydroelectric power plants—that might diminish the vital flow of water to Egypt and trigger instability there. Ethiopia, meanwhile, lacked the funds and the engineering know-how to develop its own broad irrigation network.

The disparity of fortunes dictated by the Nile geopolitics was stark. In 2003, Egypt had 8 million acres of land irrigated by thousands of miles of

Nile canals; Ethiopia had less than 500,000 acres of irrigated land. Although Ethiopia boasted vast stretches of arable land—the government estimated there were about 9 million acres that could thrive with irrigation—farmers had to rely on the erratic rains for, at best, one crop each year. In Egypt, the irrigation network using water originating in Ethiopia yielded two or three harvests annually. Egypt had harnessed the Nile to electrify the country. In Ethiopia, less than 1 percent of the nation's hydropower potential had been tapped; fewer than 10 percent of its people had electricity. Ethiopia's per capita consumption of electricity was the lowest in Africa. That had led to a massive harvest of the country's trees for fuel and, in turn, widespread soil erosion. Every evening, millions of fires were lit to prepare the evening meal and provide light. A thick blanket of smoke covered the crowded cities.

Most smoke obscures. But this nightly smoke curling up from cooking and heating fires all over the country clearly illuminated the fact that, once again, the development experts hadn't heeded the lessons of history. "There is no precedent for a country developing without harnessing its rivers and utilizing its water resources," said David Grey, the World Bank's senior water adviser.

"We've seen the writing on the wall during the famine," said Sam Nyambi, who was the head of the United Nations Development Program office in Addis Ababa in 2003. He wrung his hands and paced in his office at the grandiose UN building in Addis, built in the heady early days of African independence. The famine, he said, injected an urgency into the nascent deliberations of a body called the Nile Basin Initiative, which schemed to devise a more equitable sharing of the Nile waters among the ten countries in the basin. "The Nile for so long has been a river of conflict," Nyambi said. "We must turn it into a river of development and hope. The amount of food aid coming into Ethiopia can't continue. Something's got to be done."

World Bank officials conceded that the bank didn't want to interfere with geopolitical strategy by granting loans for dams or irrigation projects on the Blue Nile. They argued that, in any case, Egypt or Sudan would have raised objections, citing downstream impact, and blocked the projects. But as the Blue Nile rushed past the famine fields in 2003, "we began to think more deeply of the implications of the Nile usage. The international community can't go on forever ignoring the inequities," said another World Bank official. "Water and environmental degradation need to be targeted if Ethiopia is to grow. It's hard to think of the Ethiopian economy being viable without access to the Blue Nile."

Most every developed economy in the world has benefited from harnessing its waterways. America's mighty rivers, particularly the Mississippi, became an integral part of the agricultural trade; flotillas of barges laden with corn, wheat, and soybeans shuttle between grain elevators and Gulf of Mexico ports, where the crops are reloaded onto ships and dispatched around the world. Western and central Europe thrived from the commerce conducted on the Rhine and Danube rivers.

Yet Ethiopia, known across the continent as "the water tower of Africa," had remained one of the world's poorest countries and become its largest begging bowl. It defied logic. Many other places of the world—from the Middle East to the American West—faced limits to their growth and rising tensions because of water scarcities. Places such as China and India worried how their rising food production could continue while their water tables fell. But it was Ethiopia, with an abundance of water, that was the hungriest of all.

"People are very surprised when they travel around Ethiopia. You see a lot of water, we have many rivers. But yet we have drought and famine," Melese Awoke was saying as he drove alongside a rapidly flowing river while inspecting food-aid distribution sites in 2003. Before becoming a communications officer of the World Food Program, Melese was a student of Nile politics, having written his college thesis on the subject. "Ethiopia's problem is not having enough water, which is a strange thing to say in a famine," he said. "Our problem is access to the water."

Tesfahun Belachew knew that better than anyone. As he paced beside the Ribb River and his parched field, he said he was on the lookout for thieves, though there was nothing to steal. The politics of the Nile had already taken it all away.

For more than 4,000 miles, the waters of the Nile flow past some of the world's poorest, hungriest, and most war-wracked and heavily eroded landscapes. Nearly 200 million people spread over ten countries lived within the Nile basin in 2003, and that population was expected to double by

2025, making the competition for the water ever more fierce. These people, in their own ways and customs, have deified the Nile water as a god for giving sustenance and life. But they have also defiled the water with centuries of jealousy, covetousness, and fear.

"This river, the Nile, has caused a hostile environment since the creation of humans," snarled Belay Ejigu, Ethiopia's agriculture minister in 2003. He spat out his words as if they were bitter wine, seething that so many of his countrymen must starve while so much water rushes past untouched. Asked how Ethiopia's farmers could benefit from the use of the Nile, he scoffed, "Ask the Egyptians, they're the ones with the irrigation."

"For Egypt, the Nile is the main source of life," proclaimed Abdel Fattah Metawie, the chairman of the Nile water sector in Egypt's Ministry of Water Resources and Irrigation. The Nile sauntered through the center of Cairo; a few blocks from Metawie's office, a party-boat captain, dressed like a pharaoh, tried to entice tourists with a lunchtime cruise. "If we don't have the Nile we wouldn't have the pyramids. Why are there no pyramids in Libya, why are there no pyramids in Saudi Arabia? Because they don't have the Nile!" Metawie argued. He noted how the Nile inspired such architecture and aided the movement of material, how it was at the center of ancient Egyptian worship and mythology, and how the Nile's seasonal rhythms were used to record the passage of time and develop new agricultural methods. "The whole world has benefited from this. Why would you want to harm this?"

Egyptian farmer and cattleman Samir Hamed cringed at the thought of less water flowing to Egypt. "Without the Nile, I won't plant crops or raise cattle or have anything to drink," he said. He worked a 205-acre spread about a hundred miles from the Nile, a two-hour drive on a smooth, paved road. It was the last farm before the desert, where the canals surrender to the sand. He said he was limited to using 10,000 cubic meters of water a day. If he wanted to expand his operation, he would need to add on to the canals. "We are the last drop of the Nile," he said proudly.

Fifteen years earlier, this Ponderosa of the Sahara had been all sand. But in 2003, while Ethiopia starved, Hamed tended to fifty acres of apple trees; fifty acres of grapes; twenty acres of apricot trees; forty greenhouses filled with cucumbers, peppers, broccoli, brussels sprouts, lettuce, cherry tomatoes, and eggplants; and six hundred head of cattle, all thanks to the water that began as rainfall in the highlands of Ethiopia. If the Ethiopians likewise tapped the Nile, Hamed worried, "I'm sure it would affect the amount of water we can use."

Outside one of his barns, a group of water buffalo calves crowded into a pen and jostled for position under a series of sprinklers. The calves had come for their regular shower. That too was Ethiopian water. "It makes them happy, speeds up the fattening process," Hamed said, laughing at the sight of his showering cows. "Happier cows eat more!"

For Mohamed Abd-Elsalam, a farmer who tilled a much smaller plot, the Nile benefits were more existential. "The Nile is my soul, and without a soul, a man is dead," he said. He rose from a prayer rug in the shade of a tree to show off his single acre of land, which is connected to the Nile by three miles of irrigation canals. He simply turned a tap—"The Americans built this, in 1994," he said, pointing to the irrigation hardware—and water filled the furrows of his crops: wheat to feed his family and garlic for export.

He and three fellow farmers discussed the origin of their precious water. "It comes from the Aswan High Dam," said one.

"No," insisted another, "it comes from Sudan."

"No, no," corrected Abd-Elsalam. "It rains in Ethiopia and the water comes to Egypt, to the high dam and then to us."

Tension and suspicion and misinformation flowed freely along with the Nile water. The Egyptians feared that Ethiopia, perhaps with funding from Israel, was building dams to block the flow of the Nile water. In his Cairo office, Abdel Metawie confirmed that these suspicions reached into elite, educated circles. "Parliamentarians and reporters are always attacking Ethiopia, saying Ethiopia is building dams with U.S. and Israeli help, they'll take our water," he said. "As a technician here, I know it's not true." He shrugged his shoulders, conceding that technical evidence was no match for paranoid conjecture.

In Addis, Ethiopia's water minister, Shiferaw Jarso Tedecha, sputtered at such fanciful accusations. "When I visit Egypt, journalists ask me about dams on the Blue Nile constructed by Israel and other donors. Why do they ask this? There are satellites, you could see the dams, we can't hide them underground," he said. "Why would we stop the water? These are ignorant people who say this. Why would we stop the water and keep it all for ourselves? We get rain every year, we would flood!"

The Ethiopians were convinced they were under constant surveillance by Egypt. They believed Egyptian diplomats based in Addis traveled only north, to the Blue Nile region, to scrutinize water levels and spy on farmers. Ethiopians also suspected that Egyptians strategically targeted positions in international agencies to control water policy. "An Englishman once told me that in the international finance agencies, in the water departments, when you knock on the door for financing, the first person to open the door is an Egyptian, who will tell you to go away," said Teferra Beyene, an engineer in Ethiopia's Ministry of Water Resources. "This is what we hear."

To alleviate this mutual suspicion, Ethiopia had several times invited Egyptian opinion makers to visit the most wretched, hungriest places of the country. They flew government officials, parliamentarians, and journalists to areas north and east of Lake Tana where the starvation was particularly bad in 1984 and again in 2003. These were areas of deep poverty and severe land degradation, a chain of denuded plateaus where the rains carried away the soil and carved deep gullies into the ground. Peasant farmers struggled to eke out a living from the depleted land, squeezing every bit of nutrition from the anemic dirt. Hunger wasn't seasonal; it was chronic.

The Egyptians thought they had been spirited away to another planet. "After we take the Egyptians there, it convinces them," said Minister Shiferaw. "They see the drought areas, they see how people suffer. For humanity itself, these people have to improve their lives. And we showed the Egyptians the potential we have for irrigation."

Abbas Al Tarabeely went on the trip with open eyes and an open mind. An editor of the Egyptian newspaper *Al-Wafd*, he traveled to Ethiopia with suspicions and returned to Cairo with ideas. "Why not create water-storage areas for irrigation, like small dams? They would help relieve suffering while also not placing too much burden on the Nile," he said. "It is important to let Egyptians know that the Ethiopians are going through enough without making matters worse by focusing on conspiracy theories."

Metawie agreed. "They are really suffering in Ethiopia," he said. He returned from the famine tour in Ethiopia with a warning for his countrymen: Millions of starving people on Egypt's southern flank portended instability for the entire region. Without development of the Blue Nile basin, he predicted, "you have to expect a crisis in the area."

The Egyptians were also alarmed when they saw the amount of soil erosion that turned the waters of the Nile tributaries dark. Much of that would end up as silt at the bottom of the Aswan dam, reducing the storage capacity there. The misery of Ethiopia, they saw, was also exacting a toll in Egypt.

"From the helicopter, the Egyptians could see that not even a tree grows to hold back the soil. They were really surprised," said Yacob Wondimkun, the commissioner for sustainable agriculture and environmental rehabilitation in the Lake Tana region that is home to the origins of the Blue Nile. As the tour continued, Yacob pointed out that the only trees still standing surrounded Orthodox churches on what is seen as holy land. "Tree museums," Yacob joked. Then he turned serious. "Unless we have watershed management in Ethiopia," Yacob insisted, "the whole system will be hurt."

Teferra Beyene, the engineer from the ministry of water, suggested a closer inspection of the neglect, proposing an overland journey to the source of the Blue Nile, and the source of so much Ethiopian suffering and anger. It would be a bone-jarring eleven-hour odyssey over rugged roads that sometimes dissolved into dirt and gravel pathways while skimming flat plateaus or descending steep gorges. It would also be a roller-coaster ride through the politics of the Nile. "You must come to understand how we can have famine with so much water," Teferra said.

The journey began at daybreak in Addis Ababa, as legions of women—as many as 15,000 of them—headed to the hills and forests surrounding the capital. They would spend all day among the eucalyptus and fir trees, collecting branches, leaves and twigs, and other material to burn. By nightfall, the women would be trundling back down the hills in a slow, stooped trot, with bundles weighing seventy to a hundred pounds strapped to their backs. If they were lucky, a bundle might fetch seventy cents. Until more hydropower is developed, the backbreaking work of the women fuelwood carriers, as they are called, would continue to be indispensable. Biomass fuels such as wood, charcoal, and cow dung accounted for more than 90 percent of the country's energy consumption in 2003.

"Such hard work," Teferra said as he navigated past a group of fuelwood carriers trudging to the outskirts of town. "It's heartbreaking to see. Such heavy loads." He lamented the content of those bundles, too. "The biomass that people burn is needed to preserve the watershed, and the cow dung to replenish the soil," he said. "The Nile policy has so many impacts."

Teferra was a tall man in his forties with a gentle, scholarly demeanor. For him, this trip to the North was a journey back in time. "It is ironic," he said, "that the most problematic area in the country for food has been the Blue Nile and Tekeze River basin. That whole area is prone to drought. It's been cultivated for thousands of years with no irrigation beyond small projects. The land is very eroded. One of my grandfathers comes from that area. When I was young, he told me stories of forests and wild animals. Now, when I go, there aren't even bushes."

Addis's urban sprawl of little shacks with sheet-iron roofs gave way to the round thatch-roofed *tukuls* of rural Ethiopia. About fifty miles north of Addis, Teferra brought the white Toyota Land Cruiser to a stop on the road leading to the town of Debre Libanos. He walked to the edge of a cliff and pointed to a waterfall in the distance—proof, he said, of the power-generating potential of Ethiopia's rivers. In the valley below, farmers scrambled up and down the slopes, tending crops. "These are very steep slopes, all terraced to plant sorghum, beans, and teff [a staple grain]," Teferra explained. "The soil is so thin, but still the people live here and farm." He turned to walk back to the Toyota. "I feel terrible for these people," he said.

Several small rivers began in this highland area and made their way to join up with the Blue Nile. As the road descended to the lowlands, past some heavily eroded fields that looked like moonscapes with their brown barren crevices and oddly shaped outcrops sculpted by the wind and rainwater, Teferra explained his ministry's strategy: "If you have irrigation projects, you could move these people here on the slopes to those irrigated areas and give this land, the land where they live now, time to recover." By lying fallow for a couple of years, he said, the soil would replenish and the yields would improve, should the farmers move back.

A few miles beyond the town of Goha Tsiyon, and about 120 miles from Addis, the road spiraled down a canyon. At the bottom, the Blue Nile alternately meandered through straightaways or tumbled over rapids. Only two roads in the central part of the country crossed the Blue Nile, so inevitably the traffic became heavier and more ponderous, slowing to a creep, particularly on the more treacherous stretches where trucks crawled and wheezed around the descending curves.

Traffic came to a halt altogether at a dicey-looking bridge. Only one vehicle was allowed to cross at a time, and given the rickety wooden supports, even that seemed optimistic. Below, the water churned an angry brown, the color of the topsoil it had picked up along the way. The standing traffic gave soldiers a chance to peer into each vehicle and scan for bandits and smugglers.

The ministry had a plan for this gorge, too, Teferra noted while the Land Cruiser idled and waited to cross. It called for a dam to be built a bit farther down the canyon. This old bridge would be swallowed by water. The top of the dam would serve as the new bridge. "The water would fill the gorge twenty-five kilometers long or so [about fifteen miles]. No people live here, so it wouldn't displace anyone," Teferra explained. "It would be a project for hydro-electricity, but it could also pump water for irrigation. It would also provide flood and sediment control. We could export some of the power to Egypt. If we develop the project together, we both would gain." If only. Those plans had been sitting on the ministry's shelves for decades.

After a slow climb out of the canyon, Teferra suggested a break at the first watering hole to appear in the crossroads town of Dejen, the Alem Hotel. The bar was dark and cool. Posters of American actress Alyssa Milano and some international soccer stars decorated the walls. A waiter hastily cleared a table on the terrace outside. Under blue Pepsi and red Coca-Cola umbrellas—even here the cola wars raged—Teferra consulted a map and chose the road to the left. The one to the right, he said, might be quicker to Lake Tana, but it was known to be patrolled by bandits. One of his ministry colleagues had been chased by a gang on a recent trip.

The road less taken was a circuitous path, made even more so by the frequent construction detours choreographed by Chinese contractors hired by the government to rehabilitate the main stretches. But it provided the incongruous setting that Teferra desired: an ever-thicker network of creeks and streams—the source water of the Blue Nile—in a region suffering from ever-thinner production of food. Some of the waterways rushed by; some took their time. They all flowed past crops literally dying for a drop of water, all eventually ending up in Lake Tana and then the mighty Blue Nile.

"The farmers always ask me, 'How can this be?'" Teferra said as he stopped to marvel at the fast-flowing Koga River. Back in the 1960s, the Koga was one of the rivers selected by American surveyors for a network of dams that, it was promised then, would provide irrigation to the surrounding fields by the dawn of the twenty-first century. "Well," said Teferra, "the next century has come and we still don't have anything."

As the parched land gave way to marshes, the town of Bahir Dar and Lake Tana came into view. Bahir Dar hugged the southern edge of the lake, where the Blue Nile emerged. Teferra stopped the Land Cruiser as it crossed a bridge. He pointed to a metal gate in the water, right near the river's mouth. "That regulates the flow out of the lake. We've increased the level of the lake by two meters and assure a minimum flow into the Blue Nile," he explained. "We don't have a big peak of water anymore, but a steady flow. This is what the Egyptians want, so even in the dry season, there is a guaranteed minimum flow in the river."

Twenty miles downstream thundered the spectacular Tis Isat Falls, where the Blue Nile plunged over its first escarpment. Above the falls, the water lazily meandered through lush green meadows, where children tended to grazing cows and chased after herons and ibises. It was a stark contrast to the turbulent chaos at the bottom of the falls, as the Blue Nile crashed into a pool of rocks. Before the falls, some of the water was diverted to a parallel canal, which channeled the water through a seventy-meter drop that powered a hydrostation generating seventy-three megawatts of energy. (It was an amount that would electrify about 50,000 single-family homes in the United States; in Ethiopia, it was one of the few power plants in the entire country beyond the main cities.) At the bottom of the station, the water rejoined the Blue Nile and continued on its way. "See, we don't take out any of the water," Teferra wisecracked. "It's all still here."

A three-story pink building rose on the eastern bank of the Blue Nile where it emerged from Lake Tana. It was the office of the Sustainable Agricultural and Environmental Rehabilitation Commission. A poster depicting two nurses tending to a thin man lying in a bed was plastered on the front-door window: "Beware of AIDS." There was also a decal listing a dozen "principles of ethical public service": integrity, loyalty, transparency, confidentiality, honesty, accountability, serving the public interest, exercising legitimate authority, impartiality, respecting law, responsiveness, and exercising leadership.

Yacob Wondimkun, the public servant who headed the commission and who had earlier given the touring Egyptians a view of the suffering along the Blue Nile, bounded out of the building with a fistful of blueprints. They were his grand plans to irrigate a minimum of 70,000 acres on the plains east of Lake Tana. Several rivers, including the Ribb, run through the area. They originate in the mountains sixty miles to the east, where famine and land degradation had been the worst. During the seasonal rains, when the precipitation is good, the rivers flood the plains. The water stands in the fields until it evaporates, and then the farmers plant. If no further rain comes, the crops wither and die. Yacob's irrigation plan called for some of the water to be stored in a highland reservoir to control flooding during the rainy season and then to provide irrigation during the dry periods. "The amount of water saved from evaporation in the fields after the floods would compensate for the amount of water used for irrigation," Teferra explained. "So it wouldn't take any water out of the system. For the Egyptians, this should be viewed as a drainage project, because the water drained from the floods would be used for irrigation."

Yacob led the way to the Ribb, and there, standing in the parched fields, he unfurled his blueprints. Tesfahun Belachew, standing watch for intruders, came over for a look. The farmer complained that the drought and the inability to irrigate his land with the water running past his feet had made him dependent on international aid.

"This is so sad and frustrating for us," Yacob said, shaking his head. But he told Tesfahun that if the plans on his blueprints came to life, he wouldn't need food aid anymore. *If*, he emphasized. Until the world supported investment in his plans, they would remain just sketches on paper.

"Actually, this is a valley that can produce food aid for other people," Yacob noted. "Our farmers always say, 'Why not help us grow food and then buy it from us and give it to people over the mountain, just one hundred kilometers [about sixty miles] away. Is it better to feed us with food aid, or should we be helped to feed ourselves?'"

The commissioner gave Tesfahun a sympathetic pat on the back. "People downstream, in Egypt and Sudan, they must see that something must be done," Yacob said. "Your brother is without food and you have food. It's nonsense." He told Tesfahun to hold tight to the promise of his name. Be hope.

On the drive back to Lake Tana, a cluster of large brown buildings appeared on the horizon. The sun brightly bounced off the tin roofs.

"Guess what those are?" Yacob challenged his guests.

Chicken coops?

"Try again."

Greenhouses?

"No."

A sign heralded the local operation of Ethiopia's Disaster Prevention and Preparedness Commission. The buildings were food-aid storage warehouses. "They should be turned into grain processing factories instead of food aid warehouses," Yacob howled. "I'm providing you with irony."

Crossing back over the Blue Nile bridge at its Lake Tana source, Teferra pointed to another scene from Ethiopia's theater of the absurd. A blue-and-white bus had backed down the muddy bank right to the river's edge, the rear wheels standing in the water. The driver waded into the river and was washing the bus. Teferra erupted in laughter. "This is how we use our share of the Nile!" he proclaimed. "We wash our vehicles in the river and put the water right back in."

After a few minutes, the clean bus crawled back up the riverbank and rushed off. And so did the water of the Blue Nile, straight to Egypt.

CHAPTER 8

A Diet of Worms

Sudan, Swaziland, and Zimbabwe, 2003

As the Blue Nile rushed south and then made a sharp turn to the west, toward Sudan, it flowed through drought-choked fields and past remnants of another handmaiden of Africa's hunger. Rusted tanks, craters created by an exploded artillery shell, buildings with bullet-riddled walls—scenes from the fighting of the 1970s, 1980s, and 1990s that prompted, or were prompted by, famine in the Ethiopian countryside. Amid the fields of withered crops, they were monuments to the malevolent forces that often spread agricultural calamity and hunger across Africa.

In 2003, these forces were particularly devastating; not only were crops dying from drought, but farmers were being killed in unprecedented numbers as well. In Sudan, it was the government's campaign of genocide by starvation that was depopulating farming communities in the region of Darfur. In Swaziland and throughout southern Africa, it was a lethal disease—acquired immunodeficiency syndrome, AIDS—wiping out a generation of farmers. In Zimbabwe, it was Robert Mugabe's desperate bid to cling to power by using the violent confiscation and redistribution of farmland as a political cudgel. All these forces had allied with the long-term neglect of agriculture by the international community to make Africa in 2003 hungrier than it had ever been.

The sunrise attack on the farming community of Andarbrow was swift and merciless. Men on horses and camels swooped down from the golden brown hills of West Darfur and galloped into the settlement of Andarbrow. Firing rifles and slashing with swords and daggers, they killed and they raped and they leveled the village. By the count of Khamis Adam Hassen Okey, the raiders murdered 46 of his neighbors and flattened 150 houses. The survivors, about 800 people, scurried into the tall grass surrounding the village and hid from their attackers. "It was right after the rainy season. So the grass was up," said Okey, one of Andarbrow's village elders. That the grass was at its apex was their one lucky break, for it gave them cover in their flight.

But their crops were up, too. And that was bad. Sorghum, millet, sesame, peanuts, tomatoes, okra were all ready to be harvested after a summer of hard work. The raiders burned it all. They looted the food storage bins and destroyed the grains. They chopped down the fruit trees. They stole the animals. They made sure there was nothing left, nary a crumb, for the villagers to return to.

After five days of wandering through the bush—creeping under the cover of dark, lying low during the sunlit hours—Okey and the survivors stumbled into Fur Baranga, a market town near the border with Chad. There they found thousands of other farmers from other villages who had also been violently uprooted from their land. All of them were victims of the Sudan government's brutal campaign against rebel movements in Darfur, a campaign that would be branded "genocide" by many other governments around the world. As they recounted their experiences to each other, the elders of the various villages-that-were-no-more wondered why all the crops had to be destroyed. Eventually, they understood that hunger, brought on by the deliberate destruction of food and the murder and displacement of the farmers who grew it, was a vital tool of that genocide.

The shell-shocked refugees from Andarbrow settled inside the waist-high walls of the scruffy community hospital, quickly building little thatch huts around the big *lalope* tree in the center of the grounds. They took jobs sweeping up the dirt alleys of the village market and making bricks from mud. And, greatly humiliated by growing malnutrition and hunger, they held out their hands for international food aid. "We are farmers. We used to grow everything we needed," Okey said, weakly puffing out his chest with a last ounce of pride. "But if we go out from this place to plant, we will be killed."

The people of Darfur, a vast sunbaked expanse the size of France in western Sudan, were no strangers to food shortages. An estimated 100,000 had died during the drought that ravaged the Horn of Africa in 1984. The farmers who survived were largely able to recover and resume work in their fields when the rains returned. They adhered to rules of survival passed down through generations: Protect seeds for the next planting season, keep animals alive, cling to your land no matter what.

But in 2003, the hunger was willfully engineered by destroying all aspects of the agricultural system. Seed stocks were burned. Animals were stolen or killed. The implements of cultivation, such as hoes and tractors, were smashed. The farmers were driven from the land. The master plan in Khartoum was that there would be no recovery—at least not until the rebellion was quashed.

Seeking to silence Darfur rebel groups who were pressing for a greater voice in national politics and economic development, the largely Arab government in Khartoum unleashed marauding militias known as the Janjaweed—the men on horses and camels who had laid waste to Andarbrow. Composed mainly of Arab nomads and cattle herders, these militias had been skirmishing with Darfur's African farmers in a battle over arable land that had been simmering for years. Now the government escalated the enmity between the groups, sometimes even deploying helicopter gunships to support the Janjaweed's raids.

Tens of thousands of farmers and their children were killed. Those who managed to survive were herded into refugee camps inside Darfur or chased across the border into Chad. Eventually, the number of people penned up like cattle would swell to more than 2 million. In those camps of flimsy shelters, hastily set up by international relief agencies on sandy plains, child malnourishment rates soared to 40 percent.

The abandoned fields became eerie wastelands. Along a dirt path through scrub brush from El Geneina, the main city in West Darfur, to Fur Baranga on the border with Chad, one destroyed village gave way to another. The remnants of civilization were tossed every which way, as if a tornado had blown through: Shards of clay water pots. Strips of clothing. Soles of shoes. Pieces of corrugated metal roofs. Chunks of thatched walls.

Foundation stones of schools and health centers. Fields were trampled, trees burned. There were no people, only the cows, sheep, goats, and camels of the herders who had moved in to occupy the land.

"They waited until the crops were up, then the Janjaweed brought their animals to eat it all," said Abdalla Mohammed Yagob, who settled on a barren piece of land in a refugee camp just beyond the Fur Baranga hospital. "Tomatoes, onions, watermelon, peanuts, soybeans, sorghum, wheat. The animals ate it all before the harvest. Then the Janjaweed burned our villages, and stole our cattle and destroyed the food we had stored. We only came here because we had nothing to eat." Yagob scratched his head. "I don't understand. The Janjaweed don't cultivate. So who will grow the food?" he wondered. "There will be hunger all over."

That would indeed happen, as one planting season after another would pass with Darfur's surviving farmers confined in the camps. "We would like to go back to our homes and plant again," Yagob said, "but we are afraid the Janjaweed will come back and destroy the farms again."

Amid so much hunger, so many farmers were afraid to plant or harvest. This new wave of destruction in western Sudan had been preceded by two decades of fighting in the country's fertile southern region. More than 2 million people, most of them peasant farmers, died in that conflict, and millions of acres of arable farmland became a battleground. Given peace, Sudan, with its rain-blessed highland regions and its fertile land along the Nile River, could be food self-sufficient, and even a food exporter. Instead, it had become an emaciated food-aid welfare case.

Indeed, the government in Khartoum left it up to the international community to keep the farmers of Darfur from starving. Amid escalating food shortages and soaring prices, government officials would deny calls to shift grain stored in other regions to Darfur. "There is a food gap in Darfur, but it's not so significant," Ahmad Ali El Hassan, the director of rainfed (nonirrigated) farming in the Ministry of Agriculture, would later say. "Humanitarian assistance will fill the gap."

A cooling breeze sailed through his spacious office in the ministry, a two-story yellow and green building with palm trees and roses flourishing in an interior courtyard. It was a stark contrast to the crowded, sunscorched conditions in the refugee camps of Darfur. Hassan blamed the Darfur fighting on tribal conflicts and claimed that the farmers had an easier life in the camps where they could receive their food from relief work-ers rather than having to grow it themselves. Still, he insisted farming would soon recover. "Inshallah," he said. God willing.

But in the camps of West Darfur, God's will wasn't coming into play. "No way I'm going back," said Matair Abdall, emphatically shaking her head. Her village of Willo, she tearfully explained, was destroyed by the Janjaweed in late 2003. Instead of harvesting her sorghum, she sat on the dirt floor of a round thatched hut, weaving baskets with two dozen other women. In the densely packed maze of the camp, every day was the same, except some days the wind blew the sand harder than others. Their old lives were governed by the rhythm of the growing season, a constant cycle of renewal; life in the camp was consumed with worry and fear.

"We'll never feel as safe farming again," said Asha Ashagg, a thirty-five-year-old woman nursing the youngest of her five children while she crafted a basket with colored reeds. Months after being driven out of her village, she had returned to check on her farm. Hiding in a field of grass, survey-ing the destruction, she discovered that even her mango trees and banana plants had been cut down. "Don't the Janjaweed need to eat mangoes?" she wondered in her hiding place.

Suddenly, the herders who had taken over her village were running to-ward her; she had been spotted. "Why have you come back?" they shouted as they chased her through the grass. "What is your tribe?"

Ashagg ran back to her camp. There, she swore she wouldn't return to her farm until the fighting ended. And even then, she worried, could she ever get the "blood out of the soil," or the fear from her mind?

In the small, hilly kingdom of Swaziland, obscurely nestled between South Africa and Mozambique, sixteen-year-old Makhosazane Nkhambule strug-gled to bring her four younger brothers and sisters through the hunger of 2003. The Nkhambule children, barefoot and wearing dirty, shabby clothes, lived in a one-room mud-brick shack in the little village of Maphatsindvuku. They swept the floor of the house and the dirt yard with homemade straw brooms. They tried to patch holes in the thatched roof and plug cracks in the mud walls. They walked a mile to fetch water from a well. They scavenged wood for the fire. They attended an informal school in a neighbor's house.

Makhosazane said they could do everything they needed to do, except feed themselves. "I would like to plant corn and vegetables, but we have no money to buy seeds or tools," she said. And even if they had the proper implements, Makhosazane doubted she would know what to do. "My parents never had time to teach us."

Their father had died in 1999 and their mother in 2000, both of them after wasting away from what social workers and village officials believed were complications from AIDS. Makhosazane was thirteen when she became the head of the family and the Nkhambule children became part of Swaziland's fastest-growing population group: child-headed households. By 2003, in a country where more than one-third of the adult population was stricken with AIDS, some 10 percent of households were headed by children.

The Nkhambule kids knew nothing of the rituals of farming. The garden beside the shack and the two-acre field behind it hadn't been planted since their mother died. For two years, the orphans scrounged meals where they could, asking neighbors for scraps of food and waiting for relatives in distant villages to bring something to eat. Then in 2003, as drought and hunger spread across the land, their neighbors had less to share. As the World Food Program made its rounds, handing out food to those families whose crops had failed—that was the WFP's traditional criteria—it discovered the Nkhambule children and thousands of other families who hadn't planted any crops to begin with. So the WFP's list of beneficiaries swelled to include the victims of AIDS and their dependents. "The drought combined with the illness pushed people over the edge," said Sarah Laughton, who, as the WFP's emergency coordinator in Swaziland, had scoured the towns and villages for orphaned families like the Nkhambules. Even if the rains came, she said, those families wouldn't recover.

In 2003, AIDS emerged as a new agent of hunger. Researchers even came up with a name for it: new-variant famine. In famines caused by drought, pestilence, bad agricultural policy, or unrest, it was the crops that died first. In AIDS-induced famine, it was the farmers who grew the crops who died first. In an AIDS famine, recovery wouldn't come with better weather, new government policies, a peace treaty, or improved hybrid crops. Once the farmers died, no amount of rain could make the empty fields grow.

By 2003, across southern Africa, the region of the world hardest hit by AIDS, more than 7 million farmers had died from the epidemic, according to estimates of governments and relief agencies. That had left many families with no means or experience to do the farming. Chronic food shortages loomed, with a growing number of families forever dependent on food aid. Hunger and AIDS formed a deadly tag team. As AIDS increased the food shortages, malnutrition soared, which in turn made people more susceptible to diseases feasting off a weakened immune system. AIDS worsened the hunger problem; hunger magnified the effect of AIDS.

The two scourges, working in tandem, weakened economies as well as bodies. Once-vibrant Botswana, on the other side of South Africa from Swaziland, was slowed by a shrinking labor force stricken with AIDS. Construction companies halted projects because crane operators were dying; in the bush, safari camps were losing guides. Cellular phone companies advertised their services as vital for keeping up with all the funerals. The funeral industry, in fact, was one of the rare zones of growth throughout the southern Africa region. Casket makers hammered and sawed in their workshops along the main roads, advertising as they worked. They were so busy that wood shortages were reported in several countries. There was also an epidemic of stolen street signs; the slim metal placards made good handles for those caskets.

In Swaziland, the percentage of women at prenatal clinics diagnosed with HIV (the disease that causes AIDS) had skyrocketed to more than 38 percent by 2003 from just under 4 percent in 1992. That was the second-highest prevalence rate in the world, just slightly behind Botswana's. Over the same period, per capita agricultural production in Swaziland fell by a third, even before the drought of 2003 hit. The government reported a 54 percent drop in agricultural production in households where at least one adult member died because of AIDS or other reasons.

In a traditional famine, the first to die were usually the weakest, particularly children and the elderly. In the new variety of famine, AIDS struck adults in the prime of life, leaving the children and elderly to cope. In Swaziland, the government estimated that more than 15 percent of the children under the age of fifteen were orphaned in 2003; by 2010, the country had forecast, orphans could make up 12 percent of the entire population of 1 million. International aid organizations said that if 10 percent of Swaziland's households were headed by children, even more were headed by grandparents too old and too weak to work the fields.

"A drought is usually in certain areas of a country, but AIDS is all over. It is an unbelievable impoverishment agent," said Derek von Wissell, the national director of Swaziland's Emergency Response Council on HIV/AIDS during the 2003 hunger crisis. Von Wissell said aid workers discovered children who hadn't had any adult contact for months. He had encountered four siblings, led by an eight year old, wandering naked down a road. Their mother had died, and they had walked fifteen miles in search of their grandmother. Von Wissell helped them look, unsuccessfully, and then took them back to their home village, where they were put under the care of the local chief.

At a WFP food-distribution center in the southern Swazi village of Ngolgolweni, women and children gathered under a big *mopani* tree in a school yard to wait for their rations. They were "widows, women abandoned by their men, orphans—all those who can't plant, who have no resources," said Dudu Ndlangamandla, a member of the local relief committee.

Bags of food from around the world were lined up in neat rows: rice from Algeria, peas from Japan, a corn-soybean blend from the United States. A fourteen-year-old boy walked over from the school to register for his rations; he said he lived with his seventeen-year-old sister. An elderly woman with her left big toe sticking out through a hole in her tennis shoe also came down from the school and joined the line. She earned a bit of money helping to cook for the schoolchildren, but she said she couldn't grow enough to feed her own family of six children since her husband died. He had been "poisoned," his widow said, *poisoned* being one of the euphemisms for AIDS.

At a small community center close to the capital of Mbabane, a kettle of porridge cooked on an outside fire, and a big pot of vegetable soup boiled on a stove inside. It was one of a network of neighborhood locations offering a warm meal to orphans every day after school. "We had been seeing the children scavenging for food in trash cans, and we said we needed to give them a meal to eat," explained Janet Aphane, one of twenty local women, most of them retired teachers, nurses, and civil servants, who prepared the food. They began with thirty children a day and a year later were up to eighty. "We had to turn away a lot of children, because our resources limited us," Aphane said. "About 500 children would come if we threw open the doors."

Grandmothers, too. For they were going hungry in increasing numbers as they took in their orphaned grandchildren. During the famine of 2003, the WFP found Mandathane Ndzima struggling to survive in the rural Swazi village of Mpathni. At the age of seventy-three, she was caring for twenty grandchildren. Her children had been dying one by one. Her youngest son died first, of tuberculosis, a common illness of those weakened by AIDS. Then her oldest son died in a car accident. Then the middle son died, and his wife, too, of tuberculosis. In total, they left twelve children behind. In 2003, as the famine worsened, a fourth child, a forty-year-old daughter also suffering from tuberculosis, returned home with her eight children. "When my sons were alive, we had enough to eat," Ndzima said. They filled the family's plot of several acres with corn and sweet potatoes. After the sons died, the family's few oxen, which pulled the plow, were stolen. In 2002 and 2003, the grandmother and her grandchildren planted only a small portion, without fertilizer, and most of that harvest was lost to the drought. Tall grass grew over the rest of the field. Ndzima hoped to cut some and bundle it up to sell as thatch. "If I get enough," she said, "maybe I can pay someone to assist us in plowing."

She sat beside her last remaining child, Moana, on a couple of cinder blocks in the middle of their cluster of little huts. Behind them were two cylindrical grain storage bins. When her sons were alive and farming, the metal bins would be full to the brim. Now they were empty. Instead, every month, the grandmother and her grandchildren carried home their combined ration of food aid: 165 pounds of corn, 11 pounds of beans, a gallon of cooking oil, and 11 pounds of corn-soybean mixture fortified with minerals to stave off child malnutrition.

Ndzima's first priority was to make sure her grandchildren had enough to eat. Which meant that she and Moana cut back to two thin meals a day. As they did, the daughter's tuberculosis worsened. The one-two punch was devastating: hunger and disease, disease and hunger. Soon, Ndzima feared, she would be alone with the grandchildren and her empty fields.

Several days before Christmas 2003, Robert Mugabe rose before a gathering of his ZANU-PF Party. He led a Hallelujah chorus in praise of his own agricultural revolution. "Our people are overjoyed, the land is ours," he thundered. "We are now the rulers and owners of Zimbabwe."

What he was the ruler of was the hungriest country in the world. Earlier in the year, international food aid fed 7 million of the country's 12 million people, or nearly 60 percent—the highest food aid–dependent percentage of any country's population. (Ethiopia had the largest number of hungry people, 14 million, just over 20 percent of the total population.)

A scorching drought stretching into a third year had taken a severe toll in Zimbabwe. But the punishing weather was exacerbated by punishing politics. Mugabe had led his country to independence from its white rulers in 1980. He changed its name from Rhodesia to Zimbabwe and enjoyed great popular support as the economy, particularly agriculture, flourished. But as opposition parties emerged, Mugabe began using food and agriculture to demand loyalty. He pushed a fast-track land reform that confiscated, often times with brutal force, white-owned commercial farms and redistributed the property to faithful ZANU-PF supporters.

Many of the new owners were inexperienced in running large agribusinesses; by 2003, when all the food aid poured in, only a couple hundred of the 4,500 confiscated farms were still fully functioning. Harvests of food staples had plummeted by as much as 90 percent, livestock herds had dwindled, and production of the main export cash crop, tobacco, slumped badly. The resulting dearth of foreign currency led to shortages of imported seed, fertilizer, and fuel, which in turn led to a sharp drop in production on the peasant farms.

In the rural village of Pupu, hungry residents stayed alive by eating worms—roasted *mopani* worms—along with dried wild fruit. The worms, thick like caterpillars, were normally plucked from the trees and eaten as snacks. In 2003, they were often the main course. "They taste like flying termites," said one of the farmers waiting at the Pupu primary school for the monthly food-aid handouts. Everyone who heard that laughed. Another farmer volunteered: "They taste like peanut butter." That could be, if one was hungry enough; to a well-fed Westerner, they tasted like roasted rubber.

No matter the taste, in times of hunger the worms became vital for daily sustenance. Many of the farmers said they were planning a Christmas menu of food-aid cornmeal and roasted worms. "If we didn't have that, we'd be dead," said Siphatisiwe Ncube while she waited in a long line for the food-aid handouts. Barefoot and in a blue dress, she had walked two hours to the distribution site, a parched soccer field behind the school. She chewed on a small piece of dried wild fruit. "It gives you energy for several hours," she said.

Four thousand peasant farmers, a full 70 percent of the local population, had made the trek to the school field for the handouts. Drought had burned their crops. And the ravaged economy made the food that had survived too expensive to buy. Inflation had soared toward 700 percent, making goats and chickens too expensive, and too precious, to eat. A goat cost the equivalent of two hundred dollars, which would consume a teacher's monthly salary. "Even if we have a chicken for a special meal, it is better to sell it for money to buy other food," said Lahlekile Mpofu, a skinny, elderly woman who held open a ragged plastic bag to receive her ration of split peas.

The feeding of such multitudes was a shocking sight in a country that just a few years earlier was selling up to 500,000 tons of surplus food to the World Food Program for distribution to starving people elsewhere. In 2003, Zimbabwe itself was receiving that much in food aid.

As local and regional elections neared, human rights groups charged that the ruling party doled out food from the government warehouses in exchange for electoral support. The U.S.-based Human Rights Watch had released a report documenting examples of residents being forced to display a ZANU-PF Party membership card before being given some government grain. Those who didn't went hungry, the group reported. The Mugabe government also tried to take control of the international food-aid distribution in 2003, but the donors resisted, threatening to withhold their food, and the government backed down. Once viewed by its neighbor South Africa as a model for how a country could emerge prosperous and peaceful from the transition to majority (black) rule from minority (white) rule, Zimbabwe had become a nightmare. "Zimbabwe stands alone as [an example of] how one person can ruin a country," protested Tony Hall, who was the U.S. ambassador to the World Food Program and the Food and Agriculture Organization. Mugabe, he declared, had "committed crimes against humanity."

Mugabe remained resolute in the face of such condemnation, which he dismissed as the posturing of rich white nations that didn't want to see a

black African country succeed. But on the Pupu soccer field, the devastation in the Zimbabwean countryside was undeniable. Thousands of people sat in the dirt, under a baking noonday sun, waiting patiently for the
WFP and the aid organization, World Vision, to begin the distribution.
One sideline was covered with stacks of bags filled with food, a total of
thirty-five tons, from all over the world. From one of the goalposts hung a
sign listing the rations: eleven pounds of corn per person, four pounds of
peas, and three pounds of the corn-soya blend. Just so no one would get
the wrong idea about who was providing the food, a canvas banner posted
at a corner of the field proclaimed: "Food provided to the people of Zimbabwe by WFP in collaboration with World Vision to restore hope, alleviate suffering, and save lives."

"This is just about food. People must come in normal clothes, no political T-shirts," explained Zvidzai Maburutse, World Vision's deputy director of relief in Zimbabwe. In 2002, aid agencies had suspended
distributions in other parts of the country when local politicians tried to
turn the handouts to their own benefit, claiming the food was a gift of the
government rather than international relief.

The aid workers rattled off the signs of growing desperation in the country: men leaving their drought-choked farms to pan for gold, women heading to the cities to work as prostitutes, young people sneaking across the
border to find work in the neighboring countries, particularly South Africa.

Christmas in Zimbabwe was all but canceled. "We don't have enough
food to really celebrate this year," said Luke Philip Ngwenya, idly dreaming of the traditional holiday feast of roast goat, heaps of cornmeal, and
vats of sorghum beer. No one, he said, could afford a goat, the corn crop
had failed for three years, and the sorghum harvest dried up long ago.
"Christmas," he said, "will just come and go like any other day."

Ngwenya, a sixty-three-year-old peasant farmer, sat in the sparse grass,
leaning back against the trunk of a dying *msasa* tree. The rains were late,
he said. Many animals once used for plowing had died from a lack of
food and water. He had heard that some desperate farmers had begun
eating their seeds rather than wait for the rain that would signal the beginning of the planting season. So far, he and his neighbors gathered
under the tree hadn't resorted to that. But were they tempted? "Oh, yes!"
they shouted in unison.

As the food aid was doled out to the hungry farmers, women with homemade brooms scurried to sweep up every grain of wheat, every pea, every kernel of corn that fell to the ground. When the last bag of food aid had been emptied or carried away, a group of dogs—starving like their owners, they had also been patiently waiting—moved in to lick up any morsel that might have escaped the brooms of the sweepers. "This is really a sign of hunger," said Robinah Mulenga, a WFP official as she watched two brown dogs sniff the ground. "African dogs usually eat what is left over from the family meals. But now nothing is left over, because there is so little to begin with."

That would soon be the lament of much of the world.

PART II

Enough Is Enough

CHAPTER 9

Resorting to Outrage

The farmers were desperate.

"You know but very little of the state of the suffering poor," they accused. "Are we to resort to outrage? We have peaceably and quietly conducted ourselves and patiently submitted to the will of Divine Providence and cannot restrain from expressing to you our feelings, and our wrongs. Gentlemen, we fear that the peace of the country will be much disturbed if relief be not immediately, more extensively afforded to the suffering peasantry. We are not for joining in anything illegal or contrary to the laws of God or the land unless pressed to by HUNGER."

The anguished writers were not Ethiopians, or Sudanese, or Zimbabweans, or Swazis. They were Flanagans and Kellys and Monaghans and Burnes—Irish all. Twenty tenant farmers in Cloonahee, County Roscommon, penned a petition for help to the landowners, men in consort with Ireland's British rulers, who were denying them employment and, thus, food. Their supplication began at a reasoned pace and built to a threatening tone, culminating in their writing the word HUNGER in bigger, bolder script. It was August 22, 1846. The Great Irish Famine, born of potato blight and British indifference and scorn, was tightening its death grip.

"Our families are really and truly suffering in our presence and we cannot much longer withstand their cries for food," they wrote. "We have no food for them. Our potatoes are rotten and we have no grain."

The tenants of Cloonahee had been promised employment—and food for their work—by landowner Major Denis Mahon, but they had been turned away from relief services by the Board of Works supervisor. Many in the British government, too, turned away from the suffering—one official insisted the famine was God's will; others saw it as a way to thin the Irish population—and some of the London newspapers and magazines portrayed the Irish as lazy and somehow deserving of their plight. The landowners made money exporting Irish grain and meat to the United Kingdom, while food aid from a former British colony, America, was shipped to Ireland to feed the starving peasant farmers.

Within three years, the writers of the petition were gone: dead or evicted and dispatched to distant lands. The Mahon estate in Strokestown was deeply in debt, and the owner sought to relieve expenses by expelling 3,000 tenants and sending them to North America. Many died at sea, aboard rickety vessels that became known as "coffin ships." Months later, Mahon himself was shot to death, presumably by an aggrieved tenant. During the famine and the bleak years that followed, 88 percent of Strokestown's 12,000 residents departed, either through death, eviction, or emigration. Gone, too, were more than 2 million of their countrymen—1 million died, 1 million emigrated. The population shriveled by one-quarter. The Irish Famine was one of the greatest catastrophes of nineteenth-century Europe.

More than 150 years later, with hunger consuming Africa, the petition of Cloonahee read as if the ink were still wet. The rich world still knew very little of the state of the suffering poor. The death toll was still horrific, and even more so now; the equivalent of two Strokestowns were dying *every day* of hunger and malnutrition somewhere in the developing world. Those with the power to help were still indifferent. The well fed still often blamed the victims. Economic absurdities still flourished, with starvation amid plenty. An ominous threat loomed still, that those so marginalized by grinding hunger and poverty would turn to violence, in this age succumbing to the entreaties of terrorists.

But even as Western governments and world institutions dictated policies like structural adjustment that actually fostered famine and neglected the poorest of the poor, a new outrage had begun building in other sectors of society—in philanthropic circles, in communities of faith, in the business world—that such growing hunger and extreme poverty should no longer be tolerated. This new movement would first drive campaigns to forgive the debt of the poorest countries and to combat the spread of AIDS and malaria. After Africa's famine of 2003, it began to coalesce around efforts to conquer hunger once and for all.

One strong strand of outrage emerged from Ireland, channeling the spirit of Cloonahee. For the Irish, the growing hunger in the world was particularly unsettling. Had the world learned nothing from their suffering? Had they learned nothing from their own long road to recovery that they couldn't put to use on behalf of hungry people elsewhere?

Recovery on the island had been painfully slow, both financially and psychologically. For 150 years after the Great Famine, Ireland remained the poorhouse of Western Europe. Decade after decade, partly out of shame, partly out of pride, many Irish downplayed the fierceness of their famine. "It wasn't *that* bad," they would say.

But the legacy of the famine was undeniable. The suffering had inspired a yearning for landownership among Irish tenant farmers. A series of land-reform measures turned the tenants into owners, albeit of relatively small parcels of land. Still, at the creation of the Irish Free State in 1922, more than half the workforce was barely surviving on a subsistence level. As a young boy in the 1930s, growing up in Limerick, Aengus Finucane played among the remnants of the famine. The hulking workhouse loomed across the street from his home, and the paupers' graveyard was just a mile down the road. "There were still paupers in the workhouse," that boy would remember later as an old man. "There was a big high wall. We'd be playing on the road, and from behind the wall someone would let down a tin can on a string. The tin had a few coins, a tuppence and a halfpenny. With the tuppence we'd buy cigarettes for them and the halfpenny would be for us."

A century after the famine, agriculture still dominated the Irish economy, accounting for a quarter of the gross national product and nearly half of all employment. And those farmers remained very undeveloped, isolated from the modern agricultural technology emerging elsewhere in Europe and the United States. The soil was poor and fertilizer scarce. The market for Irish produce was still largely confined to Britain; under an Anglo-Irish trade agreement, 90 percent of Irish cattle exports went to Britain. And all those exports were live cattle, so Ireland didn't develop a beef-processing industry.

In the late 1950s, the Irish government determined that agriculture would be the engine for achieving the growth needed to reduce emigration and unemployment. Extension agents delivered new research and technology to the farmers. Farmers associations gained more political power. Trade markets expanded. Throughout the 1960s, Ireland negotiated its membership in the European Community, which would bring a single European market for food products and lavish support for farmers under the Common Agricultural Policy.

As Ireland finally began to gain some economic distance from its famine, many of its citizens began to feel a psychological connection to hungry people elsewhere in the world. Aengus Finucane had left Limerick for the monastery and then headed to Africa as a missionary. He was a parish priest in Uli, in the Biafra region of Nigeria, when that province sought independence from Nigeria in 1967. War erupted; famine spread.

"Parishioners were dying all around. Parents burying their children, children crying at the grave sites of their parents. You heard of cannibalism. You saw things. A man kicked to death in a market because he had stolen food. The parish house was surrounded by hungry people. The basement windows were lined with faces," Father Finucane recalled in an interview forty years later in his Dublin apartment. "You developed a horror of famine." The aging priest shivered and crossed himself. "Usually I have a drink when I tell these stories," he said. But it being ten in the morning the drink would have to wait. Leaning on a cane carved from Irish blackthorn, he hobbled to his kitchen and put on some soup instead.

"I spoke at a Sunday mass," he continued, "and I said we'd do our best to feed two hundred of the worst-off children in each of four towns in the parish. I went to one of the towns; the families were lined up around the football pitch, the children in front of the parents, the worst one in the front. I had to make the selection. I could only take one from each family, fifty from any clan. I went all along the touch line of the pitch, selecting children to feed."

The next day he returned with food. A father presented an emaciated child. "He said the one child of his family I had selected had died overnight. Could I select another one?"

Standing before that broken man in Biafra, Father Finucane believed he had stepped back in time to the days of the Irish Famine. Back then, too, selection determined who lived and who died: who got the job at the public works, who got a place in the workhouse, who got a bowl of soup. It seemed unconscionable that he was forced to make the same decisions in Biafra.

He watched an old Biafran man crawl on his hands and knees the final yards to a refugee camp, only to collapse at the gate. How many Irish people, the priest wondered, had done the same, crawling on all fours to the poorhouses, even perhaps to the poorhouse across the street from his home in Limerick?

Back in Ireland, a small flock of churchgoers who heard these tales from Father Finucane and his fellow missionaries in Biafra formed a group called Concern Africa, and devoted themselves to gathering up relief supplies to send to Biafra. Though most Irish had little to give, donations poured in; within three months, a ship filled with aid sailed from Ireland to the west coast of Africa. Then, in order to avoid detection by the Nigerian government, supplies were flown nightly into remote airstrips inside Biafra, where missionaries would collect them. Other ships followed.

Concern Africa would become Ireland's largest humanitarian organization, with Father Finucane at the helm. His abiding mantra to his fellow citizens, whether summoning assistance from his posts in Africa or while standing on O'Connell Street in Dublin holding a donation box, had been "it's the right thing to do." And they understood. "Even poor people would come up and put in money, and say, 'Ah, Father, we know what it was like to be poor and hungry.'"

Growing up in Dublin at the time was a young musician, Paul Hewson, who would later adopt the nom de rock Bono. He was from an interfaith family—his mother was Protestant, his father Catholic—in a country where, he would note, "the line between the two was, quite literally, a battle line." The Bible was the one thing both sides had in common.

And no matter which way Bono read the Scriptures, be it through a Protestant lens or a Catholic one, he noticed Jesus was always talking about the poor.

Justice for the poor would become Bono's theology, and it fused with the lyrics that grabbed him by the collar at the time: "If I had a hammer . . . It's the hammer of justice"; "How many roads must a man walk down?"; "Imagine all the people . . ." He reckoned that the Psalms of David, with their songs of praise and cries for God's presence, were like the blues. Such social awareness—piqued in the 1970s and 1980s by British entertainers donating their time and images to campaigns on behalf of Amnesty International and other human rights organizations—would also emerge in the songs of Bono's band, U2.

But the band's devotion to consciousness raising wouldn't transcend the music until famine strangled Ethiopia in 1984. Then a fellow Irish rocker, Bob Geldof of the Boomtown Rats, rallied musicians from various countries, including Bono, to form Band Aid and record a song for charity, "Do They Know It's Christmas?" The following year they staged a concert known as Live Aid that was simulcast around the world from various venues. It was an early act of an emerging new trend in business, trade, and media called "globalization." Faraway places were suddenly closer, the world smaller and more interconnected. Hunger, the ultimate act of alienation, was beamed into hundreds of millions of homes across the global village.

U2's performance in Live Aid helped fuel the band's international popularity; the famine drew Bono to Africa and launched his career as a humanitarian. Shortly after the concert, the twenty-five-year-old rocker with long hair, a beard, and an earring, and his wife, Ali, headed to Ethiopia to see for themselves what Live Aid had been about. They landed in the Wello district, a soulless zone of parched, barren landscape in northern Ethiopia at the center of the famine. For six weeks, Bono and Ali toiled in an orphanage and feeding center that was a magnet for desperate survivors of the mass hunger.

One day, an emaciated man held out his starving child, figuring the odd-looking strangers could offer a better life, if the child was to live at all. The young Irish couple couldn't help but wonder, How many Irishmen had done the same 140 years earlier?

"It stirred my soul," Bono would later say in an interview. "You wake up in the middle of nowhere and people would be traveling through the night and they would lay their children down at the gates of this camp, some dead, some not. There was barbed wire, and it wasn't to keep the people in. You do have to ask deeper questions. And then you move from charity to justice quite quickly as you dig deeper and deeper." Charity would settle for a song or a concert. But, as the rock star was discovering, it wasn't enough for justice.

As the days went by, Bono and Ali looked deeper and deeper into the eyes of the hungry. "The thing that appalled me is the look in the eyes and the complete absence of rage, acquiescence. That is the thing that I keep replaying," Bono said. "And maybe because I'm quite an aggressive character, I can't imagine having my outrage taken away. I'm always taken aback by that."

In 1846 the petitioners of Cloonahee had asked: "Are we to resort to outrage?" Bono had his answer; it would be a defiant "Yes."

The spirit of Cloonahee began to stir across Ireland, propelled in part by the responsibility of prosperity. The country's entry into the European Community in 1973 had brought its farmers the higher food prices of the European market, and the Common Agricultural Policy subsidies greatly reduced their risk of farming. Within a decade, Irish farm incomes had doubled, and farmers boosted investments in their operations. The agro-processing industry flourished, and several Irish food companies developed a global reach. Other subsidies from the EC improved the country's infrastructure. In the 1990s, the booming Irish economy came to be known as the Celtic Tiger, roaring on a number of fronts, from high-tech to arts and entertainment. Irish emigrants returned home, and Irish aid money went forth into the world to help the poor, particularly the hungry. The government's international development budget increased sevenfold from 1981 to 1996.

In light of this newfound prosperity and confidence, the 150th anniversary of the Great Famine became a moment for the Irish to embrace the suffering of the past. Books were written, speeches given, memorials unearthed and restored. At the Mahon estate in Strokestown, the old horse stable was converted into a famine museum. Images of victims of the Irish Famine were arranged side by emaciated side with images of the suffering from modern-day famines. The petition of the Cloonahee farmers was displayed to echo through the ages. Ireland found a new purpose.

"Our consideration of the Irish famine should fill us with revulsion," Father Finucane told his countrymen during an anniversary commemoration in 1996. "And that revulsion should be harnessed positively to fuel a determination to do all we can to combat the scourge of famine."

As the new century approached, concerned people throughout the world seemed to be heeding his call.

CHAPTER 10

"We Can Do Something About This"

DUBLIN AND SEATTLE

Outrage over the treatment of the world's poor erupted in two blasts on opposite sides of the globe in 1997, involving two of the world's most famous men.

In Dublin, Bono, who was fast becoming the biggest rock-and-roll concert showman of his generation, read a report from a coalition of British church groups seeking his support for a burgeoning grassroots movement demanding that the UK and other wealthy nations forgive the debts of the poorest countries at the dawn of the new millennium. It was a call rooted in the humbling parables of the Bible that Bono knew well, and in the cold, hard economics of poverty that he had always intended to know better. One fact was highlighted to grab the Irishman's attention: The $200 million that Band Aid and Live Aid had raised, a heroic sum, was dwarfed by Africa's debt payments to creditors in the rich world. In particular, Ethiopia's annual debt obligations were double that amount. Whatever aid had been coming into Africa had been going right back out in debt repayments to Western banks and financial institutions.

Bono was gobsmacked. The equation he had pondered in Ethiopia remained unsolved: What good was charity without justice? The singer was about to discover a new purpose for his famous voice.

In Seattle, Bill Gates, the Microsoft mogul who was already among the richest people in the world, and his wife, Melinda, were beginning to notice newspaper stories about the millions of children in poor countries dying every year from illnesses that could be defeated with simple medicine. One article in the *New York Times* detailed the devastation of diarrhea. They also read about one particularly deadly infection they had never even heard of—rotavirus, a common cause of severe diarrhea—that was readily treatable in rich Western countries but killed hundreds of thousands of children in the developing world every year.

Bill and Melinda asked each other, Can this be true? If it was, they agreed, it should be a priority of their growing philanthropy. They sent the news to Bill's father, Bill Gates Sr., who was running the family foundation. In an attached note, they wrote, "Dad, maybe we can do something about this."

In these two moments of revelation was born a new activism that would unite church groups, rock stars, and philanthropists; passion, buzz, and money; the sympathetic heart, the promotional ego, the calculating mind. It brought Africa to the center of a grassroots agenda, which aimed to reverse the neglect of governments and development institutions. The issues of debt and disease would initially inspire this movement, but soon a new realization would emerge: As long as hunger persisted, success couldn't be declared, or even achieved, on any other front.

When Bono and his wife left Ethiopia after their famine relief work in 1985, they vowed to remain involved in helping Africa. But celebrity pulled in the opposite direction. Back up north in the well-fed half of the world, U2's popularity was spreading. There were albums to record, markets to conquer, months-long concert tours to navigate. Bono and fellow Irish rocker Bob Geldof continued their Live Aid activism by supporting the human rights campaigns of Amnesty International, Greenpeace, and the UK's Comic Relief, an annual television fund-raiser highlighting development needs in the forgotten corners of the world. But these were mainly one-off appearances: a speech, a song, a gig to raise money for a charity.

Now in the flurry of entreaties from the drop-the-debt campaigners, Bono found a compelling signature cause. This was a crusade that merged economics and theology. Africa had piled up a mountain of debt during the Cold War, when countries from both the Western and the Soviet blocs wooed the continent's eager postindependence governments with generous loans in return for their fealty. By the 1990s, the annual service payments on that debt alone were draining tens of billions of dollars, emptying government budgets and deepening poverty and hunger across the continent. In Zambia, for instance, per capita debt was more than $700, which was twice the average annual income. In Mozambique, the debt was four times the country's gross national product.

As economic disaster approached, so did the millennium. Christian groups seized on the biblical idea of the Jubilee Year, where every fifty years debts are forgiven and slaves set free. It was right there in the Old Testament book of Leviticus, chapter 25. Verse 13: "In the year of the jubilee, you shall return every man unto his possession." Verse 35: "If your brother becomes poor and cannot maintain himself, you shall maintain him . . . you shall not lend him your money at interest, nor give him your food for profit." And there were the teachings of Jesus in Luke 4:18–19: "The Spirit of the Lord is upon me, because he has anointed me to preach the gospel to the poor; he has sent me to heal the broken-hearted, to preach deliverance to the captives and recovering of sight to the blind, to set at liberty them that are bruised. To preach the acceptable year of the Lord."

The year 2000 would be a Jubilee Year writ large. And in the mid-1990s, from the pews of churches and the lecture halls of universities arose the UK Debt Crisis Network, channeling the eighteenth-century spirit of William Wilberforce. Wilberforce was a legendary English social reformer—a fervent Christian, philanthropist, and politician—who dedicated his life to the abolition of the slave trade in the British realm. After four decades of crusading, appealing to both the high and mighty in their fancy salons and the commoners on the street, he succeeded in ending slavery in the empire.

The campaigners at the end of the twentieth century saw themselves as the new abolitionists; to them, debt was the new slavery. But they didn't have decades to accomplish their goal; they had only a few years. They needed an accelerant, a fuel to set the grassroots ablaze.

ın 1995, Jamie Drummond, a development activist at the British faith-based humanitarian agency Christian Aid, headed to Ethiopia to look at the impact of the Live Aid concert ten years on. He saw some positive developments that had come from the money that had been raised: community projects, some health investments, some agricultural improvements. But he also discovered that the onetime donation by an enthusiastic global audience was overwhelmed by Ethiopia's annual debt obligations. Although the country owed some $400 million a year, it could afford to make only a fraction of that payment. The debt transfers to the Western creditors were more than the government was spending on either health, education, or agriculture. Here, Drummond thought, were the shackles of the poor. "I'm going around in Ethiopia, I'm getting angry at all I'm seeing, and then the penny dropped. You could see there was a structural cause of poverty in Africa," Drummond would later recall.

Debt was an arcane, theoretical subject, unlikely to fire up the masses. But Drummond's travels in Ethiopia had conjured up a stark image of debt devouring aid. And it gave him an idea: Make debt relief tangible by illustrating what debt payments prevented countries from doing—inoculating children, building clinics, paying teachers, feeding families—and then a populist campaign might gain some traction.

When he returned to London, Drummond and his fellow debt crusaders began lobbying those in the music industry in England and Ireland who had staged the Live Aid extravaganza. A single concert wasn't enough, they told them; what was needed was concerted action. They sent faxes and letters and knocked on doors. Bono, because he had been to Ethiopia, was their top target. "Could you champion a campaign that attacked the structural cause of poverty in Africa?" Drummond asked him in 1997.

Bono understood immediately, for here he saw his path from charity to justice. And the Jubilee idea played to his two personal theologies, one honed from the Bible, the other in Ethiopia: care for the poor, equality for Africa. It also appealed to his seriously wonkish side, which had been well disguised by the blasé rock-and-roll veneer. He told Drummond that the juxtaposition of the Live Aid money with the debt payments was powerful. But he wondered if the time was truly ripe for such a campaign, given the Asian financial crisis that had erupted in mid-1997. He noted that Asian economies were in free fall at the time, rattling the world's financial structures. Doesn't that make debt cancellation by 2000 fanciful? Bono asked.

Drummond told him the Asian crisis made it all the more necessary to relieve the debt burden on Africa, for squeezing money out of the continent would only worsen the countries' economies. The debt campaigners believed they had the economic and theological angles covered and were beginning to make progress on those fronts. What they needed, Drummond told Bono, was somebody to provide the populist edge. "If you get behind the campaign," he promised the rock star, "we could do something even more spectacular."

Bono formally joined Jubilee in early 1998 and used his celebrity to gain access to European politicians and put debt relief on government agendas. The doors readily opened, for the Continent's politics were turning in Jubilee's favor, swinging from right to left. The conservative governments in London and Berlin that had backed the strict structural adjustment policies were falling out of power. Tony Blair and his Labour Party moved into Number 10 Downing Street in London in 1997, replacing the Conservative Party. In Germany, Gerhard Schroeder, leader of the liberal Social Democrats, became chancellor in 1998, sending the Christian Democratic Union to the sidelines.

The sweep of European culture was turning in Jubilee's favor as well. The ascendancy of the Labour Party after many years in opposition ushered in an era of Cool Britannia, a pun on the patriotic song "Rule Britannia," where things coming out of Britain were hip again. Jubilee made debt relief cool. In May 1998, Jubilee organized 80,000 people into a human chain surrounding the summit meeting of the heads of state of the leading economies known as the Group of 8, or G8, in Birmingham, England. They did the same thing the next year, at the G8 meeting in Cologne, Germany. World leaders at that summit promised to write off 90 percent of poor-country debt and a portion of debt due to the international financial institutions, such as the World Bank.

Jubilee was making progress. But Bono and his fellow activists knew that the debt relief movement would succeed only if the Americans came on board, for the United States was the world's financial superpower. It controlled the purse strings of the major institutional creditors and could

, move the needle on debt forgiveness. American leadership was crucial, yet on this issue the most obstinate.

For much of 1999, Bono relentlessly shuttled between Dublin and Washington, D.C. He bent the ear of President Bill Clinton and was often seen with administration officials. But he realized that the "real Elvis" in Washington, as he put it—the one body that did the crucial moving and shaking, at least when it came to passing legislation—was Congress.

And it was in Congress where the debt relief skeptics resided. There was a strong bloc, mainly anchored by conservative Republicans such as Senator Jesse Helms, that believed foreign aid was a waste of money; they claimed it was corralled by corrupt dictators to prop up repressive governments. And on the debt issue, the doubters insisted that forgiveness would only encourage the beneficiaries to engage in more fiscal irresponsibility.

Many of those members of Congress were also deeply religious, and this is where Bono hit them. He could Bible-thump with the best of them; he pointed out that there were more than 2,100 passages about caring for the poor, and together they would search the Scriptures for them. Sometimes he would tell his driver to continue circling Capitol Hill and the White House while he selected the proper Bible passage, so he would have one ready for the meeting. He stood beside U.S. faith-based groups like Bread for the World, Mazon, and the Catholic Bishops Conference and refined his lobbying message: The Jubilee debt cancellation was the right thing to do, the moral thing to do. After reading the Bible with Senator Helms, who had led the congressional chorus against foreign aid, the gentleman from North Carolina proclaimed the error of his ways and began singing the praises of the debt relief movement.

But for all of Bono's high-profile lobbying, it was the efforts of a couple of genteel church ladies in Birmingham, Alabama, that clinched U.S. backing for the Jubilee debt forgiveness. They became Exhibit A of the power of individual actions in changing the world, and proof, as Bono would say, that God works in mysterious ways.

One evening in early 1999, Pat Pelham's phone rang while she was preparing dinner at her home in the Birmingham suburbs. "Hello," she answered with a pinch of irritation in her voice. She didn't like getting calls at dinnertime.

"Hi Pat, it's David," said the familiar voice of David Beckmann, the president of Bread for the World. "Guess who's chairman of the relevant subcommittee for debt relief?"

In the newly seated 106th Congress, conservative Republican Spencer Bachus had been tapped to head the domestic and international monetary policy subcommittee of the House Committee on Banking and Financial Services. From that rather technical perch, he would be the gatekeeper for any legislation on debt relief. Bachus was the representative for the district where Pat and her friend Elaine VanCleave lived. For the past couple of years, they had been two of his most persistent and persuasive constituents, twisting his arm to support Bread's agenda for feeding the hungry in America and abroad.

Beckmann, who had positioned Bread at the vanguard of the Jubilee movement in the United States, told Pat and Elaine to pack for a trip to Washington. They had an assignment on Capitol Hill.

Pat and Elaine were no idealistic firebrands. They were two young mothers in the upper-middle-class suburbs who met two Tuesdays a month in a women's study group at the Independent Presbyterian Church. They would talk about kids, husbands, the community—and, wistfully, about changing the world.

A few years before Beckmann summoned them to Washington, before they even knew him, Pat was at home watching a rerun of *Designing Women,* a television sitcom about the lives of four southern women running an interior design firm. It was one of Pat's favorite shows; she most identified with the character Suzanne Sugarbaker, played by Delta Burke, a onetime beauty queen who later struggles with her weight. Pat had long felt a similar pressure growing up in the comfortable suburbs of Birmingham: One could never be too thin.

In the episode Pat was watching that day, entitled "They Shoot Fat Women, Don't They?" Suzanne fusses over what to wear to her high school reunion, wondering which outfit will best hide her additional weight. Still, she suffers the stares and snide comments of her old classmates. At the same time, Suzanne's friends participate in a two-day fast to focus on world hunger, which, they are told, kills as many people every seventy-two hours as died in the wake of the Hiroshima nuclear bomb. A boy from Ethiopia, who says his entire family died during a famine, tells Suzanne that she is beautiful, extra weight and all.

Back at the reunion, Suzanne wins the "Person Who Has Changed the Most" award. Shocked, she tells her former classmates: "Last night I got my feelings hurt because I came to this reunion thinking I was beautiful, and what I find out was that I'm fat, at least you think I am. . . . I met a little boy from Africa tonight whose family died of starvation, and I realized that I spent the whole day at home worrying about the fact that I had too much to eat. I'm not sure the old Suzanne would have appreciated the absurdity of that, but this one does."

Pat did, too.

"It was as powerful a moment in a sitcom as there can be," she would later say. "It reached out of the TV screen and grabbed me by the collar: 'Listen to this!' The paradox of that really got me thinking."

Later, out for a walk in her neighborhood, she stopped in the middle of the sidewalk, paralyzed almost, and began weeping. A passage from the Bible kept repeating in her mind. It was from Isaiah. "Here am I, Lord. Send me."

Pat, a psychiatric nurse practitioner, told her women's study group at church about her Sidewalk to Damascus moment. "I really believe God reached out to me and said, 'Make something of this.'" For the group, everything they had been discussing over the months suddenly came together. They had been reading a book, 'Tis a Gift to Be Simple, and mulling its message: Simplify life, let go of the things that don't matter, embrace those that do, and change the world, make it a better place.

The women knew what they must do. "We all said, 'Let's answer this call, let's start a hunger ministry,'" Elaine recalled later. "As mothers of young children, we couldn't imagine being a mother and not being able to feed your child. The image of a little child crying from hunger and not being able to stop it because there was nothing to eat . . . I couldn't imagine any pain worse than that."

Their pastor steered them to Bread for the World. Elaine did the research and signed up for Bread's mailing list. One day came a notice that David Beckmann, Bread's president, would be speaking at Birmingham's Our Lady of Sorrows Catholic Church, hosted by Father Martin Muller. Pat and Elaine arrived early and sat in the front row.

Beckmann, a lanky, winsome man with a preacher's gift for storytelling, said Bread could use Birmingham's help in ending world hunger. Raising money and collecting cans of food was important, he said, but what was absolutely vital was changing public policy and stirring political will. Pat noticed that this unassuming man talking about the poor had a hole in his shoe. They were hooked. As they left Our Lady of Sorrows, Pat and Elaine were ready to enlist in Bread's army of citizen lobbyists.

They aligned their church with Bread's network of congregations. Next step, in good Presbyterian tradition, was to host a church dinner. Beckmann was invited to be the guest speaker, and Pat and Elaine ambitiously dispatched invitations to Alabama's senators and congressional representatives, state officials, and the mayor. They didn't really expect any of them would come.

The hosts nearly fell over when they saw Congressman Bachus and his wife walk through the door. Bachus represented Alabama's Sixth District and had a reputation as one of the most conservative members of the House of Representatives. Pat and Elaine put him at the same table with Beckmann, who went into lobbying overdrive. "We'd be grateful if you'd consider co-sponsoring a piece of legislation to end childhood hunger," he pressed the congressman.

At the end of the evening, alone at the church, Pat and Elaine were uncertain if the gathering had made an impression on Bachus. They laughed at the audacity of their invitation, and at the notion that they would ever hear from him again.

The next night at five o'clock, as Pat was preparing dinner, her phone rang. Who, she wondered, would be calling at that hectic time?

It was Congressman Bachus. He would be proud, he said, to champion Bread's agenda in Congress. "And thank you," he added, for the introduction to the hunger cause. "The issue of hunger had always been out there," he would later say. "It just took someone to call it out for me."

Pat and Elaine had their entrée to public policy. From that moment on, the ladies peppered Bachus with a steady stream of letters, keeping him posted on Bread's activities.

In 1998, Bread jumped into the worldwide Jubilee campaign and cranked up its lobbying effort to push for debt relief for the world's poorest countries. It was an issue close to Beckmann's heart. He had degrees from Yale and the London School of Economics, and had worked at the World Bank in the 1980s, where he had a front-row seat to the burgeoning debt crisis in the developing world. He knew every dollar spent paying down debt was one dollar less the poor countries had to spend on food or agricultural development. Relieving the debt burden was a crucial front in the war on hunger.

When the committee assignments came out for the new Congress, Beckmann was delighted to see that his dinner companion from the Birmingham church would be the steward of debt relief legislation. His first call was to Pat, who then called Elaine. They booked a flight to Washington.

The two women knew the capital only as tourists. Beckmann and others from Bread transformed them into Capitol Hill lobbyists with virtually around-the-clock briefing sessions. Over dinner and then breakfast the following morning, with only a few hours of sleep in between, Pat and Elaine and two fellow members of their Birmingham church learned all they could about debt relief.

After breakfast, they hustled over to Bachus's office, only to be told he was in the committee chambers. They hurried through the underground passageways of Capitol Hill, Pat and Elaine racing on high heels, to make their appointment. Before they entered the committee room, they stood in the hallway and said a prayer. Pat looked down and saw her skirt had twisted backward, so fast had she walked.

Bachus greeted his constituents warmly and asked them to educate him on debt relief. "Pretend like I don't know anything about it," he said. "Tell me why you're here."

For an hour, they talked. The delegation from Birmingham handed over a petition calling for debt relief carrying several hundred constituent signatures gathered by Father Muller. Pat cited the biblical imperatives. Elaine spoke as a mother: "There are thousands of children of mothers dying of hunger and disease every day," she told her congressman. "I can't do anything as one person, but working with you we can do something together."

Bachus got the message. "We all value children," he said. "Children get our attention." Without hesitation, to the giddy delight of Beckmann, Bachus promised his constituents he would take up the banner of debt relief.

And he did so with great passion, holding forth the image of a mother unable to feed her child. He introduced legislation. He summoned committee hearings. He brought rare moments of emotion and poignancy to the Banking Committee deliberations.

"Doing the right thing, whatever the material cost, should always be the imperative," Bachus exhorted his Banking Committee colleagues on June 15, 1999. Then he delineated the material cost of the three-year $970 million debt cancellation bill: $1.20 for each American citizen each year. "It is the cost of an ice cream cone," he said.

Like Elaine, he mentioned children. "Today, in dozens of poor countries all over the world, little boys and girls are born into poverty, disease and hunger. . . . For the people living in these poor countries, their suffering is temporal. It will end with their lives. For us, the decision will follow us. We will not only live with it in this life, but we will live with it in the next life."

Amazed to hear such emotion coming from Banking Committee deliberations, members of the Clinton White House and cabinet attending the hearings reported back to the president. They urged that the United States provide international leadership on debt forgiveness. If conservative Republican Bachus was talking about hungry children in Africa, they said, the White House could count on support in Congress far beyond the usual liberal Democratic ranks.

As Bono had suspected, where the United States led, other Western countries followed. By the dawn of the Jubilee Year, world leaders had agreed to cancel 100 percent of the debt owed to their countries by the poorest nations. Billions of dollars would remain in Africa to help feed the hungry. Beckmann told the general assembly of the United Nations Food and Agriculture Organization in Rome a few years later that it might never have happened if Pat and Elaine "had not so effectively lobbied their representative in Congress."

On the other side of the world, the two genteel ladies from Alabama blushed. "Soccer moms watching soap operas and sitcoms go to Washington," laughed Elaine. "We can all do something. There are no acts too small."

Bono often said that a lobbying alliance of rock stars and soccer moms was a surefire recipe to get politicians quaking in their boots. Now they were joined by another force rallying attention to the inequities of extreme poverty.

As software mogul Bill Gates began to focus on philanthropy, he initially set out to bridge the digital divide between rich and poor. Computers and access to the Internet, whether in Seattle or Senegal, could be the great equalizer. But when he and his wife and father began researching the global health issues they had stumbled upon in their reading, they discovered an even bigger divide: Some lives were seen as worth saving, and others weren't. Why were millions of children in the poor corners of the world dying of diseases that had long ago ceased to be killers in the rich world? Why didn't their lives matter?

In 1998, the Gates family began pumping money into efforts to research children's vaccines. That year, Bill Sr. spotted the work of the International AIDS Vaccine Initiative (IAVI), a New York–based nonprofit agency founded two years earlier to work on the development of a vaccine to prevent HIV infection and AIDS. He forwarded a report on the organization's ambitions to Bill and Melinda, noting in the margins: "I don't know what we can do about this. But if this isn't what philanthropy is for, I don't know what is." In the spring of 1999, the foundation gave $25 million to IAVI, which, at the time, was the largest charitable gift targeting the AIDS epidemic.

Those were the first drops in what would become a torrent of money flowing into global health to bankroll research on diseases primarily afflicting the poorer precincts of the world. In 1999, the Gateses made an initial gift of $750 million to the Global Alliance for Vaccines and Immunization, a coalition of development organizations such as UNICEF, the World Bank, and the World Health Organization working to broaden access to immunizations in developing countries. The next year, they consolidated their philanthropic efforts into the Bill and Melinda Gates Foundation, which they endowed with an initial blast of $16 billion and this philosophy: "Every human life has equal worth. The life of an impoverished child in a developing country is as precious as the life of a middle-class child in a developed one."

Three diseases in particular—AIDS, tuberculosis, and malaria—were fingered as those that disproportionately struck down lives in the developing world. The newest of the three, AIDS, was the most terrifying as it rampaged across Africa, particularly the southern tip. In the 1970s and 1980s, before a common worldwide label was attached to the disease, Africans called it "Slim." People were mysteriously wasting away, stick figures seemingly populating whole villages. Doctors and nurses, as well as traditional healers, noted that it was especially prevalent in certain sectors of the population: traders, truckers, traveling teachers—mobile vocations that required a lot of time away from home. They carried the sexually transmitted disease into the general population and across borders. By the 1990s, it had exploded on a horrific scale. As the twentieth century rushed to a close, AIDS was savaging Africa like the Black Plague of the Middle Ages had ravaged Europe. In the bucolic countries of Botswana and Swaziland, where nearly 40 percent of the women in prenatal clinics tested positive for HIV, an entire generation faced extinction.

For the Gateses, AIDS was an especially acute case of the value-of-life divide. The antiretroviral drugs that were saving the lives of AIDS sufferers in the rich countries were rarely available in Africa. And when they were, few people could afford them. The Gates Foundation spending on this health divide acted like a magnet, attracting additional funding from other philanthropies and aid agencies, as well as the talent and energy of the scientific world to develop vaccines, and of the development community to modernize public health systems. In 2002, the United Nations created the Global Fund to Fight AIDS, Tuberculosis, and Malaria. Pledges amounting to billions of dollars rolled in.

Bill Gates knew that money alone wouldn't be enough to bridge the health divide. Like debt relief, AIDS relief would need a global movement to build political will. Gates had never been to a U2 concert, but he knew Bono's voice. It was a siren call even the richest man in America couldn't resist.

Bono had met Bill Gates in Davos and at other stops along the rich-and-famous circuit, and the rock star kept hammering away at an idea he had to keep the grassroots momentum of the Jubilee campaign rolling. Throughout 2001, Bono and Gates huddled with Bob Geldof and Bobby Shriver of the Kennedy clan to create a new organization that would target the "extreme poverty" of the African continent in the new millennium. In 2002, they launched the cleverly named DATA. The initials projected two meanings: "debt, AIDS, trade, Africa" as well as "democracy, accountability, and transparency in Africa." As one word, it also conveyed the image of a fact-driven, policy-oriented organization.

Based in Washington, D.C., the DATA staff, along with other policy and lobbying groups like Oxfam and Bread for the World, kept the pressure on the White House and its new occupant, President George W. Bush, and other world leaders to keep their nations' promises to increase aid levels made at the G8 meetings and other summits. There were advances and setbacks. In March 2002, with Bono's applause, President Bush announced the creation of the Millennium Challenge Corporation and a steep increase in annual development assistance for the poorest countries in the world; the MCC would funnel new aid money to the most accountable governments, which would take part in designing the aid programs. The president also called on the world's richest countries to step up the offensive against AIDS. But later that spring, Congress passed and Bush signed the 2002 Farm Bill that expanded subsidies for American farmers and increased the inequities in global agricultural trade.

After the terrorist attacks of September 11, 2001, Washington was full of talk about the need to use the soft diplomacy of development assistance to spread American ideals abroad. But, Bono wondered, did America really get it? When he pushed Congress beyond the debt relief issue, especially on the urgency of combating AIDS and unfair trade practices, he and his colleagues were often told, "Nobody in Middle America is clamoring about these issues. Nobody out there cares."

Bono's response: You want clamor, we'll get clamor. He and his DATA associates studied the political map, and saw that many of the key members of the congressional committees overseeing the funding for development aid were from the Midwest. That, then, would be where he would get people talking. It would also be his personal Frank Sinatra challenge. If he could succeed there, he'd succeed anywhere. No New York, New York. This would be Des Moines, Des Moines.

"I felt there was a kind of decency in Middle America that is very attractive to me," Bono would later say in an interview in his New York apartment. His fondness for the Midwest went back to his early tours with U2. "Even though I was standing there in my tartan trousers and pierced ears, even though we were getting strange looks, I just loved the honesty of the people in the Midwest. There is a moral compass, this is where America is. If you can disprove the cliché that people in Middle America don't care about what is going on in the rest of the world . . ."

That was the challenge: Get them to care. The truckers, the waitresses, the students, the factory workers. The churchgoers. Especially the evangelicals, the spiritual descendants of Wilberforce, and the evangelical megachurches with their huge flocks. "They are an army waiting to be well-mobilized, and they have leaders. It's a no-brainer," advised Jamie Drummond, who became DATA's executive director.

Their strategy: Motivate these Christian soldiers to march in a new direction, away from the bedroom issues of the old Moral Majority and toward the issues of how we treat the poor, the issues of a new constituency. "You could call them narrow-minded idealists, blinkered idealists, fundamentalists," Bono said. "But if you widen the aperture of their ideals, these people, they really are a resource."

When he first came to the United States carrying the banner of the Jubilee campaign, he was mystified: Where was the church on these issues? "The sleeping giant of the church was an anomaly to me," he said. "I found it very difficult to accept the lack of good judgment and the judgmentalism that was around. In 2000, only 6% of polled evangelicals felt it was incumbent on them to respond to the AIDS emergency. It just completely confounded me."

Bono had come to see AIDS as the new leprosy, and Jesus healing the lepers, he said, "is at the heart of Christianity." But in America, if evangelical congregations were talking at all about AIDS, it was as divine retribution for immoral behavior. "This holy huddle, this bless me club, is so dangerous, it contradicts the whole purpose," he said. "There's two main things from my reading of Scripture: personal redemption and social justice. Second to personal redemption is how we treat the poor. I don't want to take away from the top line, but the counter point is definitely justice following on the heels of truth. And in a religious country like America, that's a fantastic thing. If you could harness that energy to go out and actually live your life like that . . ."

On November 29, 2002, Bono embarked on the Heart of America tour, a wintry bus ride over the cold and bleak midwestern highways, far from the bright lights that usually follow him. He hit seven states in eleven days to talk to Americans about fighting poverty in Africa. The first stop was Lincoln, Nebraska. Then it was on to Omaha, Des Moines, Iowa City, Davenport, Dubuque, Chicago and nearby Wheaton, Indianapolis, Cincinnati, Louisville, and, finally, Nashville on Dec. 9. He traveled not with his mates from U2 but with Agnes Nyamayarwo, an HIV-positive nurse and activist from Uganda, the Gateway Ambassadors youth choir from Ghana, and a cadre of international AIDS activists and experts.

Bono bounced off the bus at truck stops, greasy spoons, college campuses, and churches and ascended the pulpits, podiums, and bar stools of the Midwest, intent on shaping a new moral majority in America. He was the antithesis of the slick, silver-haired televangelists who had long captained the religious Right. His vestments were a leather jacket and sunglasses. He laced his Scripture-quoting homilies with an occasional expletive. He only half-jokingly confessed to having a Messianic complex. He came not to sing and play, but to preach and pray.

He told his audiences that the country was missing the point with all the righteous fulminating on personal morality by what he called "God's second-hand car salesmen on the cable TV channels." He recited his favorite statistic: The Bible mentions poverty—"not sex, not immorality"—more than 2,100 times. "It's not a coincidence," he would say. "It's not an accident."

Bono relished the challenge; there were hard-core doubters like Jesse Helms wherever he spoke. "There was a truck stop, I think somewhere in Iowa, I was speaking to the people having their coffee," Bono recalled. He told his roadside crowds that truck drivers in Africa, migrating up and down the continent, were particularly afflicted with HIV/AIDS. "There was this guy," Bono said, describing a caricature of the American open road straight out of a Monty Python skit: burly, tattoos, fearsome, sitting off to the side, nursing a coffee. "I had spoken about how to turn these issues into an American necessity, which is to say to make caring about other people in the world a patriotic act. I'm walking by this guy on my way out . . ." Retelling the story in New York, Bono rose from his couch and re-created his walk, a wary sidestep on tiptoes, making himself thin as if to avoid the tattooed one. As he recounted the conversation, his brogue gave way to a flat Iowa accent. "'I'm a trucker,' he says to me. 'I just wanna talk to you here now a second. You say that all these people, these truckers, are going to die in Africa, or half of them are?' I said, 'That's right, 50% are HIV-positive, and if they don't get the medication they are all going to die.' He said, 'I don't know anything about politics, I don't know anything about anything, but I know that's not right. I'll give you my name. I don't know much, but I can drive. If you want me to drive for you, I will drive.'"

"There it is!" Bono shouted in New York, springing from his couch. "That's the America that the world needs to see. The turning points for me were Jesse Helms and the trucker, because they're the people you don't expect. Tough as old boots. You underestimate Americans."

As he neared Chicago on his tour, Bono stopped first to meet with Bill Hybels, the pastor of megachurch Willow Creek and an influential teacher of other pastors. Hybels didn't know this traveling troubadour, but Bono had kept pestering him for a meeting. The two prayed together, and soon Hybels's congregation would be raising money for AIDS work in Africa and Bono would be addressing Hybels's network of pastors across the world on the Christian call to help the poor.

Bono then laid siege to the citadel of evangelical learning, Wheaton College. Wheaton was where Billy Graham, the great and tireless preacher of the gospel, saver of souls, had studied. Whatever was discussed in the lecture halls and dormitories of Wheaton would soon spread to evangelical communities across the country. This was the Heart of America tour's boldest foray.

To thunderous applause from a crowd of nearly 2,500, Bono bounded onto the stage of Edman Chapel, where the students regularly gathered to ponder spiritual matters. What was about to happen on the cold, starry night of December 4, 2002, was truly radical, mind-blowing stuff. Wheaton was a deeply conservative school where, as one professor described it, the "only action open to the students was protesting abortion and saving souls," where "historically we've separated love of God from love of God's people." And here now was a rock star—a rock star, of all people, at a school that didn't even allow dancing on campus—being enthusiastically welcomed to their chapel (their *chapel!*) by the college president. The assembled actually prayed that the Almighty "use these words to energize us."

And what words they were.

"Equality is a pain in the ass," Bono bellowed from the chapel lectern, just a short walk from the Billy Graham Center. "It won't sit still, it's constantly evolving."

"Pain in the ass" wasn't exactly a passage from Deuteronomy or Lamentations or anywhere else in the Bible.

But this was: "Love thy neighbor," Bono said. That wasn't a suggestion, he added in admonition, "It's a command."

And who were thy neighbors? The hungry, the poor, the AIDS afflicted of Africa, he said. Love them, he implored, as you would the person sitting in the seat beside you. "Distance has disappeared," Bono explained.

He returned to the Bible: "Jesus said, 'I am come to bring a sword.'" And with that, Bono brandished a sword of his own—a metaphorical one, of course, a challenge to confront and rally the reticent into a crusade for social justice in Africa.

"We're waiting for a miracle in Africa," Bono said. He paused, a show-man setting the hook. "I think it is much more likely that God is waiting for us to act. God is on his knees to the church, to us, to act, to turn around the supertanker of indifference to our brothers and sisters in Africa."

The crowd hung on every syllable of his Dublin brogue. He recited verses from Matthew 25, perhaps the most powerful and poetic of those passages where Jesus addresses caring for the poor. "For I was hungry and you gave me food. . . . Whatever you do for the least of these my brethren, you do for me."

"In Africa right now," Bono said, "the least of my brethren are dying in shiploads, in container loads. And we are not yet responding. Wheaton College, will you sound the alarm?"

He challenged the campus, and by extension the entire evangelical movement, to save the physical soul as well as the spiritual one. "The prob-lems we can solve, we must," Bono urged. "We're not here looking for charity. We're looking for justice and equality. Justice and equality are at the heart of America. We need students to sound the alarm," he pleaded. "Will you sound the alarm for us?"

The audience, Sunday-morning silent, exploded like a raucous Saturday-afternoon football crowd. Epiphany tipped toward ecstasy. Sandra Joire-man, head of Wheaton's Department of Politics and International Relations, saw scales fall from eyes throughout the chapel. "For the stu-dents, the entire evening was shocking," she said. "Bono comes and they see there's a different way we can embrace this. All of a sudden, wow, he's using Scripture and it is embraced by the school. It's showing them a dif-ferent practice of evangelicalism than they had seen. The old evangelical model was: we care about your soul, not about your hunger. We've been brought forward to where social justice can be discussed."

In Bono's wake, students flocked to a class called Third World Issues; enrollment would quadruple, forcing a move to the biggest lecture hall on campus. A program called Human Needs and Global Resources, or HNGR, which sent students on six-month internships in developing countries, also grew in popularity.

"Bono's coming changed the whole school," Professor Joireman said; students had a new prism with which to view Christianity and the world. "Repent, be saved, live a sanctified life. That's viewed as insufficient by young evangelicals. They're now also asking, 'What about the other people?'"

Bono had barely left the lectern in Edman Chapel when Professor Joireman and Sister Sheila Kinsey from the Wheaton Franciscans formed the DuPage Glocal AIDS Action Network (*Glocal* being a combination of *Global* and *Local*), a community organization in surrounding DuPage County, to rally residents to lobby government representatives on poverty issues. And Bono's words were still echoing across campus when a group of Wheaton College students founded a chapter of the Student Global AIDS Campaign. The student government passed a resolution calling for the funding of the global AIDS bill before Congress at the time. Professors and students came together to draft a theological statement on AIDS. The college administration contacted Wheaton alumni in national think tanks, in Congress, and in the White House to urge action on poverty reduction matters.

From the heart of America arose a clamor: Do something, and fast.

A little girl, carrying her sister on her back, waits outside an emergency feeding tent in Boricha, Ethiopia, 2003.

Hagirso and his father, Tesfaye Ketema (center), wait for deliverance while sitting on a mattress on the floor of an emergency feeding tent in Boricha, Ethiopia, 2003.

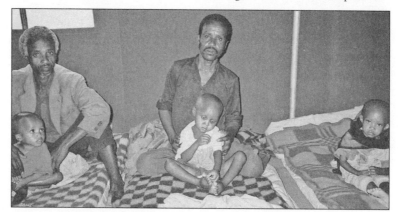

Chombe Seyoum (center, white T-shirt) with neighboring farmers on his parched fields near Adami Tulu, Ethiopia, 2003. Chombe turned off his irrigation system when prices collapsed following bumper harvests the year before the famine.

Norman Borlaug, father of the Green Revolution, takes notes on promising plants in his wheat plots. *Courtesy of the International Maize and Wheat Improvement Center.*

Henry A. Wallace studying results of corn-breeding experiments. *Courtesy of Pioneer Hi-Bred, a DuPont unit.*

Norman Borlaug with villagers in Ghana, where farmers saw their harvests multiply when they used his new techniques, 1988. *Courtesy of Christopher R. Dowswell, Sasakawa Africa Association.*

Kenneth Hood, Mississippi cotton farmer and chairman of the National Cotton Council, in 2002.

Members of the Sangare family in Mali plow their cotton field in 2002. This photo was taken the same day as the photo of Kenneth Hood.

Jerman Amente is dwarfed by sacks of Ethiopian-grown grain in his warehouse in Nazareth, Ethiopia, 2003.

Two Ethiopian lentil farmers stand beside the Djibouti-Addis Ababa road as trucks carrying American food aid, including lentils, barrel past, 2003.

Tesfahun Belachew (with scarf twirled into a turban on his head) on patrol beside the Ribb River, part of the source waters of the Blue Nile. His family was receiving international food aid in 2003 while his crops died in the drought. Tesfahun, whose name means "be hope," was unable to use the water for irrigation; it was meant to flow unimpeded to Egypt.

The wide Blue Nile near its source in northern Ethiopia during the famine of 2003.

Egyptian farmer Samir Hamed gives his calves a shower with water from the Nile River while the Ethiopian famine raged in 2003. Some 85 percent of the water in the Nile comes from Ethiopia.

Makhosazane Nkhambule, age sixteen (on right), and her younger siblings were unable to farm the family land after their parents died of what neighbors and aid workers said were complications from AIDS, 2003.

Zimbabweans in the town of Pupu await distribution of U.S. food aid, 2003.

Father Aengus Finucane, CSSp, a founder of Concern Worldwide, at Concern's Unaccompanied Children's Center in Rwanda, 1997. *Courtesy of Concern Worldwide Library.*

Flanked by AIDS activists, Bono takes his "Heart of America" tour to Wheaton College, December 2002. He was accompanied by American entertainers Ashley Judd and Chris Tucker. *Courtesy of Wheaton College.*

Bono and an African choir perform at Wheaton.

Dr. Joe Mamlin, who began handing out food along with medicine to HIV/AIDS patients in Eldoret, Kenya, 2007.

HIV/AIDS patients at Dr. Mamlin's clinic in Mosoriot, Kenya. Salina Rotich, the first patient to receive food, is in the center, 2007.

Ethiopian farmer Chombe Seyoum today runs the country's John Deere dealership, 2008.

Students at the Magada Primary School in rural Malawi gobble up a porridge made of corn and soy beans grown by local farmers, 2007. Hungry students make up one of the biggest markets for Malawi's small farmers.

A market stall mural beckons customers to try orange sweet potatoes, which are rich in vitamin A, in the Mozambique village of Milange, 2007.

A mother feeds her severely malnourished child Plumpy'nut in a refugee camp in Darfur, Sudan, 2005.

After photographing this starving girl in northern Ghana in 2000, Howard Buffett plunged into the fight on hunger. *Courtesy of the Howard G. Buffett Foundation.*

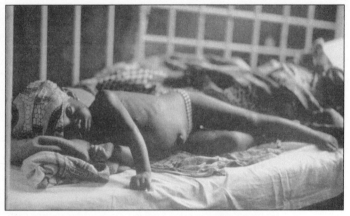

Howard Buffett teaching farmers in a Burundi corn field. *Courtesy of Melissa L. Hickox, 2009.*

Eleni Gabre-Madhin rings the brass bell to open trading at the Ethiopia Commodity Exchange in Addis Ababa, 2008.

Susan Kanini presents a green pepper to Jim Rufenacht of Archbold, Ohio, while Reverend Cosmas Mwanzia looks on (above). The pepper is part of the first harvest from a field irrigated with rain water stored behind the Mercy of God Dam (below) built by local farmers with funds provided by the residents of Archbold, 2007.

Norman Borlaug, at ninety-three years of age in 2007, returns to where it all began, Mexico's Yaqui Valley.

CHAPTER 11

Take with Food

MOSORIOT, KENYA

Far from the padded seats of Edman Chapel, in a rudimentary health clinic in Kenya's western highlands, another clamor for urgent action was building. The doctors and nurses were losing a patient. The AIDS medicine wasn't working as it should, and they didn't understand why.

A few months earlier, a boy had rushed into the clinic carrying what appeared to be a skeleton. It was his mother, Salina Rotich. She had wasted away to little more than skin and bones. Her weight had plummeted to seventy pounds. The oxygen level in her blood was minimal. "There's more oxygen in a rock than what she has," Dr. Joe Mamlin whispered to his colleagues.

Running a series of tests, Dr. Mamlin discovered that his patient was suffering from pneumonia, tuberculosis, and diarrhea. Further blood work confirmed their worst suspicion: Salina was dying of complications from AIDS at the age of thirty-four.

Dr. Mamlin went to work. He cleaned out her lungs and got her breathing better. He treated the diarrhea and controlled the tuberculosis. As Salina's health stabilized, Dr. Mamlin put her on the antiretroviral drugs that were beginning to trickle into Africa and to his clinic, thanks to the new money from governments and philanthropists targeting AIDS. The doctor had seen the drugs work wonders in reviving other AIDS patients, and he expected the same for Salina.

She returned to her home and faithfully followed the drug treatment, adhering to its precise regimen. When she returned to the clinic for a checkup a few weeks later, the nursing staff was shocked. Rather than measuring her recovery, they charted her stubborn deterioration. She had only slipped closer to death.

Stumped, Dr. Mamlin threw out an idle question. "Salina, what have you been eating?"

"Nothing," the patient said weakly. She was living alone, she explained. Her five children had left home to be cared for by other relatives. She was too ill to work to earn money and too weak to till her fields to grow her own food. Her cupboards were bare.

Nothing?! Salina's answer was both stunning and revelatory to the doctor who, approaching retirement, had moved to the Kenyan highlands from the flatlands of Indiana. "Of course," he told himself in his eureka moment, "the AIDS drugs won't work for hungry, malnourished patients." In fact, the drugs were so potent they could actually do more harm than good in a malnourished body.

It should have been an obvious observation, not only for Dr. Mamlin but for everyone working in the AIDS field. After all, for years back home in Indiana, Dr. Mamlin had been dispensing the standard doctor's advice when prescribing medicine: Take with food. Yet the obvious had been obscured in the furious scramble to attack AIDS in Africa. In 2002, international treatment protocols made no mention of feeding AIDS patients. The focus was on getting affordable drugs into Africa, and accelerating efforts to develop a vaccine.

In the small clinic in Mosoriot, Dr. Mamlin saw that effort being trumped by a simple reality: Long before there was AIDS, there was hunger. Salina's answer, so soft and weak, was a screaming alarm for Dr. Mamlin and his team in Kenya—and for health officials toiling in clinics across the continent: AIDS can't be conquered unless hunger is, too. What good were the billions of dollars being donated to get AIDS drugs to Africa when the patients didn't have a few coins to buy something to eat, or the strength to grow food themselves?

Dr. Mamlin reached into his pocket and pulled out some Kenyan shillings to buy eggs, milk, and cornmeal for Salina. Week after week, the doctor gave his patient money for food. And week by week, she gained strength. Finally, the antiretroviral drugs began to work.

"Once I started eating," Salina reported, "I started to get better." After six months of receiving food from Dr. Mamlin, she had gained seventy pounds. She returned to her fields to grow her own corn and other vegetables and fruit.

Salina wasn't alone in her hunger; Dr. Mamlin was finding that many of his AIDS patients weren't responding to the drug treatment because they had no food at home. "For 80% of people on anti-retrovirals, their health improves within six to eight weeks," he said. "But 20% don't come up. They're the ones without enough food."

(A report by the International Food Policy Research Institute in Washington, D.C., would later confirm his anecdotal evidence: An adult with HIV requires 10 percent to 30 percent more energy, or calories, to avoid losing substantial weight; children with HIV need up to 100 percent more calories.)

Dr. Mamlin knew he couldn't keep feeding patients himself, so he started his own Green Revolution, pioneering a merger of medicine and agriculture. If his network of clinics were to save their hungry AIDS patients, they would have to grow their own food. The high school in Mosoriot provided a plot to the clinic to start a garden. After that, Dr. Mamlin began organizing farms anywhere he could get a slice of land.

The doctor became a farmer. Back in Indiana, he had authored papers on blood pressure and bacterial endotoxins. Now, he began reading up on the life span of passion-fruit vines. He surveyed the construction of a tomato hothouse. He studied the application of fertilizer and the distribution of seeds. He analyzed the benefits of drip irrigation. He began breeding chickens. Of the 3,500 chickens in his program, he would proclaim, "Any one that can't lay an egg becomes a contribution to our meat stock."

One of the farms stretched more than two acres just beyond the morgue of the Moi Teaching and Referral Hospital in the main western highlands city of Eldoret. Dr. Mamlin would regularly make the rounds of the verdant garden of carrots, onions, cabbage, collard greens, and fruit trees, just as he would inspect the wards of AIDS patients inside the hospital. "How much food are we harvesting today?" he would ask the staff in the same urgent manner he would quiz them about a medical diagnosis. "How many people are we feeding?"

Every morning a truck would stop by the farms, pick up the freshly harvested fruit and vegetables, and then deliver it to a network of clinics in western Kenya. There, the doctors would hand the patients a prescription for drugs *and* a ration card for food.

"In the U.S., I could sit in my office and write a prescription. But here, amid hunger and such poverty, I can't just write a scrip," Dr. Mamlin would explain. "There are no calories in the drugs."

A tall, rangy man with a crown of white hair, Dr. Mamlin was often compared to Dr. Albert Schweitzer, whom he resembled not only in appearance but in his dedication to a medical practice in Africa. He had been revered as a professor of medicine at Indiana University and the chief of medicine at Wishard Memorial Hospital in Indianapolis, where he created a neighborhood health-care system for the inner-city poor. In 1989, he and other doctors from Indiana formed an academic exchange program with Moi University in Kenya—medical students from each school would travel to the other for training. In the early 1990s, Dr. Mamlin spent two years in Kenya as a visiting professor for the program. In 2000, he returned to Eldoret to head up the university partnership.

This time, he noticed a drastic difference from his previous stint in Kenya: Patients in the hospital wards were dying at a much faster rate and at a much younger age. AIDS was exploding across the country and the continent. "We find ourselves in the middle of maybe history's worst pandemic," Dr. Mamlin told his colleagues.

One night, walking the corridors of the hospital, Dr. Mamlin spied one of the fifth-year medical students sitting on a bed cradling an emaciated patient and feeding him with a spoon. "What are you doing?" the doctor asked the student. "This is my classmate," the student replied.

A chill raced through Dr. Mamlin's body. The epidemic had struck at the heart of his program. The deathly ill patient was one of the Kenyan medical students, Daniel Ochieng. Dr. Mamlin scrambled to come up with a treatment; Daniel became the partnership's first patient to be given the regimen of antiretroviral drugs. "It took six weeks, but we saw Lazarus come back from the dead," Dr. Mamlin later recalled. "We thought, if that can be done for Daniel, how many more can we save?"

No longer, he knew, could the partnership remain a purely academic program. "To stay and do what we were doing would have been absurd," he said. "It would have been immoral to walk around oblivious to what was going on around our feet."

While the student exchange continued, a new purpose and urgency seized their work: The partnership would become a practicing health-care network working with government clinics throughout the region. Dr. Mamlin joined other practitioners on the continent in the mad rush for drugs. Initially, he corralled enough money from the partnership's benefactors in the United States to treat forty patients, then hundreds. Then Salina was carried into the clinic in Mosoriot.

What emerged, the Academic Model for Prevention and Treatment of HIV/AIDS, or AMPATH, was the first and most comprehensive food-and-drug treatment program in Africa. Dr. Mamlin's formula: Distribute food to patients on the antiretrovirals for the first six months while the medicine gets them back on their feet. One of the doctor's orders: Provide enough food to feed not only the patient but the entire family as well. "You can't just feed the patient when there's no food in the house," Dr. Mamlin insisted. "How can you feed just the mother and not the children?"

Once the patients recovered their strength, AMPATH would keep them on their feet by helping them to grow their own food or to get another job that would earn money to buy the food. The same *Shamba la Ukiwima*— "AIDS farms," in Swahili—that provided the food for the patients would become their training grounds.

"It gives the patients a sense of not only getting well but of also being able to control their own food security and income," Dr. Mamlin said. "When a patient first comes to me wasted and dying, the eyes look up and ask for medicine. After two months, when they are a little more powerful, those eyes look up and say, 'I'm hungry.' After six months, those eyes look up and ask, 'How do I get a secure life, be independent?'"

Standing at the deadliest crossroads in the world—where AIDS intersected with hunger—Dr. Mamlin could see the traffic of aid moving in both directions. He was grateful that such big money was flowing into

AIDS research and drug distribution in Africa. But he was dismayed that it was ten times more than what was being spent on agricultural development. Compared to the billions targeting health care, the mere millions in Norman Borlaug's Sasakawa Africa budget to improve the continent's farming was statistically irrelevant.

But some of the big spenders were beginning to notice, too. As they traveled the world to visit their health projects, Bill and Melinda Gates saw how malnutrition was negating the efficacy of some of the medicines they had been supporting. In 2002, the Gates Foundation helped launch the Global Alliance for Improved Nutrition, a public-private partnership focused on fortifying staple foods like corn, wheat, and soybeans with micronutrients missing from most diets in the developing world.

And the World Food Program began hitting up its donors, mainly the rich-world governments, to provide funds for its nascent programs to feed orphans whose parents had died of AIDS or were too sick to operate their farms. "We cannot win the battle against AIDS by focusing on drugs alone," Robin Jackson, chief of the WFP's HIV/AIDS service, would argue. "Funding anti-retrovirals with no thought to food and nutrition is a little like paying a fortune to fix a car but not setting aside money to buy gas."

Still, the world health community greeted Dr. Mamlin's model merger of medicine and agriculture with a great deal of skepticism. When the partnership appealed for funding, it was often told that adding food requirements to the recommended AIDS treatment protocol would increase the burden on doctors and clinics and distract the focus from the priority of getting drugs to Africa. And where, Dr. Mamlin was asked, were the clinical studies showing that good nutrition was vital for successful HIV-AIDS treatment?

Dr. Mamlin howled at such excuses and ignored the footdraggers. "While the HIV world awaits definitive studies proving the role of nutrition as an essential component of HIV care, we are willing to simply say, 'Food is good for sick people, especially very sick people who have very limited or at times no food security,'" Dr. Mamlin wrote in his notes. "We prefer to be caught giving food when someone discovers it is not necessary, rather than found not giving food until someone determines it is essential."

Simple common sense, Dr. Mamlin thought. "I take it as a given that food is good," he would tell his colleagues in Kenya. "At the end of the day, when in doubt, I'll feed the hungry."

By the beginning of 2003, the intersection of AIDS and hunger in Africa was more deadly than ever. Kofi Annan, the UN secretary-general, dispatched his two top lieutenants on the issues to examine the "unprecedented crisis": Jim Morris, the head of the World Food Program who was also Annan's special envoy for humanitarian needs in southern Africa, and Stephen Lewis, a veteran Canadian diplomat who was the secretary-general's special envoy for HIV/AIDS in Africa. From January 22 to January 29, 2003, they visited four of the hardest-hit countries in southern Africa: Lesotho, Malawi, Zambia, and Zimbabwe.

Wherever they went, the two men saw and heard what Dr. Mamlin and medical practitioners on the ground already knew: Without food, the battle against AIDS will be lost, and both scourges will worsen. Of that revelation, and of one particular encounter, Lewis would later write: "Malawi was a touchstone for me. It was at the Lilongwe General Hospital, stumbling through wards late one night in blighted darkness, that I recoiled with horror at the pain and suffering of the AIDS pandemic. And it was in the Malawi hinterland that I most vividly remember the impact of poverty and hunger, particularly on women, most particularly on grandmothers. I had always believed that people living with AIDS would clamor for drugs. I was wrong; they clamor for food."

While Morris and Lewis were in Africa, on the evening of January 28, 2003, President Bush rose before Congress and threw open the funding floodgates for the provision of AIDS drugs to Africa. "Tonight, I propose the Emergency Plan for AIDS Relief—a work of mercy beyond all current international efforts to help the people of Africa," the president said in his State of the Union address. He asked Congress to commit $15 billion over five years to, among other things, treat at least 2 million people with the antiretroviral drugs.

The clamoring from Middle America had succeeded. DATA and Bono had been heavily lobbying the president and his administration for a big AIDS initiative, and the pleas from Wheaton College ensured that such a proposal would have the support of the president's evangelical base. The president's plan would be hailed as one of his major foreign policy achievements.

"Today, on the continent of Africa, nearly 30 million people have the AIDS virus. . . . More than four million require immediate drug treatment. Yet across the continent, only 50,000 AIDS victims are receiving the medicine they need," the president said. "Ladies and gentlemen, seldom has history offered a greater opportunity to do so much for so many."

He didn't mention food, the one thing, as Morris and Lewis were hearing, Africans were clamoring for more than any other. By the time 2003 was over, the multitude of Africans on the verge of starvation would far surpass the number suffering from AIDS.

CHAPTER 12

Two Steps Forward, Two Steps Back

AROUND THE WORLD

Kofi Annan had finally seen enough. For the head of the United Nations and the highest-ranking African in the world of statecraft, the hunger of 2003 was doubly painful: It represented the failure of the world community he led and the failure of his beloved continent.

While Ethiopian children still battled for their lives in feeding centers, Annan summoned Africa's heads of state and international development specialists to Addis Ababa in July 2004. He discarded the usual diplomatic niceties. Standing under a banner blaring "A Call to Action," the UN secretary-general recited a litany of woes that left the assembled embarrassed and ashamed. Behold, he said, what Africa had become: "Nearly a third of the men, women, and children in sub-Saharan Africa are severely undernourished. Africa is the only continent where child malnutrition is getting worse rather than better. We are here together to discuss one of the most serious problems on earth: the plague of hunger that has blighted hundreds of millions of African lives—and will continue to do so unless we act with greater purpose and urgency."

Previous food summits under the UN banner stretching back to 1974 had failed, Annan acknowledged. The UN's lofty Millennium Development Goal of halving hunger by the year 2015 appeared to be "more a far-off fantasy than an achievable target" for dozens of countries, he lamented. Africa had become a continent of Oliver Twists holding out their bowls to the world, begging for more. The humiliation and misery of 2003 had to be a watershed, a catalyst for finally doing right by the poorest people of Africa, Annan insisted, or all the suffering would have been for naught. "Let us all do our part to help Africa's farmers and their families take the first steps out of chronic poverty," Annan urged. "Let us generate a uniquely African green revolution—a revolution that is long overdue, a revolution that will help the continent in its quest for dignity and peace."

There it was: a demand for the Green Revolution to finally be brought to Africa. It was a call to reverse two decades of international development theory and practice and to strike a death blow to structural adjustment. Surely, Annan suggested, the hunger of 2003 proved that agriculture was the key to lifting Africa out of such poverty, that its farmers were part of the solution, not the problem. "We are here," he told the gathering, "as part of the movement for the rural and agricultural transformation of our beloved continent."

Annan was keenly aware that a quorum of African leaders saw that far worse times were coming if something didn't change. Several months before Annan's call to action, many of those leaders had gathered in Maputo, Mozambique, and pledged to spend at least 10 percent of their budgets on agriculture and rural development—a vast improvement over the miserly amounts previously thrown toward the farmers. And shortly before the Addis summit, at a conference of international hunger fighters and African ministers in Uganda called "Assuring Food and Nutrition Security in Africa by 2020"—Vision 2020, for short—a new realpolitik emerged. There, African voices clamored for Africa to take charge of feeding its own people.

One of the most passionate of those voices came in a higher octave than is normally heard in top-level discussions on the continent. Graca Machel, the former minister of education in Mozambique who had married South Africa's legendary leader Nelson Mandela, bluntly rebuked her fellow Africans: Start the feeding and stop the fighting. "We have a proliferation of small arms on this continent," she said. "In certain places, it is much easier to get a pistol than to get a book for a child."

Researchers at the International Food Policy Research Institute, the Washington, D.C.–based agency that had convened the Uganda conference, counted more than 37 million people in twenty-two countries of sub-Saharan Africa who were in need of food assistance directly because of conflict at the turn of the millennium. They were scrounging for food either during wars, after wars, or while fleeing wars as refugees. The total number of hungry and malnourished people in those twenty-two countries—where the preoccupation of the population was surviving the violence rather than growing food, and the priority of government spending was procuring guns rather than distributing seeds—was 198 million.

"Conflict, refugees, internally displaced people and food insecurity are closely interlinked," Machel said. "We are quite aware, as Africans, that none of our projects to change the status of this continent are achievable without resolving conflict. Not only are there movements of people, but people have lost land, they have lost everything they had, they have lost even the strength and capacity to work because they have been in a debilitating situation for many, many years."

No matter which direction she looked from the podium, she saw a manifestation of her words. Uganda had been hideously scarred by conflict, particularly the murderous lunacy of dictator Idi Amin. Even during the conference, just several hours' drive to the north, government forces battled the Lord's Resistance Army, a group of rebels who talked about installing rule based on the Ten Commandments while murdering, raping, and pillaging in the countryside. The fighting had uprooted nearly 2 million people, rendered farming impossible, and left nearly half of the children in the region chronically malnourished.

Machel's passion built to a crescendo. "We need to reprioritize our resources toward development," she exhorted. "Resources that were once concentrated on armies, on so-called 'security,' must now be diverted to human security, one of whose basic aspects is food and nutrition." There can be no higher goal for a country, she said, than to feed its children. And no greater shame than the failure to do so.

Machel's message reverberated down to the shriveled cornfields in the skinny southern African nation of Malawi. The region's drought had stretched on through 2004, and food production in Malawi fell precipitously. More than 5 million people—nearly half the population—went hungry. Bingu wa Mutharika had become president in May 2004, and one of his early official acts was to formally declare a state of emergency so the UN could launch a special appeal for food aid. The country held out its begging bowl, and $110 million worth of emergency food rushed in to fill it. Countless lives were saved, but Mutharika felt humiliated that he couldn't feed his own people. Enough is enough, the president told his countrymen. Malawi couldn't continue to live on food handouts every year. "If we are to make hunger a thing of the past," he said, "we need to make serious changes. No longer business as usual."

So Mutharika, a development economist and diplomat, brushed aside two decades of dictums from outside advisers and declared that Malawi, a former British colony, was starting its own program to subsidize the provision of seeds and fertilizers to the country's farmers. Such subsidies had been eliminated in the early 1990s under pressure from the World Bank. Now, the bank and Britain's Department for International Development howled in protest at Mutharika's plan, which was the first substantial challenge to the discipline of structural adjustment. The bank threatened to withhold new lending if the president persisted.

The president persisted. "These are Malawi's children who are starving, not the World Bank's," he told his cabinet. "As long as I'm president, I don't ever again want to go begging for food."

Mutharika's government introduced a $55 million fertilizer and seed subsidy program for 1.4 million small farmers in 2005. That year, Malawi's production of corn doubled to 2.6 million metric tons, yielding a surplus of several hundred thousand tons above the national demand. The next year, the subsidy program was expanded—partially paid for with money saved when a big portion of the country's international debt was canceled—and the corn harvest topped 3 million tons. In 2007, Malawi would sell surplus corn to Zimbabwe for $120 million, and, in a stunning turnaround, would even donate corn to the World Food Program to feed the hungry elsewhere in Africa.

"We wanted to make a statement: With good policies, you can feed your country and you can help others in need," said Patrick Kabambe, permanent secretary in the ministry of agriculture.

The subsidy program also helped expand Malawi's nascent democracy into the countryside. As it crafted the procedure for distributing the fertilizer and seeds, the government for the first time consulted with farm organizations and the agricultural private sector. And it brought the rural areas into development discussions. "This has become a politically burning issue," said finance minister Goodall Gondwe. "Our political foes are saying there's hardly any money around. They mean around in the cities. We're making rural life more attractive. That's where the votes are. But don't write that!" He erupted in laughter and leaned across a table in his office. "Today in Malawi, you really, really have to pay attention to the farmers. All the politicians now know that."

Once the World Bank and British development officials saw the economic benefits of the homegrown subsidy system—it actually made money for the country through the export of surplus crops—they offered their financial help to extend the program. In doing so, the bank's actions repudiated two decades of its development theory and sparked a reconsideration of the practices of structural adjustment, at least those that applied to farming.

At the same time, a change in leadership at the bank set the table for a new attitude toward agriculture. James Wolfensohn retired after his second five-year term as president and was replaced in mid-2005 by Paul Wolfowitz, President Bush's deputy secretary of defense who was best known as a mastermind of the Iraq war. Although Wolfowitz was criticized by humanitarian activists for a lack of experience on development issues as well as for his hawkish record, he brought a fresh curiosity about agriculture's ability to lift economies. He had seen firsthand how the Green Revolution benefited Asia while serving as President Reagan's ambassador to Indonesia in the 1980s. Several months after becoming World Bank president, he and other officials decided that for the first time in twenty-five years the bank's annual *World Development Report*—a seminal study that often sets development priorities for years to come—would focus on agriculture as a potential engine of poverty reduction in the developing world.

While the report was being prepared, the bank's conscience was pricked by scathing criticisms from within. In 2007, a critical internal evaluation report blasted the bank for neglecting African farmers by reducing spending on agricultural development. A glossy booklet the bank itself published, *Fertilizer Use in African Agriculture: Lessons Learned and Good Practice Guidelines,* bluntly blamed the structural adjustment demands that governments abandon fertilizer price controls, end subsidies, and dismantle state distribution agencies for increasing hunger in Africa. "Although these reforms had generally positive impacts on government budgets," the authors found, "they resulted in significant reductions in overall levels of fertilizer use and increased food insecurity among many rural households."

Wolfowitz made agriculture a top priority—along with cutting off lending to corrupt regimes—but his tenure ended in June 2007 with allegations that he used his position to help his girlfriend, a bank staffer, get a better job. Fortunately, his successor, Robert Zoellick, who had been President Bush's top trade representative, continued to push the bank's farm policy in the same direction. His work on the Doha trade talks had schooled him on the importance of agriculture in the developing world, particularly the role of subsidies. He quickly embraced new World Bank research that showed agriculture could be far more effective at raising the incomes of the world's poorest people than any other sector of the economy. In October 2007, the *World Development Report* called for the bank to quickly boost its investments in agricultural development and to create the conditions for a Green Revolution in Africa. Malawi's program was hailed as a model to follow, a worthy case of "smart subsidies."

It was then that Kevin Cleaver, the World Bank official who argued that Borlaug's methods weren't appropriate for Africa, acknowledged that the bank's past strategy for African agriculture—a strategy he helped articulate—hadn't worked out as expected. "My error was I thought that if the government got out the private sector would go in," Cleaver said minutes after participating in a panel discussion on the report's findings.

As the conference room cleared, the lanky economist lingered at the head table. He had left the World Bank to work at the UN's International Fund for Agricultural Development as an assistant president in 2006. He wanted to make clear that part of what had motivated his trust in Africa's private sector was his distrust of Africa's public sector. He had seen too much government corruption and ineptitude. In the early 1970s, in Zaire, he had worked in the Ministry of Finance of President Mobuto Sese Seko, who routinely used the public treasury as if it were his own. At the bank, Cleaver despaired as agricultural projects that flourished in Asia, Latin America, and North Africa withered in sub-Saharan Africa.

"What's changing," Cleaver said as he hailed the return of World Bank support for agriculture, "is now we see African governments are starting to care more."

At the same time that Malawi was implementing its subsidies, another African voice, on the other side of the continent, also rose to challenge the old development order. In the West African nation of Liberia, Ellen Johnson-Sirleaf became Africa's first elected female leader. After her election in 2005, and after nearly two decades of civil war had ravaged her country, President Johnson-Sirleaf told all who would listen that it was time to put down the guns and pick up the plows. "African leaders need to prioritize agriculture," Johnson-Sirleaf said in an interview with *The Wall Street Journal* shortly after assuming office. "We have spent so much on security and defense. Agriculture has to come first, that will be the basis for our industrialization. That's the way it has happened in every developed country in the world. If we don't get food security and agriculture development first and foremost, we'll never get to our industrialized objectives.

"We have to be careful about food imports," she continued. "To those who want to give us aid, we must say, 'Give us seeds and tools instead of food.'" She blasted the World Bank and the International Monetary Fund for not allowing African governments to support their farmers; that, she said, had led to woefully undeveloped agriculture across the continent and a dependence on international food aid. "Rethink subsidies," she urged. "Support farmers more, rather than using money to import food. We must do our own subsidies to bring agriculture back to full food security, to export."

To show the way, President Johnson-Sirleaf planted high-yield rice in a swamp behind her home in the capital of Monrovia. This action recalled images from four decades earlier when India's Indira Gandhi tore up a flower bed to plant Norman Borlaug's new wheat strain as the Green Revolution took root in Asia. That dramatic gesture became an enduring symbol of the political will that was vital for the success of the Green Revolution. Johnson-Sirleaf was hoping to convey the same message. "We all have to get involved in production," she said. "We all have to try to feed ourselves to the extent possible."

The assertive voices of Africa crying out that food must be a priority were becoming a chorus. In a letter to the White House in May 2005, health ministers from Kenya, Zambia, and Zimbabwe thanked President Bush for his $15 billion AIDS program, and then passed on a piece of bush wisdom. That great gift, they warned, would be lost if there wasn't an equal amount invested in agricultural development. Giving AIDS medicine to a patient who doesn't have enough to eat, they told the president, "is like washing your hands and then drying them in the dirt."

All these calls to aid the African farmer stirred action within the United Nations and Western capitals. Jeffrey Sachs, a Columbia University economist and UN special adviser on the Millennium Development Goals, crafted a series of Millennium Villages in ten African countries, where simple agricultural, health, and educational initiatives would be launched. The goal: Prove that an investment of roughly $110 per person per year in those villages could lead to food self-sufficiency and even surplus production for the market. To expand such initiatives across the continent would require a doubling of aid spending by the fraternity of developed countries. That, in turn, would be reachable if those countries would invest just 0.7 percent of their gross national income on the development of the world's poorest countries. At the time, their development assistance generally amounted to between 0.1 percent and 0.5 percent of income.

That aid target was also coming into the sights of British Prime Minister Tony Blair as he watched the empire's former colonies sink deeper into poverty and misery. Back in 2003, as hunger spread, Blair and Bob Geldof had established the Commission for Africa to draw up a blueprint to reverse Africa's slide. The commission recommended increased public aid and private-sector investment for the continent to support the work Africans were doing themselves. "We are storing up trouble for the future," the commission warned in its 2005 report. "The longer Africa's problems are left unaddressed the worse they will get."

International activists hailed the report and designated 2005 as the Year of Africa to shine a light on the problems of hunger, disease, and debt. They zeroed in on the summit meeting of the Group of Eight in Gleneagles, Scotland, that Blair would be hosting that summer. Bono and Geldof organized Live 8 concerts, reprising the Live Aid concerts held during the Ethiopian famine of 1984–1985, and other organizations rallied 31 million people around the globe to send text messages or e-mails to the G8 leaders. The grassroots movement, A Global Call to Action Against Poverty, attracted 120 million signatures.

At the summit meeting, Blair pushed his fellow heads of state to heed these calls. The year before, meeting on Sea Island, Georgia, the G8 leaders had endorsed a plan promoted by President Bush grandly titled "Ending the Cycle of Famine in the Horn of Africa, Raising Agricultural Productivity, and Promoting Rural Development in Food Insecure Countries." The document begins: "We are united in our belief that famine is preventable in the 21st century." At Gleneagles, Blair urged his fellow leaders to put up the money to achieve that goal. After two days of talks, they agreed to a doubling of aid by 2010, which would mean an extra $25 billion for Africa, and to writing off as much as $55 billion in debts of the world's poorest countries.

The British prime minister—who had earlier described Africa as "a scar on the conscience of the world"—injected a moral, as well as economic, urgency for ending the hunger in Africa. "If what happens in Africa happened in any other continent in the world, there would be a complete and total outcry," he told *The Wall Street Journal* in an interview in 2005. "It's just so cruel and tragic." He was in Davos, Switzerland, after he had given the opening address to the World Economic Forum. The prime minister had changed from his dark suit into jeans and a polo shirt and was drinking a local Alpine beer, Monsteiner Huusbier. Relaxing in his hotel suite, he made a rare (for a British politician) connection between religion and public policy: "You can't be a person of any faith and see what happens in Africa and not be ashamed at the world not doing anything about it."

The next day in Davos, at a press conference with Bill Gates and Bono, Prime Minister Blair said, "All of us feel the moral force of what happens in Africa, but also an enlightened self-interest." Such wretched poverty, he worried, would be a breeding ground for anti-Western sentiment. For the sake of Western security, he said, "It isn't sensible to let Africa stay in this shape."

Not all the self-interest in the West, though, was so enlightened. There remained many people who failed to heed the lessons of the 2003 famine. The guilt for Africa's hunger problems, they continued to believe, wasn't theirs. They pointed to the actions of Robert Mugabe in Zimbabwe and Omar al-Bashir in Sudan and said, "There, those are the guilty ones."

So, despite the pledges from their heads of government, some politicians in the United States and Europe didn't follow through with support for Africa, electing instead to continue their self-interested policies. They remained firm in supporting their own farmers with agricultural subsidies that tilted trade in their favor; in the Doha round of world trade talks, there was little movement to scale back Western subsidies and create an even plowing field around the world, even though African negotiators insisted subsidy reform was their top issue. The American Congress refused to consider reforming the U.S. food-aid policy, despite growing evidence that it had become outdated. Both the United States and Europe plunged deeper into programs to turn food into biofuels, despite signs that world grain stocks were diminishing as the demand for food soared from burgeoning middle classes in emerging powers such as China and India. And the wars against terrorism in Afghanistan and Iraq tapped the treasuries of Western countries for ever-greater amounts. That spending prompted a budget squeeze, jeopardizing those lofty promises to increase aid for international development, particularly to Africa. The 0.7 percent target of the rich countries receded further and further into the distance.

"The G8 are way off track with their commitments to increase effective aid, the kind that we know works," concluded a 2007 report by DATA, Bono's advocacy organization that monitored the progress of the Gleneagles promises. "The G8 were right to make bold promises—and profoundly wrong to let them slip."

Writing in the report, Liberian President Ellen Johnson-Sirleaf scolded: "The G8's commitment to Africa seems to be faltering. . . . If these promises are not kept on both sides, we cannot realize our collective dreams for Africa."

It was the unenlightened self-interest in the United States, Britain, and other rich countries—the exact opposite of what Blair called for—that made hollow the rhetoric of the G8 leaders, betrayed the effort of Africans to help themselves, and propelled the world toward a greater food crisis.

Andrew Natsios, the administrator of the U.S. Agency for International Development, had craved the flexibility to buy surplus grain in Ethiopia during the famine of 2003. He knew it would get to the hungry faster, and it would be cheaper, than bringing in food from the United States. He also knew that any suggested change to the policy of shipping only U.S.-grown food would be met with fierce resistance from the Iron Triangle of food-aid interests and their allies in Congress.

But as the G8 leaders intensified their focus on Africa, Natsios thought he saw an opening. He suggested to President Bush that reforming the decades-old food-aid program would complement his initiative to end famine in the Horn of Africa. In early 2005, the White House sent the next fiscal year's budget to Congress with the proposal that one-quarter of the $1.2 billion Food for Peace food-aid money be used to buy African crops to feed starving Africans. The administration argued it would save time on shipping, save money on the cost of commodities, and save lives—as many as 50,000 a year.

"Who could oppose that?" Natsios wondered.

He unveiled his proposal at the annual conference of the food-aid industry in Kansas City in April 2005. All the players were there: the farmers, the grain storage operators, the commodity brokers, the shippers, the humanitarian groups. Grain marketing executives in suits mingled with relief workers in blue jeans and T-shirts. Processors of everything from raisins and soybeans to salmon and buckwheat bellied up to the food-aid trough.

The 2005 gathering convened under the slogan "Strengthening the Food Aid Chain." Natsios essentially challenged his audience of eight hundred to do just the opposite. Citing the experience of Ethiopia in 2003, he asked them to loosen their grip on the food-aid money for the sake of the world's hungry. "The fact that U.S. farmers and shippers are able to benefit from the Food for Peace program is an important but secondary benefit," he said. "The primary objective is to save lives."

The audience was aghast. It was as if Natsios had asked a roomful of New York Yankees fans to renounce Babe Ruth. "He didn't make friends with his speech," said Robert Zachritz of World Vision, a nondenominational Christian aid group that had long distributed U.S. food aid. Natsios wasn't given to such understatement. "Hostile" is how he labeled the reception he received.

In the politicking that ensued, shouting matches erupted and epithets flew. When faith-based aid groups, like Catholic Relief Services and World

Vision, rejected the proposal, Natsios, who once worked for World Vision, fumed that their opposition was "morally indefensible."

After all, just inside the lobby of Catholic Relief's headquarters in Baltimore at the time, the words of Jesus jumped off the wall. The biblical verse Matthew 25:35—"For I was hungry and you gave me food. I was thirsty and you gave me drink"—was engraved on a plaque that greeted all visitors. Inspired by these words, Catholic Relief had fed millions of starving people around the world over the past half century. Pope John Paul II blessed the organization's feeding of the multitudes and extended his "profound gratitude." Mother Teresa wrote to say she kept the organization in her prayers.

In World Vision's lobby in Washington, D.C., giant wall art depicted a shepherd in blue jeans and a baseball cap walking in a grassy meadow beside still waters. Workers and visitors waited for the elevator alongside these other words of Jesus: "I have come that they may have life and have it to the full."

The White House figured its proposal would provide a chance to feed an additional 50,000 people. That, Natsios reckoned, should be enough to win over the aid agencies. But he didn't depend on divine intervention; he also offered a barrage of secular evidence. He pointed to the harmful effects of U.S. food aid on the Ethiopian market in 2003 and the disincentive to farmers. The World Food Program that year had calculated that transportation and handling costs from the United States to Ethiopia added nearly $200 to each ton of grain. Similar evidence came in from other parts of the continent. The United States had spent $57 million in 2003 delivering 100,000 tons of grain to Uganda to feed hungry people displaced by fighting in the northern part of that country. John Magnay, the chief executive of Uganda Grain Traders Ltd., estimated that the United States could have purchased nearly three times more grain if it had shopped locally and purchased surpluses produced by Ugandan farmers in other regions of the country.

In a June 2003 report to the U.S. Senate on the hunger crisis in southern Africa, the General Accounting Office (GAO) said that local production shortfalls were exacerbated by a lack of timely food-aid donations. "WFP officials estimate that in-kind contributions take three to five months from the time donors confirm the contribution to the arrival of food aid at its final distribution sites," the report said. "However, according to WFP officials, when contributions are made in cash and procurement is done within the region, the process can be reduced to one to three months."

The GAO also reported that Zambia had rejected 76,000 metric tons of American corn, fearing that it contained biotech products that could harm the health of the food-aid recipients, interfere with the country's agricultural biodiversity, and impact its ability to export its own agricultural products to other countries wary of biotech contamination. Some African countries required that U.S. whole-kernel corn first be milled before crossing their borders so none of the biotech kernels would end up being planted by local farmers. The GAO quoted WFP estimates that milling the corn in South Africa added another $80 per ton to regional distribution costs.

Armed with this mounting evidence on the benefits of local-purchase flexibility, Natsios counted on the support of the charities, particularly the faith-based ones, to carry the debate in Congress. He planned to approach legislators with this line: "The humanitarian people need this to save lives and fight famine."

But over the years the charity organizations had become one side of the Iron Triangle of farming, shipping, and humanitarian interests that benefited from feeding hungry people. Several dozen relief organizations participated in the distribution of food aid; in fact, it was a central part of their operations abroad. For Catholic Relief, donations of commodities and transportation costs, which came largely from the U.S. government, totaled $281 million in fiscal year 2004, or just over 50 percent of its budget. For World Vision that year, donations of U.S. Food for Peace commodities and associated transportation costs amounted to $166 million, or about one-fifth of its revenues.

No side of the Iron Triangle had an interest in seeing less American food shipped abroad. In fact, they wanted more. Relief agency officials had come to the Kansas City convention wearing white buttons displaying a simple black "2"—as in $2 billion, which was the food-aid funding level they were seeking from the federal government. That amount would nearly double the spending from the previous year. Natsios's proposal, however, spread fear that the food-aid budget would actually shrink. Humanitarian aid officials argued that a cash item in a budget would be easier to cut in the future than a food item that would keep money in America.

Warned Michael Wiest, Catholic Relief's chief operating officer who had spent two decades in Africa: "The largest crisis in the history of the food aid program is upon us."

The relief officials cautioned that slashing funds spent on U.S. commodities would erode the farm sector's interest in food aid. Arguing from a humanitarian perspective that food aid should be funded because it is the right thing to do—that feeding the hungry is the American thing to do—wouldn't be nearly enough. Only economic self-interest, they believed, preserved food-aid funding. "If you break up the coalition," Wiest argued, "we will be less able to help poor people around the world than we are."

Natsios scoffed at such a rationale. "If you can get more food for the money, why not do it?" he asked. "Just to protect the cartel?"

The "cartel" was a cottage industry with outposts scattered throughout the American economy. There were the lentil farmers on the Palouse whose biggest customer was the food-aid program. There were the commodity-processing giants like Bunge Limited, which sold cornmeal to the government. There were the companies that made the patriotic-labeled sacks that held the food aid. There were the forty-five government employees working at a nondescript suburban Kansas City office park who dispatched e-mails and faxes to commodity suppliers, inviting bids on food-aid orders for everything from flour to dehydrated potatoes. And there were men like Dwayne Jordan, who filled those U.S.-themed bags with Palouse-grown wheat at the Port of Lake Charles, Louisiana, which handled upwards of 400,000 tons of food aid each year.

Jordan didn't much like the White House proposal. "If you start spending the food aid money overseas, you start losing jobs here," he said, wiping the sweat from his forehead on a blistering-hot Louisiana afternoon. He noted that his pension was tied to how many hours he worked; the less food aid he packaged, the smaller his pension. "You won't find many people here in favor of that," he said.

There weren't many to be found in Congress, either, when hearings were conducted on Natsios's proposal. All sides of the Iron Triangle rallied to oppose any change. The testimony featured a steady drumbeat of concern—not over how many additional lives the proposal would save but whether it would be good for the American farm industry.

Sourcing food aid overseas "would deprive the U.S. agricultural community of their sense of pride and compassion," testified John Lestingi, vice president of Rice Company, a Roseville, California, exporter, during a House hearing in June 2005.

"It is our right to provide aid in the form of food instead of cash," chimed in Jim Madich, vice president of Horizon Milling, a joint venture with commodity-processing giant Cargill, Inc., whose units and ventures did big business selling grain to the U.S. government for use in foreign food-aid programs.

Bob Goodlatte, Republican chairman of the House Agriculture Committee, said last rites over the cash proposal. "Moving funds into foreign markets, into the pockets of U.S. farmers' competitors in the global market, is not a good use of taxpayer money," he argued. Food aid, he insisted, "must come from American farmers" so the benefits would continue to "circulate through the American economy."

The White House proposal to shift one-quarter of food aid to cash, for the sake of saving time and money and lives and helping African farmers, failed in 2005.

And in 2006.

And in 2007.

And in 2008.

The Partnership to Cut Hunger and Poverty in Africa, a Washington, D.C.–based advocacy group, tried to broker some movement toward reform. "Meeting the food needs of hungry people must be the priority driving U.S. policy on food aid," it argued. Several aid agencies, like Catholic Relief and World Vision, accepted the need for some local-purchase flexibility. And Congress did approve a token pilot project—just $60 million over four years—in the Farm Bill. But still the Iron Triangle was able to hold back any significant reform with its same mantra, as conveyed by the U.S. wheat industry in its congressional testimony: "Our philosophy is simple: Keep the food in food aid."

One big obstacle to reforming U.S. food aid was that most of the money for it was controlled by the agriculture committees in Congress rather than the committees dealing with foreign policy. This was a legacy of food aid's original purpose: disposing of surplus crops. Members of the House and

Senate agriculture committees jealously protected the interests of their farming constituents, rather than prioritizing what was best for U.S. foreign policy—or the world's poor.

Similar political self-interest doomed any chance for reform of the U.S. agricultural subsidies in the Farm Bill, even though the time had never been more ripe for change. The Depression-era formula for doling out federal aid based on per-bushel production was no longer fulfilling the original purpose: putting money into the pockets of poor Americans, many of whom at the time were farmers. The concentration of the agricultural business from smaller family farmers to bigger operations had reached the point that most of the subsidy money was collected by the larger farmers. The more bushels a farmer produced, the bigger the subsidy check. Fighting poverty by the bushel wasn't effective anymore. In 2004, for instance, the U.S. Department of Agriculture sent $807 million in government checks to farm operators with annual incomes exceeding $200,000. By 2006, the largest 10 percent of U.S. farms in terms of sales reaped more than half of all government payments. And the bulk of that money flowed to just 22 of the 435 congressional districts, according to the Environmental Working Group, Washington, D.C.–based critics of production-linked subsidies.

During the Depression, farmers' income was half that of nonfarmers. In 2007, the average household income of farmers was $86,233, which was 27.5 percent greater than the average income of all U.S. households, according to the USDA. It had been the same story every year during the life of the 2002 Farm Bill. The average household income of farmers grew by 31 percent between 2002 and 2007, compared to just 16.9 percent for all American households.

The financial advantage that farmers had over the typical U.S. family was even greater when it came to wealth, a function of the fact that farmers control much of the nation's land. According to the Federal Reserve System, the median net worth of U.S. households was $93,100 in 2004. The comparable figure for U.S. farm households was $456,914; that amount rose to $533,975 in 2007. The gap likely expanded through 2008, a year in which the net worth of the U.S. farm sector hit $2.1 trillion. The average farmer was now better off financially than the people he fed; still, the government continued to tax the latter to subsidize the former.

Emboldened by these economic realities, a number of taxpayer groups began mobilizing against subsidies. They were joined by antihunger activists, like Bread for the World, who saw how Western subsidies contributed to the African hunger crisis of 2003. Strange bedfellows—from Oxfam on the Left to the libertarian Cato Institute and the National Taxpayers Union on the Right—formed the Alliance for Sensible Agriculture Policies to campaign against the subsidy system. They even began winning converts in the Farm Belt.

In Iowa, one of the most heavily subsidized states, a lanky, mustachioed Republican running for state agriculture secretary in early 2006 told farmers they should get smaller federal checks. Mark W. Leonard, who campaigned in a white cowboy hat, explained to a group of farmers gathered in a building on the Iowa State University campus how federal payments spurred overproduction, depressing prices for growers overseas. "From a Christian standpoint, what it is doing to Africa tugs at your heartstrings," Leonard told them. He had come to this conclusion after Oxfam arranged for him to escort a Mali cotton farmer to church gatherings near his farm in Holstein, Iowa. At every stop, Leonard had listened to tales of how U.S. cotton subsidies undermined the livelihoods of African farmers.

The antisubsidies coalition also enlisted environmentalists, who believed that the system of paying farmers by the bushel encouraged growers to work their land too hard in order to get as much federal money as possible. It was hardly a coincidence, they noted, that four of the crops Washington had chosen to favor—corn, wheat, cotton, and soybeans—consumed 60 percent of all of the nitrogen, phosphate, and potash fertilizers used in the United States. Farmers certainly didn't want to waste any fertilizer, on which they spend roughly $10 billion annually. But despite increasingly precise application methods, chemical-tainted runoff from the fields seeped into the waterways that eventually funnel into the Mississippi River. A toxic stew had spawned a dead zone in the Gulf of Mexico that in some years has been bigger in size than the state of Massachusetts. The U.S. Environmental Protection Agency reported that excessive nitrogen and phosphorus in the water had fueled a population explosion of algae, which used up so much oxygen that fish and other marine life couldn't survive.

At the same time, growing pressure on the federal budget from Washington's war on terror prodded the White House and Democratic leaders in Congress into a rare consensus: Farm subsidies cost too much. The president, who had signed the 2002 Farm Bill sweetening subsidies, now wanted to get serious about reform. Not only were farm subsidies a drag on his budget, but he had gotten an earful on the damage that Western subsidies were inflicting on African agriculture during his two trips to that continent. Subsidies, he was told, were undermining the goodwill generated by his AIDS initiative.

And there was pressure from the Doha round of negotiations at the World Trade Organization, through which the United States and European Union hoped to win more access to developing countries for their industrial goods and financial services. While developing countries had in the past meekly ratified global trade deals negotiated by the Western powers, now China, Brazil, and India had rallied a bloc of developing nations to demand a big cut in the subsidies paid to farmers in the United States and the European Union. No farm subsidy cuts, no new markets for Western companies, they insisted. The White House, fending off lawsuits within the WTO to stop U.S. subsidies, feared international trade relations would be gravely harmed.

Then domestic politics intervened. The Democrats won control of both the House and the Senate in the 2006 elections, and the party leadership's ardor for subsidy reform faded. Rather than lead the charge, they retreated. The Democrats were anxious to solidify their control of Congress in 2008—as well as win the presidency—and so wanted to avoid putting any seats at risk. And changing farm subsidies might just do that in the Midwest and the South, where the farm lobby was the most powerful.

The farm industry had invested wisely in lobbyists over the years. Because almost every state has farmers, virtually all one hundred senators were susceptible to pressure from farming interests. In the House, meanwhile, legislators from farm districts had a history of putting farm interests before their party even as partisan bickering grew more toxic in nearly every other policy area. And the legislation behind farm subsidies had been structured to make it unusually hard to undo. Unlike many laws, which automatically expire on a predetermined date, the laws underlying subsidies weren't programmed to end. Instead, if Congress didn't craft and enact a

new farm bill every five years or so, the law reverted back to the Agricultural Adjustment Act of 1938 and the Agriculture Act of 1949, which contained even sweeter payments to some farmers.

Thanks to this cunning bit of lawmaking, the farm lobby hadn't had to
justify the existence of the subsidies the way it would have if the programs
were automatically slated for extinction. Rather, Congress was often in a
race to avoid that chaotic leap back in time.

In the Darwinian world of Congress, the longevity of the Farm Bill had
given it time to evolve survival skills. Over the decades, the USDA extended
its reach into many new areas, creating political currency for the congressional agriculture committees even as the farm vote shrank to less than 1
percent of the U.S. population. The farm bill setting the USDA's budget
grew to include money for food stamps, school lunches, meat inspectors,
rural utilities and housing, soil conservation, export credit guarantees, crop
insurance, and the fighting of forest fires. Less than a third of the money
spent by the USDA would end up in the pockets of farmers; most would go
to nutrition programs for low-income families, children, and elderly.

The expansion of the USDA's responsibilities empowered farm-state
legislators by giving them something to swap with lawmakers who couldn't
tell a heifer from a steer, let alone a countercyclical payment from a loan-
deficiency payment. Legislators who wanted more money from the agriculture committees for nutrition programs aimed at the poor had to go
along with handouts to farmers living in far better circumstances.

And so, when the 2002 Farm Bill came up for renewal, it didn't matter that the markets had been going through enormous changes in 2006
and 2007 that would have made it relatively painless to wean many farmers from their supply-based subsidies. A new push for corn-based ethanol
fuel was in effect subsidizing demand for all sorts of crops. As farmers raced
to plant more corn to make ethanol, prices of the crops they nudged aside
also rose. Processors of everything from soybeans and wheat to popcorn
and lentils had to raise their prices in order to keep farmers interested in
growing enough of their crops.

At the same time, U.S. agricultural exports were soaring to record levels. A weak dollar was making U.S. exports more attractive to foreign buyers as the swelling middle class in countries such as China and India were
able to spend more and more on food.

Many U.S. farmers reaped the most profitable years of their careers between 2004 and 2008. Net farm income, the USDA's rough measure of profitability, hit a record $86.8 billion in 2007, up 48 percent from 2006. In 2008, net farm income edged even higher, to $89.3 billion.

As the grain markets boomed, the size of subsidy checks shrank. Although some of the federal payments to farmers wouldn't change from year to year, much of the subsidy money was linked to market prices. Crop by crop, Washington had established a per-bushel price (or in the case of cotton, a per-pound price) that bureaucrats calculated would allow growers to recoup their investment and stay in business. For example, the government's target price in the 2002 Farm Bill for a bushel of corn was about $2.60 and for a bushel of soybeans $5.80. When market prices fell below these targets, which was usually the case, the government was obligated to make up the difference. By late 2006, however, market prices had climbed above the levels that automatically triggered price-support payments. And many economists were beginning to forecast that growing demand for crops around the world would lift the prices of America's subsidized crops to a new plateau.

Opponents of the crop-subsidy system hoped this outlook would do more than anything to get farm groups to go along with the reform movement. It seemed to be in the financial interests of farmers to finally break away from the old production-linked system and tie their payments to another formula, such as environmental practices or past levels of financial support.

But it didn't happen. Farmers simply didn't believe that commodity prices would stay high for long enough to make their traditional subsidies worthless. They had heard such talk before. Amid an export boom to Asia in 1996, a Republican-led Congress anxious to cut the federal deficit passed legislation to wean farmers from subsidies over seven years. But Washington backed off after a few years when Asian exports suddenly cooled, and the U.S. farm economy entered one of its cyclical tailspins.

And so the agriculture committees of Congress did what they do so well. To overcome a rising wall of opposition, which included the White House, the farm-state legislators offered a bigger batch of political goodies to their nonfarm colleagues. The result was the most bloated Farm Bill in history.

The Farm Bill that was finally enacted in June 2008 had 672 pages, 60 percent more than the 2002 Farm Bill. According to Congressional Budget Office forecasts, the federal government will spend about $104.2 billion during the life of the five-year bill on programs that put money into the bank accounts of farmers. The amount covers everything from crop–price support payments to land-idling checks to crop-insurance subsidies. The bill's pork included an authorization to sell National Forest land to a ski resort and money for desert lakes. In exchange for a big increase in spending on nutrition programs, farmers won an increase in the subsidy rates for several crops, the lengthening of the list of anointed crops eligible for support, and the creation of a "permanent" disaster fund for livestock and crops.

President Bush, who had tried to keep the Doha talks alive by offering America's trading partners a reduction in the U.S. spending cap on certain subsidies by 60 percent over five years, took the extraordinary step of vetoing the Farm Bill. But it didn't matter. Congress easily approved the legislation a second time with a veto-proof vote.

Farm groups applauded the 2008 Farm Bill for providing "stability" to agriculture. The Doha round of trade talks sank deeper into a coma, Mark Leonard lost his race for Iowa agricultural secretary, and critics of the subsidy system could only complain about a squandered opportunity for reform. "The pigs at the trough continued to promote generous handouts from taxpayers," said Oxfam. Added Craig Cox, a vice president of the Environmental Working Group: "The staying power of subsidies is remarkable."

Another burst of American self-interest was turning food into fuel at an ever-accelerating pace, even as global stocks of grain were dwindling and world hunger growing. Despite the 2003 famine, which portended ever-greater strains on the world's food supply, Washington politicians ignited a boom in the ethanol industry—which uses corn to make a gasoline additive—and it became a major competitor with the world's hungry for food. About 30 percent of the 2008 U.S. corn crop was destined to go into cars.

Once again, a subsidy put the hungry at a disadvantage in the competition with energy companies. Ethanol had been a sacred cow for Washington since the 1970s, when the Arab oil embargo hobbled the U.S.

economy and ensnared it in the Middle East's ancient conflicts. Ethanol was an easy answer to the challenge to develop alternative forms of fuel because it was simple to make from grain, which the United States often produced in great abundance. Corn kernels proved to be a rich source of the sugar loved by the yeasts and other microorganisms good at making the ethanol brew, which was basically the same thing as the beverage alcohol that had long been distilled from corn and other crops. But the ethanol industry isn't economically viable on its own because ethanol is more expensive to make than gasoline. So since 1978, the U.S. government had given oil refiners a tax credit for every gallon of ethanol they added to gasoline. The government also moved to protect the industry from Brazil's cheaper sugarcane-derived ethanol brew with a per-gallon tariff of fifty-four cents. These incentives grew to be worth billions of dollars annually.

After a cooling of oil prices in the 1980s and 1990s chilled investor interest in ethanol, American political interest in alternative fuels swelled again in the new century when oil began a steady climb and the war on terror and the costs of the war in Iraq increased the political appeal of a home-grown energy supply. In the Energy Policy Act of 2005, Congress mandated that the petroleum industry use renewable fuel, and set amounts that increased each year. Since corn-derived ethanol was the only renewable fuel of any size, it benefited most from the act. The mandate called for 4 billion gallons of renewable fuel in 2006, escalating to 7.5 billion gallons by 2012.

These incentives fueled an ethanol-plant building boom across the Corn Belt. In what was the biggest investment movement to sweep rural America in decades, farmers and their neighbors raided their nest eggs to pour billions of dollars into local ethanol companies. By the end of 2007, the ethanol industry had grown so big that its 134 plants were capable of producing 7.2 billion gallons annually, far more than the federal estimates of what the country would be needing for several years. And dozens more plants were under construction or on drawing boards.

To keep up with this dizzying expansion, Washington ratcheted up the mandates, compelling the petroleum industry to use even more ethanol. Congress passed the Energy Independence and Security Act of 2007, which mandated the use of 9 billion gallons of renewable fuels in 2008 and 36 billion gallons by 2022.

In 2004, about 1.2 billion bushels of corn, or 11.6 percent of the country's harvest, was turned into fuel. Just two years later, ethanol plants used 1.6 billion bushels, or 14.4 percent of the crop. By 2007, 20 percent of the nation's corn was being turned into ethanol—the equivalent of an Iowa corn harvest.

This demand pushed corn prices skyward. It also scrambled the amount of other crops being grown; so many farmers abandoned their traditional crops to grow corn for the ethanol industry that prices of soybeans, sorghum, and barley climbed sharply, too.

The United States wasn't the only country feverish with biofuel mania. Food-to-fuel mandates proliferated around the globe. About 40 percent of Europe's fourth-largest crop by hectares—rapeseed—was diverted to make biodiesel after the EU set a target of getting 10 percent of its motor fuel from biofuels by 2020. The needed crops would occupy about 15 percent of all the arable land in the EU realm. In Asia, Thailand and other countries adopted the policy of encouraging the use of biodiesel made from the oil of a local tree called the oil palm, widely used in the region for cooking oil. The push contributed to a near doubling of the price of palm oil in the country in 2007, forcing the Thai government to allow the import of 30,000 tons. In India, the government began offering subsidized loans to sugar mills for building ethanol plants. Brazil encouraged its consumers to use sugarcane-derived ethanol by taxing ethanol-containing fuel at a lower level than gasoline. Canada, China, and Indonesia also adopted mandates or targets for biofuel production.

Critics scoffed that it was all counterproductive. In their eagerness to reduce, by even a little, their dependence on high-priced foreign oil, these countries inadvertently coupled the price of several major crops to the price of petroleum, making their economies even more vulnerable to the nonrenewable resource. In the West, in particular, the motor-fuel business is so big that a huge share of these crops must be consumed to make even a small dent. The United States used about 20 percent of its record 2007 corn harvest to make an amount of ethanol that displaced only about 3 percent of the 142-billion-gallon gasoline market. Not only does a gallon of ethanol push a car fewer miles than a gallon of gasoline, but the growing and harvesting of corn consumed a lot of petroleum in the first place. U.S. corn farmers applied natural gas–derived fertilizer on their fields, ran their tractors and combines on diesel, and operated natural-gas heaters to dry their crops.

For the hungry of the world, though, this was the bottom line: Filling a twenty-five-gallon fuel tank of a sport utility vehicle with a blend containing 85 percent ethanol—the highest mixture available at commercial pumps in the United States—would consume about eight bushels of corn, which contained enough calories to feed a person for a year.

Jean Ziegler, the then-UN special rapporteur on the right to food, did the math as forecasts indicated the United States would soon be pumping billions of bushels of corn into cars. What it added up to, he charged, was a "crime against humanity."

CHAPTER 13

The Missing Links

KENYA AND GHANA

That hunger was on the rise in an era of technological wonder was the shock that history needed to repeat itself. Six decades after the Rockefeller Foundation—which was then the world's largest philanthropy—formed the Office of Special Studies, the Gates Foundation—now the largest private philanthropy—launched its Strategic Opportunities initiative in January 2005 with the immodest goal of divining how its money could have the greatest impact on reducing the greatest inequities in the world. And just as the Rockefeller scientists in the 1940s focused on reducing hunger after seeing their work on malaria and hookworm disease undermined by malnutrition, so did the Gates staffers turn to agriculture, as they saw that hunger was the core cause of many of the illnesses and deaths they were trying to prevent. Failed crops and underachieving agriculture trumped the vaccines and drugs. They, like Dr. Joe Mamlin, found themselves working at the deadliest intersection of disease and hunger.

"When you visit a rural clinic in Africa, you see all the patients are farmers," said Rajiv Shah, a veteran of the Gates health program who directed the Strategic Opportunities review. "And you see that malnutrition is tied to poor harvests." How could we make inroads on major health challenges, they asked themselves, without simultaneously working to reduce rural poverty to sustain health?

The reemergence of big-time philanthropic investment in agriculture and improving the incomes of poor farmers was vital if hunger was to be conquered. The political will for such an assault by governments and statesmen flourished primarily in rhetoric, the promised deeds so often defeated by narrow domestic self-interests. If Kofi Annan's call for an African Green Revolution was to be realized, it would need the firepower of a battalion of well-funded social entrepreneurs in Africa and beyond determined to create new institutions, develop markets, and improve products to end hunger and help Africa feed itself. The Gates money, as it had done in the health field, would attract talent, energy, and a new set of business skills and economic know-how to the long-neglected space of African agriculture.

In its hunt for strategic opportunities, the Gates team looked at more than forty potential investment targets around the world, from farming to sanitation to finance. "What is the driver that helped communities move out of poverty?" Shah asked his team. "Where are the biggest inequities in the world, where are the biggest levers to resolve them?"

No matter where they looked, he would later explain, "we always came back to agriculture. We saw it was a big problem, it was getting worse, the global effort was getting less. That looked like a crisis to us. And we saw that agriculture is tremendously important for reducing poverty."

Once they settled on agriculture, they dug deeper. As they poked around Africa, the Gates project scouts saw noble efforts with great potential: scientists bent over in fields nurturing new seed varieties, efforts to fortify staple crops with micronutrients like zinc and vitamin A, tinkering on basic, affordable irrigation systems. But many of these efforts were occurring in isolation, starved for funding and struggling to gain the traction necessary to make an impact beyond a single community.

Always the Gates team asked these questions: Could its efforts on agriculture be scaled up quickly to benefit millions of people, particularly the small farmers of the developing world? Could progress be sustained, financially and environmentally, if the foundation funding stopped? And, the biggest question of all: Is hunger really solvable?

The Gates scouts studied the successes of agricultural transformations throughout history: in the United States, Europe, and Japan, and the Green Revolutions in Mexico, India, and China. And they also studied failures, most recently the market busts that triggered Ethiopia's 2003 famine.

In Africa, they discovered a convergence of forces opening the door to a new agricultural revolution. More national governments were making agriculture a top priority so they could feed their people. And, particularly attractive to the Gates crowd, new technologies were spreading across the continent, like hybrid seeds to boost yields and cell phones to disseminate market information. Villagers who never had landline telephones jumped a generation of technology straight into cellular phones, which were peddled and serviced by entrepreneurs in tiny kiosks sprouting up along Africa's main byways like flowers in the Sahara after a rain.

After sixteen months of exploration, the Gates Foundation had its answer: Yes, hunger could indeed be conquered. African farmers had the potential to lift the continent out of poverty. In contrast to health care in the developing world, which is largely a humanitarian act, agriculture is economic empowerment. Shah, who had been the foundation's deputy director of policy and finance for the global health program and before that was the health care policy adviser on the 2000 presidential campaign of Al Gore and a policy aid in the British parliament, explained the critical difference: Health is a public good; someone, somewhere, has to pay for it. Agriculture is a market enterprise that can be self-sustaining; it generates revenues and creates wealth, along with feeding people.

In April 2006, the Gates Foundation restructured to include a global development division. In June, one of the world's other richest men, Warren Buffett, pledged to donate 10 million shares of Berkshire Hathaway, Inc., stock to the Gates Foundation to be delivered over time in annual installments; at the time, the gift was worth about $31 billion. In September, this new philanthropic money hooked up with old money as the Gates Foundation joined with the Rockefeller Foundation, which was already in Africa working on new seeds and improving soil but making little headway. Together they would take up Kofi Annan's call in Ethiopia and launch the Alliance for a Green Revolution in Africa (AGRA). It would be based in Nairobi, Kenya, and be led by Africans (Annan would later become the chairman). The initial investment was $150 million. It was just the kind of history-changing, millions-of-lives-to-be-saved challenge that aroused the passion of the twenty-first-century philanthropists. By coupling agricultural investments with the foundation's health work, they believed they could dramatically move the needle on African development.

The Gateses knew the plunge into agriculture wouldn't be without controversy. And it started with the name of their cornerstone venture: Should it include the words *Green Revolution*? In some circles, particularly among environmentalists, that phrase evoked the overuse of fertilizer and the strain on water resources that were consequences of Asia's Green Revolution. The foundation said a main focus of its Strategic Opportunities research was to learn from the past; it studied the abuses of fertilizer and water and decided that its efforts to boost crop yields would focus more on using better seeds than on applying more fertilizer. They would look at growing crops that return nutrients to the soil, and using farming methods such as crop rotation and no-till agriculture that renew soil without chemicals. And they would focus on projects that harvest rainfall rather than tapping groundwater and aquifers. They would embrace the words *Green Revolution* for the promise they conveyed. That promise became their mantra: feeding millions, saving lives, reducing poverty.

The Gates global development team also encountered criticism from antiglobalization activists wary that all ideas and wisdom for Africa would henceforth descend from Seattle. Indeed, the foundation offices on the shores of Lake Union were about as far away as you could get, geographically and materially, from hungry, drought-plagued Africa. To defuse this argument, Shah set out to attend development conferences around the world and tell audiences that the foundation had few ideas of its own to implement on the ground in Africa and rather was expecting that ideas would come to the foundation. The foundation wouldn't be operating its own programs, he said, but would instead be funding and enabling others to do the work. And that funding, the foundation hoped, would act as a magnet to attract more money to African agriculture, just like its health funding did for global health issues. Worldwide investments by various sources to fight AIDS, for instance, exploded from just $250 million in 1996 to $10 billion a decade later.

"There is an African proverb," Shah would often say. "If you want to go fast, go it alone. If you want to go far, go together."

The agricultural proposals flooded into Seattle by the thousands. During the selection reviews, Shah's team primarily asked for two things: Did the proposed projects have a clear path to markets for whatever goods would be produced, keeping in mind that the failure to develop markets in Ethiopia had crushed farmer incentive? And did the proposals include consultations with the local communities as to how they could best benefit the peasant farmers and their families?

In his small, tidy foundation office in Seattle, Shah, the director of agricultural development, drew inspiration from a photo hanging on the wall behind his desk. A little African girl was crouching in a blue wash bucket. Only her head was visible above the bucket's rim. She, and not the mighty Bill Gates, was the one they all answered to, Shah said. "We're working to benefit her. She's the boss."

To reach her, AGRA would need to forge a sturdy chain linking the African scientists creating new seeds in their laboratories to entrepreneurs selling the seeds in their tiny shops to farmers planting the seeds in their fields to consumers shopping for food in the markets. In Alliance parlance, this was called the "value chain." During Asia's Green Revolution, Shah knew, such a chain "pulled hundreds of millions of people out of poverty." In Africa, structural adjustment policies had broken so many links in the chain that it wasn't pulling anyone out of the mire.

"It's the seeds, stupid!" Joe DeVries proclaimed while barreling through the Kenyan bush in a four-wheel drive. "Farmers plant seeds."

DeVries, a Rockefeller Foundation plant scientist based in Nairobi, had been working for several years to repair the first link in Africa's agricultural chain. But conjuring up new seeds for Africa was a lonely pursuit, and frustration over the lack of additional support was mounting. "We felt that among private donors we were working in obscurity taking a serious swing on ending hunger," DeVries said. "Ending hunger went out of fashion."

So serious was the international neglect of African agriculture that even when DeVries and his colleagues did make a breeding breakthrough, the new seeds mainly languished on the laboratory shelves, collecting dust rather than poking through dirt in the fields. National governments and international institutions showed no interest in, and had little funding for, distributing the seeds to farmers or driving markets for the crops. Instead of forging a strong chain, the scientists felt like they were "pushing rope," DeVries said.

The formation of the Alliance for a Green Revolution in Africa allowed the Rockefeller team to shift their Program for Africa's Seed Systems into high gear. PASS had already prepared the intellectual soil: The scientists had come to realize that one magic seed wouldn't do as much for Africa as Norman Borlaug's dwarf wheat strain did for Asia. The continent's growing areas were too varied, ranging from rain forests to deserts, for a one-seed-fits-all approach. "Jump in your car and go 100 miles," DeVries noted, "and you're in a different agro-ecology area."

Which is precisely what he did on a bright Saturday morning in early 2007. Jumping in a Toyota Prado, DeVries set out from the lush Nairobi highlands for the much drier southern plains, home to many a drought and to one of the main breeding labs of the Kenya Agriculture Research Institute. "In Asia, the Green Revolution took place in a big bang," DeVries said while navigating around gaping potholes that threatened to swallow vehicles on the main national highway running from Nairobi to the Indian Ocean port of Mombassa. "Here, it'll be more of a rolling revolution than a big bang. You'll need lots and lots of scientists and lots and lots of research. Instead of one or two Borlaugs, we need to train up a whole generation."

One of the would-be Borlaugs, James Gethi, enthusiastically greeted DeVries at the research station. The two shared a common mission, for Gethi's life, too, was all about seeds. A scholarly Kenyan, Gethi had studied plant breeding in Canada and the United States and then returned home dreaming of scaling Borlaugian heights, inspired to spark a revolution.

Toiling in the national research lab, deploying his nation's scarce scientific resources, he often felt overwhelmed by the weight of responsibility: Kenya's farmers, he believed, were counting on him to develop the next generation of hybrid corn seed and ease the hunger of their families. But he worried that he wouldn't have the funding to follow through on his research, or if he did develop a new hybrid, that the discovery would rot in his lab for lack of interest to get it out to the farmers. The Gates-Rockefeller assault on hunger electrified him and his work. "Now I know I won't be dropped in the middle of my research," he told DeVries.

The excitement was palpable at the agricultural research station. Gethi ushered DeVries into his lab on the second floor of a two-story building designed for the stifling African heat. The open-air corridors captured even the slightest breeze and funneled it through all the offices. Similarly, the breeders working there had caught the fresh air of the Gates-Rockefeller funding and turned it into a whirlwind.

Gethi was working to breed crops for three growing ecologies—coastal, hills, drylands—while wrestling with several riddles: water stress, corn blight, weak soil, and postharvest susceptibility to weevils and other pests. Just outside the lab stretched a vast test field. Even on a Saturday, scientists were bent over their crops, scribbling into notebooks. They were inspecting new strains of sorghum and cassava, two sturdy crops that had been utterly neglected throughout Africa during the previous thirty years. They were even tending an experimental plot for a plant that produces a chemical for combating malaria.

Gethi led the way to his particular corner, a patch of tall, strong corn stalks. "We want to give the farmers something better than what they have now," he said while admiring a couple of succulent ears being bred to resist drought. "This is coming along nicely."

He walked to another patch that was testing for pest resistance. As he waded into the long rows of corn, he rubbed against some leaves, and three larvae attached themselves to his khaki pants and brown shirt. "We don't spray the trial crops, we want the worms here so we know what to breed out," he said, flicking the pests off his clothes. Sometimes, he said, the breeders become so familiar with the pests that they give them names. Particularly persistent and strong beetles had been named "Scandia," after the sturdy Scandinavian trucks that survive Africa's rugged roads. Others that were especially destructive had been christened "Osama."

The test fields revealed how much catching up there was to do in Africa. Gethi was working to improve some corn varieties that farmers had been using for fifty years despite ever-lower yields. They had passed the seeds down from generation to generation with no breeding updates to adapt to changing soil or weather conditions or new pests. The most recent corn variety being used by peasant farmers in the area, he said, had been introduced in 1995. "The efforts hadn't been put into developing new seeds," Gethi complained, "or, if they did, those efforts didn't come to fruition because funding dried up."

The Alliance injected a new urgency and purpose. DeVries told Gethi he was impressed by the new corn varieties on display in the test plots, and urged him to move to the next link on the chain with haste. "Let's get the seeds to the farmers as quickly as possible," DeVries said. The quickest way to end hunger, he insisted, was to "get the research out of the laboratory, off the shelves and into Africa."

But, as the Alliance discovered, that was no simple matter. Indeed, moving the latest advances in agricultural technology from Africa's research labs to the fields of its peasant farmers had long been one of the missing links of Africa's agricultural revolution.

It was also one of the continent's greatest mysteries. No matter where one roamed in Africa, be it a sandy settlement in the Sahara or a village deep in the thick equatorial bush, someone would be selling Coke, Pepsi, Fanta Orange, Guinness stout, or the beer from the national brewer. But why were the latest seeds and fertilizers rarely to be found in these distant outposts? "Too many people figured that African farmers are limited in capability, financially and intellectually," DeVries concluded. "There's been such a long time of selling them short."

The result was that most producers of seed, fertilizer, and farm implements didn't bother to sell to them at all. They believed there was no market in subsistence farmers tilling only a few acres. Those farmers might be able to afford a Coke or a beer, went the corporate calculations, but how could they afford more than a handful of hybrid seeds or a thimbleful of fertilizer? The competitive hustle driving the soft drink and beer distributors to penetrate the deepest bush—Coca-Cola's slogan was "a Coke within arm's reach," and it had achieved the goal almost everywhere—was a foreign notion in the agricultural sector. The farm supply companies, be they government monopolies or private enterprises, were largely content to drop their wares in the larger towns and cultivate business with the bigger, wealthier commercial farmers. The seed and fertilizer dealers for the most part sat in their shops sipping the ubiquitous Cokes, believing that the small farmers, if they wanted something, would come to them.

DeVries knew that if the labor of scientists like Gethi was to put a dent in Africa's hunger problem, the Alliance would also have to forge the next links in the value chain: the seed companies who would turn the new hybrids into commercial products, and the small shopkeepers in the bush who would sell them to the peasant farmers. DeVries met with the handful of private seed companies in Kenya and struck a bargain with them: The Alliance would bankroll the development of new seed strains if the companies would put the discoveries into production and then market them. "Don't worry about the seeds. That's what we're doing," DeVries said.

Saleem Esmail, for one, jumped at the partnership. He was the chief executive officer of Western Seed Co., Ltd., based in western Kenya. As one of Kenya's newest private seed companies, Western—slogan: Bringing Technology to the Farmer—saw an opportunity to reduce its own research expense, and thus lower the cost of its seeds. In contrast to the big international seed companies, Western had zeroed in on the poor growing ecologies and the poor farmers who live there. That, Esmail decided, is where its profits would be found. "The private sector needs the poorer areas to be successful and sustainable. Then the private sector can start making sustainable profits," he said. The peasant farmers would sell their surpluses produced from the better seeds, and the seed companies would meet the farmers' growing demand. "That," said Esmail, "is a phenomenal power!" He continued, "If you give the farmer what he wants, then he's well on his way. He wants what gives him better yields, more food, better storage." But there was one catch: "The farmer has to have what he needs, on time, and he has to be able to afford it."

That was the next link in the chain needing repair, so the Alliance, through its funding of the Agricultural Market Development Trust (AGMARK), began cultivating a network of shopkeepers, called stockists, to sell seeds, fertilizer, and other farming necessities alongside their other goods. Most of them were young, well-educated, and entrepreneurial. The majority were pharmacists or veterinarians who cleared space beside the deworming medicine and tick powder; a few were proprietors of hardware stores who stocked the farming essentials beside saws, nails, paintbrushes, and Super Glue. "This is the new breed that will change things in Africa," said Caleb Wangia, East Africa regional director of AGMARK, as he set off on a tour of his clients. An affiliate of CNFA, a Washington, D.C.–based agency that aids rural entrepreneurs, AGMARK trained stockists to sell the latest farming technology, taught business and accounting skills, and provided credit guarantees to help the stockists establish trustworthy relationships with the agricultural supply companies. Above all, AGMARK encouraged shopkeepers to take up posts off the beaten paths, to get the farming materials closer to the farmers. "These stockists can play a big role in the food security of Africa," Wangia said. "The small farmers want to use the best inputs, the hybrid seeds, the fertilizers, to be more productive and grow more food, but the distances have been so great. The rains come, they want to plant, but they can't get to the city shops. So they just planted any old seeds they could get. The vicious cycle continued. They never got ahead."

The gregarious Wangia talked nonstop as he drove through the western Kenyan highlands, near the border with Uganda. He turned off the main paved road onto a narrow dirt strip that was deeply rutted and studded with jagged stones. Though the terrain was flat, bicyclists often dismounted and pushed their way over particularly rugged passages, tiptoeing past voracious potholes. Even the ubiquitous *matatus,* the colorful daredevil vans packed with people that serve as Kenya's main mode of transportation, wouldn't venture on this road. After cruising down the paved highway, Wangia slowed the four-wheel drive to a crawl on this perilous washboard, leery of scraping bottom and leaving a muffler or exhaust pipe behind.

Three bumpy miles down from the last patch of pavement, Wangia pulled to a stop in the small village of Nalondo and approached a row of hovels made of wood and corrugated metal sheeting. Gregory Wanjara Wayongo peered out from behind the counter of a shop lit only by the sunlight rushing through the front door. The shelves behind him groaned under the weight of cans and sacks of seeds: onions, collards, watermelon, tomatoes, cabbages, and, most abundantly, hybrid maize. Bags of fertilizer lined the floor. Backpack sprayers and small irrigation pumps added to the clutter.

Wayongo, an earnest man in his midthirties who had studied veterinary science in school, was a true pioneer in these parts, a Kenyan Johnny Appleseed. Before he set up this shop, bringing seeds and fertilizer to this isolated village, the farmers were forced to go on a long trek to gather their essential elements. "Eight kilometers, ten, twenty," said Wayongo. Five miles, six, twelve. That was the distance, depending on where you lived, to the outskirts of Bungoma, the main city of this district on the Ugandan border. The seed companies and other agricultural suppliers would travel the paved road to Bungoma and unload their products there. For the farmers, it would be an all-day journey to the shops, two days if it rained; if it rained hard, the trip would be canceled altogether.

Wayongo, who was running a veterinary service in Nalondo, watched the seasonal migration of farmers trekking for their supplies. "I noticed that farmers were going into the big town to buy what they needed," he said. "I saw an opportunity and decided to open a shop." He would do the traveling for the farmers. "I'm too much off the main road to have the suppliers come here," he said. "So I hire a vehicle to go to them in Bungoma."

With their travel time cut in half, at least, farmers from Nalondo and neighboring villages flocked to Wayongo's shop. If they got an early start, they could pick up their supplies and be back home planting and tending to their fields all in the same morning. "Before, the farmers didn't use the hybrid seeds and fertilizer so much. They didn't bother if they couldn't get into town in time," Wayongo said. "Now they come to me and are interested in what's best for their farm. They come to me for technical advice. They have lots of questions."

Wayongo had plenty of questions himself. He signed up for an AGMARK seminar and learned about seed science and soil nutrition, as well as bookkeeping skills and inventory management. He learned to cater to his customers, whether that meant repacking seeds and fertilizer into smaller amounts for farmers with only one or two acres or forming savings groups with his farmers so they would have enough money when planting season came around. He displayed the certificate from the training course prominently in his shop, behind the counter. Beside the front door he posted another AGMARK sign: "Trained in Business Management Skills and Product Knowledge and Safe Use of Farm Inputs."

The sign became a customer magnet. Wayongo told Wangia he was averaging 300,000 Kenya shillings (about $5,000) in monthly sales; during the main planting season, in March and April, he would sometimes rake in 30,000 shillings a day. This made him a veritable mogul in a rural area where many people lived on only a few dollars a day. To drum up more business, he planted a trial plot with a new hybrid maize seed that had been bred for the region's short rainy season in September. When the corn was about to tassel, he invited farmers to come and inspect the tall, robust crop. They came with little notebooks and pencils, and took copious notes as Wayongo told them about the seeds. "The farmers were impressed. Seeing

is believing!" Wayongo said. Sure enough, after the demonstration, orders
for the next planting season poured in. As bigger harvests arrived, he began
connecting farmers to consumers, and he contemplated becoming a buyer
himself; with AGMARK, he had his eye on purchasing a mill so he could
turn the farmers' corn into flour. When violence followed nationwide elections in late 2007, disrupting the flow of supplies to many rural areas in
western Kenya, Wayongo would go out of his way to get the necessary seeds
and fertilizer for his farmers.

"You are the pride of your community!" Wangia proclaimed, wrapping
an arm around his former student. "It's great you're here, in the interior of
the country." He turned to address the crowd that had gathered in Wayongo's shop. "See here, this is the new breed bringing the Green Revolution to Africa."

Meanwhile, on the other side of the continent, another American philanthropist retraced Norman Borlaug's footsteps.

Howard Buffett's dusty SUV pulled into Fufuo, the village in the
Ashanti region of Ghana where Borlaug had struggled to sustain a Green
Revolution two decades earlier. The burly Illinois farmer, accompanied by
Ghanaian agronomist Kofi Boa, hurried into a large cinder-block building
where thirty farmers had been waiting, sheltered from the sun.

"Would you please let them know that we are sorry we are late?" said
Buffett. He had flown that morning from Ghana's capital city, Accra,
where he and former U.S. President Jimmy Carter had visited Ghanaian
President John Kufuor. Then he bounced over rough roads from the city of
Kumasi, dodging potholes the size of cars and a careening logging truck
with "Only God Can Judge Me" written under the front window.

"Do you still have time?" the fifty-two year old asked politely.

Back home, Buffett owned eight hundred acres of corn and soybeans
and a fleet of the most modern John Deere implements. Now, standing
before these farmers who scratched the dirt with sticks and machetes, he
hoped to learn something from them. Fufuo's brush with Borlaug had
shown the villagers how new ways of farming could improve their lives.
Having tasted prosperity, they were experimenting again. Boa, the agronomist, was coaching them to replace slash-and-burn farming with a practice he called "no-till."

In many African villages, poor farmers—who are often women—had traditionally made room for their crops by chopping down the brush and trees on a few acres of tribal land. They let the debris dry for a few days and then burned it to expose the ground. In much of Ghana, the soil was so low in organic matter that a farmer could cultivate such a plot for only a few years before it was exhausted and yields plunged. Then it was time to hack another plot out of the bush.

Boa knew that slash-and-burn farming is hard on the environment and the farmer. It's a lot of work to cut brush and then burn it, which removes organic matter vital to the health of the soil. Farmers have little incentive to take good care of the soil when they move on like this every few years. Beneficial insects are destroyed, and the land is laid bare to erosion. In some parts of Africa, slash-and-burn farming is eating away at forests and destroying wildlife habitat.

This type of farming is done in places where there isn't enough fertilizer to recharge the soil nutrients taken up by the crops. Synthetic fertilizer is expensive, and livestock manure is in short supply. Insect-borne diseases limit the raising of cattle in some parts of Africa, and the livestock that do live on the continent are as malnourished as the people. The spent plots are reclaimed by the bush, where it takes five to ten years for the soil to recuperate.

The agronomist could see that slash-and-burn farming was becoming an ever-bigger problem. Africa's, and Ghana's, growing population was increasing the demand for farmland, which meant farmers were giving the land less time to recover. As the soil deteriorated, farmers worked harder and harder to produce food.

Boa preached that Fufuo's farmers should disturb the ground as little as possible. Other than poking holes in the dirt to plant their seeds, the ground was not to be hoed or vegetation burned. Organic residue—such as leaves, stalks, and roots—was valuable, not trash.

Fufuo's farmers were taught to make room for their seeds shortly before planting time by squirting the competing vegetation with Chinese-made glyphosate weed killer dispensed from backpacks. Glyphosate, which kills nearly all things green on contact, is widely used in the West. It quickly breaks down in the environment and is one of the least-toxic pesticides to animals. In the United States, glyphosate is better known as Roundup, which is made and marketed by Monsanto. In Fufuo, glyphosate gave the farmers' corn a jump on the weeds. With their head start, the leaves of the corn plant could make a canopy that starved the weeds of sunlight.

The village quickly discovered that no-till plots yielded bigger crops with far less labor. The mulch acts as a sponge when it rains, banking water for crops, and then breaks down into plant food. The time the farmers saved by no longer hoeing weeds and cutting brush was time for moneymaking endeavors. Some started to raise cocoa trees, a crop prized by Ghana's government for its export earnings; others began to raise chickens, feeding them with their surplus grain. They sold eggs to neighboring villages for extra money.

"How many seeds of corn do you plant on a hectare?" asked Buffett as he peered through thick eyeglasses and jotted down answers in a notebook while his son circled with a camera. "Can you farm more land now?" he continued, fascinated by the impact of no-till. "How much corn did you harvest? What are you paid for it? How much herbicide do you use?"

Buffett was hungry for evidence that could help him convince farmers elsewhere in Africa that no-till, a version of which he practiced on his Illinois farm, could boost their food security. His mission was to find sustainable ways for poor farmers to feed their families that didn't depend on expensive infrastructure or inputs. His foundation was spending tens of millions of dollars a year on projects such as developing a disease-resistant sweet potato, drilling wells, educating farmers, and providing microcredits.

As the queries piled up, the farmers in the room looked at one another. It had been a long time since an American had asked them so many questions. As Buffett prepared to leave, he surprised the farmers by shaking hands, African style. He extended his right arm, which bore a faint scar from a cheetah bite, and then launched into a rapid combination of finger snapping and palm slapping.

The SUV that drove off that day in February 2007 carried the man slated to one day become the chairman of the board of insurance and manufacturing conglomerate Berkshire Hathaway. As dust swallowed the vehicle, the farmers were told that their visitor was the oldest son of a billionaire named Warren Buffett.

Howard Buffett is the likeliest of philanthropists. It was ordained that he and his two siblings would see the family fortune given away rather than have it to spend on themselves. His father, who lives far below his means in a modest Omaha house, has argued publicly that it does little good for society when children inherit great wealth by virtue of an "ovarian lottery." The multiplier effect is far more powerful, the argument goes, if fortunes are used to help the less fortunate rather than to suckle a bloodline of trust funders.

It is a philosophy possible in part because of an unusual perspective on money. Howard's father is a genius stock picker who values the amount of money he makes as a way to keep score of his performance, not so much for the luxuries it can buy. Handing down more than a fraction to his descendants makes no more sense to him than allowing the children of great athletes to inherit their records on the gridiron or baseball field. Warren Buffett went to Congress in November 2007 to argue *in favor* of the estate tax, saying it counters an unhealthy concentration of wealth.

For Howard Buffett and his older sister and younger brother, their father's philosophy meant they would have to earn a living. He didn't know it at the time, but the career he built would prepare him for helping Africa's hungry. He would do it differently than anyone else.

Unlike his father, who is happiest working alone in an office pouring over reams of corporate data, Howard Buffett is gregarious and likes working outdoors. When he was twenty-three years old he cashed in stock from his grandfather to buy a bulldozer in order to start an excavating business. What he really wanted to do was farm, but he didn't have the money. His father agreed to buy a modest Nebraska farm for his son, but in classic Buffett fashion, he charged him rent at the market rate.

As the grandson of a congressman, Howard appreciated the value of public service. He became chairman of a state agency aimed at encouraging the construction of ethanol plants in Nebraska and then won election to the Board of Commissioners that governs the county in which Omaha sits. Howard's grasp of farm politics, as well as his last name, put him on the radar of Dwayne Andreas, the cagey chairman and chief executive of grain-processing behemoth Archer-Daniels-Midland Company in Decatur, Illinois.

Buffett joined ADM's board and became a corporate vice president, posts that gave him a global perspective on agriculture as he began buying land for an Illinois farm. Buffett left ADM in 1995 to avoid becoming embroiled in a price-fixing scandal and joined a nearby manufacturer of steel grain bins called GSI Group. Soon he was off to South Africa to drum up business from its large grain farmers.

It wasn't long before Buffett was smitten with Africa. At home, his interest in photographing wildlife had helped to make him a conservationist. In short order, Buffett bought land near Johannesburg for a cheetah preserve, where he soon lived nearly four months of the year. He established a small foundation to funnel money to causes such as protecting gorillas and cheetahs.

His concerns changed the longer he stayed in Africa. In late 2000, while traveling in Ghana on GSI business, he brought his camera to a hospital near the northern city of Tamale at the invitation of World Vision. He photographed a child lying motionless on her side, her belly distended by the malnutrition that was allowing malaria and meningitis to kill her. Through his lens he peered directly into the eyes of the tiny girl. Her helplessness surged into the father of five. Buffett snapped a picture and then steadied himself.

"I remember it so well still. Her mother was sitting in a chair watching hopelessly. I put my hand on her shoulder and told her how sorry I was," he said.

As journalists do in these situations, Buffett told himself that he could accomplish some good by bearing witness. Publishing her photo could help call attention to the plight of hungry children. He continued walking through the hospital and then encountered another severely malnourished child, this time a boy. The surge of emotion happened again in Niger, where he photographed a girl with a swollen belly and stick-thin legs. She died three days later.

The hungry kept jumping into his mind, even as he was photographing migrating wildebeest and zebra on the Serengeti from a rickety plane. Trying to position his camera for a picture, he saw scars on the ground where farmers had used fire to clear the land. Just as the Gates people had figured out that they had to attack hunger in order for their health campaigns to succeed, Buffett realized that he couldn't protect Africa's environment without first fighting human misery.

"I'm watching this thinking, 'They are going to destroy the last forest,'" Buffett later recalled. "It was an epiphany for me: The hungry can't worry about conservation. I realized you can't save the environment unless you give people a chance to feed themselves better."

The death of his mother, Susan Buffett, from a stroke in 2004 helped to crystallize his focus on the world's most desperate people. It also gave

him the means to make a difference. The Buffett children had always expected that their mother's foundation would oversee the distribution of
their parents' vast wealth. She had long supported medical research, education, and abortion rights, and had encouraged her children to take so-
cially progressive views. She brought young Howard along when she went
into Omaha's housing projects to help a Cub Scout troop.

Her death at age seventy-two forced Warren Buffett to confront how to
start giving away a fortune then worth roughly $40 billion. He settled on
directing the bulk of his Berkshire Hathaway shares to the Gates Foundation. He trusted Bill Gates, a Berkshire Hathaway board member who
played bridge with Buffett regularly. What's more, the Gates Foundation
had the infrastructure to handle a gift of such size, as well as a philosophy
that matched his own.

On top of this, Warren Buffett promised each of his three children's
foundations annual gifts of stock initially worth $50 million, far more than
they had ever expected. For Howard, the gift meant that giving by his
foundation, from which he didn't draw a salary, could increase at least
eightfold. "He's got my money and his mother's heart," his father said.

With one foot in American agriculture and the other in Africa, Howard
Buffett sees more clearly than most why the continent needs a Green Revolution unique to it. As he traveled from Ghana to Togo and Benin by
SUV, Howard told his traveling party how the monoculture practiced in
Asia and the West, in which farmers specialize in just a few crops, would be
dangerous in Africa. The only insurance many poor farmers have against
fickle weather and pests is to grow as many different crops as possible—
such as millet, sorghum, maize, cassava, and sweet potato—to better the
odds that there will be something to harvest.

On most of Africa's farms, Buffett had noticed, the woman's most important chore is stretching her family's food so that it lasts until the next
harvest. Adding to the misery of what farmers call the "hunger season" is
that they have the least to eat at exactly the time they work the hardest in
their fields. The smallest miscalculation means death.

"First the cattle eat less, then I start cutting rations in half, and then I
make a soup from tree leaves," a rail-thin woman who feeds seven children
in the Togo village of Borgou told Buffett.

Later that night, Buffett told a delegation from CARE, an American humanitarian agency traveling with him, that he wanted to focus on looking for ideas that would help the families of poor farmers survive the hunger season. "What is more ironic than a farmer who can't feed himself?" he said. "We can't count on mechanization or infrastructure or fertilizer reaching these people. It has got to be simple, like no-till, or better seeds. If we can double their yields this way we can make a big difference for families trying to make it through a three-month or four-month starvation period."

For Buffett, the hunger fight is all consuming. He flew 178,000 miles in 2008 to eleven African countries as he looked for ideas to go along with the dozens of projects he already had under way. Among other things, he helped organize and finance a project that will give African breeders royalty-free access to Monsanto's biotechnology for drought-tolerant corn.

He rarely stops thinking about Africa even when he is tending his farm in Illinois. He invites politicians, scientists, entertainers, and corporate executives to squeeze into the cab of his Deere tractor, where he can have their undivided attention as he navigates corn and soybean fields with global positioning technology. One of the few people he has allowed to drive his harvesting combine, worth hundreds of thousands of dollars, is Shakira, the bombshell pop singer from Colombia who has an education foundation.

A visitor to his farm asked him if he believed he is making a difference. Buffett pondered for several minutes from atop his combine. "Africa is not a lost cause," he said finally. "Sure, sometimes I ask myself: 'What am I accomplishing other than trying?' You know, maybe that is enough."

After all the hunger Africa had endured, this was no time to give up. On a number of fronts, particularly the long-neglected markets, new initiatives were finally taking off.

CHAPTER 14

The Opening Bell

CHICAGO TO ADDIS ABABA TO QACHA'S NEK

As her taxi turned on to LaSalle Street in Chicago's Loop, Eleni Gabre-Madhin was confronted with the vision that had driven her ambition since Ethiopia's famine of 2003. "Wow, there it is. It's right in front of us!" she shouted, startling the driver. The art deco tower of the Chicago Board of Trade loomed straight ahead, just a few blocks away. Under a bright morning sun, the statue of Ceres, the Roman goddess of grain, beckoned from the pinnacle. Eleni was as wide-eyed as Dorothy approaching the Emerald City in *The Wizard of Oz*.

A reception committee from the Board of Trade ushered the Ethiopian economist into the vast trading chamber, where a chaotic gathering of men and women in brightly colored jackets waved their arms and flashed signals with their fingers to initiate trades in the wheat, corn, and soybean pits. Prices on all sorts of commodities blinked on big boards hanging high around the room. "This is what it really is—the color, the people, the excitement, the numbers," Eleni marveled, savoring the flurry of commerce on that early spring day of 2007.

Since the failed markets she had long warned about plunged Ethiopia into famine in 2003, Eleni had been on a single-minded mission to create an African version of the Board of Trade. The famine had confirmed her jeremiads: The country's farmers could never thrive, could never navigate agriculture's boom-bust cycles, as long as they bore all the risk in a way that virtually no other farmers in the world beyond Africa did.

After two decades outside her country crying in the wilderness of international institutions and global conferences, Eleni had moved back to Ethiopia in 2004, determined to reform its agricultural markets. She campaigned tirelessly for the formation of a commodities exchange, jousting with top government officials to persuade them to endorse and support it rhetorically and financially. She listened triumphantly as the country's president declared in a speech that such an exchange would be the most important financial project of the new millennium (which, on the Ethiopian calendar, began in September 2007).

Eleni also recruited a team of specialists from within the country and from Ethiopia's diaspora to help shape her vision. To her surprise and delight, she discovered that there were a number of Ethiopians already working in financial markets around the world, particularly in the United States, who had expertise on trading-floor operations, securities regulation, and information technology. Eleni and her team traveled to India, China, and South America to study exchanges in other developing countries, analyzing the impact on small farmers and their production.

The greatest lessons, and inspiration, came from the most sophisticated and most famous exchange of them all: the Chicago Board of Trade. In a conference room overlooking the trading floor, officials described life for the Midwest farmer in the 1840s, before the Board of Trade opened. A lack of price discovery, an absence of reliable buyers, and a scarcity of storage capacity made farming a very risky proposition. The visiting Ethiopians nodded knowingly to each other. "That's pretty much like our farmers today," Eleni told them. They grew their crops and had very few choices when it came time to sell.

Eleni and her colleagues returned home convinced that the Board of Trade innovations that had transformed American agriculture—fair price discovery, uniform quality standards, futures contracts that would share the risk of oscillating prices—could also transform Ethiopian farming. There would be no stopping them now. Eleni began constructing the legal framework and shaping a partnership between the government and the private sector to manage and finance the exchange. The government agreed to put up a substantial portion of the fund that would protect exchange participants against trade defaults, and it also kicked in $2.4 million of the $21 million startup budget. Eleni scrounged the rest from the World Bank, various UN agencies, and individual countries such as the United States and Canada.

The skeleton of a trading floor began taking shape on the second story of a new sleek glass building in Addis Ababa, down the street from the St. George brewery. The site was surrounded in mud, and boys played soccer with a ball made of tightly wound cloth in the neighboring vacant lot, when Josette Sheeran, the new executive director of the World Food Program, stopped by. It was Sheeran's first trip to Africa after assuming the helm of the WFP in the spring of 2007. Her first visit wouldn't be to a food distribution site but to this construction zone for a grain trading exchange. Her first interviews wouldn't be with hungry food-aid recipients but with traders and farmers who could potentially supply the food aid. The inspection of Eleni's work in progress would emphasize one of Sheeran's top priorities: Use the WFP's purchasing power to support small-scale farmers, and use the markets to drive agricultural development. The WFP should be in the business of famine prevention, she told Eleni, not just famine recovery. "Part of the cycle of hunger is the lack of connection between the farmers and markets," said Sheeran, who had been deputy U.S. trade representative and undersecretary of state for economic, business, and agricultural affairs. "This exchange has the potential to make that connection and break the cycle. And it could be a model for other countries."

The WFP had become one of the largest grain buyers in Africa; in 2007, it bought nearly 900,000 tons for more than $245 million from twenty-six countries. Most of its transactions were with larger traders and farmers who had the capacity to meet the WFP's bid requirements on quantity, quality, and delivery. In Ethiopia, where the WFP bought 53,412 tons in 2007 for more than $18 million, it routinely dealt with about two dozen clients. Sheeran wanted to know if the exchange could help the WFP widen its purchasing base to reach the smallholder farmers and put more money, and incentive, in their hands.

"Absolutely," Eleni declared. Helping small farmers market their surpluses was precisely the aim of the exchange. Rather than putting out a bid to buy an amount of food, like 1,000 tons of corn, that only the largest farmers could meet, the WFP could purchase the accumulated production of a number of small farmers that would be sold through the exchange. That corn would be brought into exchange warehouses and its quality certified under the exchange's grain grading standards. The delivery schedule would be guaranteed by the exchange contract. Such a transaction, Eleni argued, would be more reliable, more transparent, and possibly cheaper because the WFP could buy at the market rate instead of the asking prices of the proffered bids. "It's time to think of pro-poor, democratic market purchases," she told Sheeran. "The exchange allows anyone with grain to sell it."

With the construction of the exchange well under way, Eleni became the leading African voice for a message rarely heard on the continent: Markets matter. As word of her initiative and passion spread, she was invited to address a group of big thinkers and entrepreneurs from around the world who had gathered in Arusha, Tanzania, in June 2007 for the TED Global conference, a marketplace of ideas where TED stood for Technology, Entertainment, Design. "Africa today is not the Africa that is waiting for aid solutions or foreign cookie-cutter policy prescriptions," she told the assembled. "Africa is learning, though perhaps too slowly, that markets don't just happen by themselves. In the 1980s, it was fashionable to talk about 'getting prices right,' which was mainly about getting governments out of the market. We now recognize that unleashing the power of the market is about getting *markets* right, which involves investing in the right infrastructure and developing the necessary market institutions. When conditions are right, we are seeing that the power of innovation is alive and ready to explode in Africa just like anywhere else."

Denouncing the misguided advice of so many development experts down through the years who neglected the potential contribution of the African farmer to the continent's development, she said, "The real question is: How can markets be developed to harness the energy of the individual farmer's drive for innovation and entrepreneurship? . . . If one thing is clear, it is that Africa *is* open for business, and that agriculture is business."

The Ethiopia Commodity Exchange opened for business on April 4, 2008, with a launch at an elaborate national forum in Addis Ababa's vast conference center. "Anything worth having, worth achieving, worth fighting for, starts with a dream," Eleni proclaimed.

Beside her stood Ethiopia's prime minister and his deputy, a raft of parliamentarians, and an assortment of ambassadors and diplomats from around the world. And before them stood 1,200 curious and proud Ethiopians. The hall was festooned with declarations of the exchange's mission: Empower farmers' choices, grow our agriculture, and transform Ethiopia. "The idea of the Ethiopia Commodity Exchange started as a dream. A dream to change Ethiopia. A dream to do something concrete about the real problems faced by real people every day," Eleni told the crowd. "Our dream is nothing less than to revolutionize the agricultural economy of our country through the market institution that we are launching." It was 160 years and one day since the first formal meeting of the Chicago Board of Trade (April 3, 1848).

For the next two weeks, the exchange conducted mock trades with its members, who by then numbered nearly one hundred, to work out any bugs. And farmers deposited more than 5,000 metric tons of corn and beans in exchange warehouses scattered around the country, ready to be sold. On the morning of April 24, Eleni reached above her head for the brass bell hanging over the exchange trading floor. She shook the chain a couple of times, and the clarion ringing opened the first day of trading.

In the trading pit, a sleek corral of lacquered wood and polished glass, a barrage of staccato shouts and a flurry of waving hands commenced the exchange's "open outcry" trading in corn and beans. That day, 185 tons of corn were traded, with the price rising nine birr (about one dollar) per 100 kilograms, from its opening; 20 tons of beans also changed hands, with the price holding steady. (Wheat and other grains and oil seeds, such as sesame, would later be added to the trading mix, as would coffee.) It was a moment Ethiopians had, literally, been dying for. Eleni's dream had been born of the nightmare of mass starvation that was triggered by the absence of an institution like the commodities exchange. Now a nation fervently hoped that the bell opening the exchange—and an era of more price transparency and more incentive for farmers—also tolled for the end of Ethiopia's ruinous cycle of feast and famine.

It was also a big moment for Africa. The proliferation of commodities exchanges in India, China, and South America that solidified the gains of their Green Revolutions had bypassed the vast interior of Africa north of the Limpopo River, South Africa's northern border. Now, finally, an opening bell was ringing on the world's poorest and hungriest continent, and it was reverberating in Malawi, Uganda, Ghana, and other countries that were tinkering with their own commodities exchanges. If an opening bell could ring in a land of epic hunger and starvation, shouldn't it carry the promise and potential of a Green Revolution across Africa? On the launch day, the continent swelled with giddy expectation that Africa was a step closer to feeding its own people. Eleni's grander dream was that the exchange would pave the way for a Pan-African trading platform. Then, perhaps, no longer would anyone starve in one corner of the continent while food piled up, unable to find a market, in another.

Eleni knew that the exchange by itself wouldn't eliminate the threat of drought or pestilence that could plunge the country—or the continent—into another hunger crisis. And a legacy of Marxist thinking and the deep scars of poverty, such as ragged telecommunications and regulatory infrastructure, presented many challenges to such a sophisticated tool of capitalism. But in addition to the commerce that would be conducted on the trading floor, the exchange stood as a remarkable symbol of possibility amid the poverty. It exuded optimism, like the street vendor who operated below the trading pit. He sold books such as *The Power of Positive Thinking* and *You Can Win* from a plastic tarp laid on the dirt and broken sidewalk pavement in front of the exchange.

The exchange's mark of success would be greater innovation and entrepreneurship among the country's legion of peasant farmers, and thereby an increase in national production. The vast bulk of Ethiopia's total agricultural output, 95 percent by some estimates, came from smallholder farmers working a couple of acres by hand. In the past, producing surpluses had only exposed them to the risks of Ethiopia's unsophisticated market: gluts, fickle demand, wild price swings of as much as 80 percent within just a few months.

The commodities exchange aimed to tame that volatility by offering a place for fair price discovery, a place where production gluts could be absorbed and distributed, a place where farmers could finally share some of the risk, a place where they could obtain a futures contract that locked in price even before planting, a place where they could be directly connected to the consumers of their produce rather than through a series of middlemen who would pocket two-thirds of the final price. A place that for the first time in their lives would give the farmers choices. "Well-functioning markets offer choices," Eleni said on the floor of the exchange. "And choices mean freedom."

Eleni and her staff barnstormed Ethiopia, explaining to smallholder farmers how they had become prisoners of their poverty. If they produced a surplus, they would likely sell it at the time of harvest when prices were lowest because everyone else was selling then. Loans were due, long-term storage facilities were scarce, the pressure was on to sell. And they usually sold to the first person who came by their farm, a person they knew, because they feared there might not be another offer. Then, later in the year, during the lean season, or the hunger season, when the family's household provisions might be running low and the next harvest was still a few months away, and when prices were at their highest, the farmers usually needed to buy.

The exchange, Eleni explained to gatherings up and down the country, would free the farmers from these bonds of time and place. A film illustrating the ins and outs of trading opened with a split screen showing a farmer walking behind an ox-drawn plow while a spinning satellite in space beamed down market information. Prices from the trading floor in Addis would flash on some two hundred electronic boards in market centers around the country. Farmers would take their surplus to one of the exchange warehouses for weighing and quality certification, and they would receive a warehouse receipt for their goods that they could sell whenever they chose. They could use the receipt for collateral to get loans for the next planting season's seeds and fertilizer or, perhaps, to install a small irrigation system. "Changing the marketing system is our hope for the future," the film's narrator proclaimed. "We must emancipate ourselves from years of traditional farming."

Demere Demissie, the general manager of the Lume-Adama Farmers Cooperative Union in the delightfully named town of Mojo, was already feeling liberated. In the co-op's concrete warehouse, dozens of women sat on the floor and prepared the harvest for market as their ancestors had done down through the ages. With fast-moving hands, they plucked weeds, stems, and pebbles from several tons of white pea beans and then tossed the beans into the air to shake off any remaining dirt, catching them in reed baskets. Demere waded into this backward scene, looking forward. "Soon, we'll be connected to the world," he announced to everyone.

He had signed up the co-op to be a member of the exchange so he could trade on behalf of his 19,000 members, most of them smallholder farmers who still walked behind their ox-drawn plows and harvested by hand. He relished the choices he would have. "If a trader in Addis offers us, say, 200 birr," he said, citing the Ethiopian currency, "we can say 'No, Chicago is at 250, London is even higher.' Before we have to take the Addis offer. Now we will know what's out there."

He anticipated his farmers boosting production. "Only price creates incentive to produce as much as possible."

Larger farmers like Bulbula Tulle and Chombe Seyoum also rushed to grab applications to become exchange members, and to embrace the promise of choices they didn't have in 2003. As crop surpluses in 2001 and 2002 triggered a catastrophic price collapse, they had no choice but to cut expenses, to leave thousands of acres of land idle, to forego fertilizer and premium seeds on the little land they did plant, and to shut off irrigation systems. They couldn't afford to do otherwise. "If we had the exchange then, maybe we wouldn't have had the famine," Bulbula confided to friends in the week of the exchange's launch. "Maybe China or Chicago could have bought the surplus grain and kept the price from falling. If we had known we could sell our surplus, we would have planted as normal. Instead, we were blind."

"It was awful, we had no choice but to do what we did," Chombe echoed. He was sitting in his Addis office, which he had transformed into the country's John Deere dealership after almost going bankrupt from his farming in 2003. "The problem then was that we weren't even able to get anyone to take away our grain. If we had the exchange, we could have taken the grain to the exchange warehouses and got a receipt and the banks wouldn't have hassled us to pay right after harvest. We wouldn't have been desperate to dump our grain," he explained. "We were all scared, the price was falling, so we all dumped our grain and made it worse. If we had the exchange, we could have kept the grain in the warehouse and used the receipt for credit, we would have kept on planting. I wouldn't have had to turn off the irrigation."

Both men said it had taken the past five years to recover from their losses. But they were still haunted by their actions in 2003: Bulbula leaving so much land idle, Chombe turning off his irrigation, while their countrymen held out their hands for food. "The impact is still there, financially, psychologically, morally," Chombe said.

Eleni hoped the exchange would be a catalyst to change both attitudes and infrastructure. Bringing technology and market information to the peasant farmers, she envisioned, would spur a demand to improve rural education. The market incentives to increase production would increase the urgency to develop irrigation projects from the country's bountiful water resources. The network of electronic price boards would prod the telecommunications ministry to roll out fiber-optic cable farther into the countryside. Pavement would smooth the rutted dirt farm-to-market roads. And entrepreneurs would devise a more efficient and safe long-haul delivery system to replace the transportation network of meandering donkey-drawn wagons and maniacally driven five-ton Isuzu trucks—called "al-Qaedas" for the way they terrorize other traffic. "This is what market-led development is all about," Eleni said, marveling at the possibilities.

That, too, was the evolving vision of the World Food Program. The WFP had been one of the early buyers on the exchange, and Sheeran was determined to do more business. The WFP's cash donations were increasing, particularly from private donors (even though the U.S. government continued to donate food only), enabling it to buy more of the commodities it needed from farmers in Africa rather than relying on food donations. In April 2008, shortly after the Ethiopian exchange was launched, she visited Eleni for a second time. Together they stood in the trading pit, believing they could change the course of Africa. "This right here is what we need," Sheeran declared, throwing wide her arms as if to hug the entire operation. "A market revolution to spur the Green Revolution."

The Ethiopian exchange had also spurred the imagination of the Gates Foundation and the Alliance for a Green Revolution in Africa, for the continent's underdeveloped markets were one of the weakest links on their value chain. Scientists could breed better seeds and shopkeepers deep in the bush could stock them, but if the small farmers couldn't find markets for their improved harvests, incentive would disappear and demand for the improved seeds would decline. The entire chain would disintegrate.

Eleni's opening bell was heard all the way in Seattle. If Ethiopian farmers were now dealing with sophisticated market devices, the Gates team reckoned, perhaps they could be introduced across the continent. The foundation took up Sheeran's call to help develop a program she called Purchase for Progress, in which food-aid purchases would create a market and income for Africa's small farmers.

The program would contract with farmers for three years to purchase a certain amount of grain or beans at a guaranteed price level—the same sort of futures contracts that Eleni was introducing on the Ethiopian exchange and that had long been the basis of farming in the United States and other developed countries. Africa's farmers could use these contracts to get financing to buy the necessary seed, fertilizer, and farming essentials to improve their harvests. The WFP and the Gates Foundation hoped that the incentive of a reliable market would lead to greater production that would bring the continent closer to food self-sufficiency. And, they hoped, commercial interests, like the world's big food companies, would one day use this contract model to purchase from Africa's farmers.

These big ambitions grew from a tiny transaction. A group of twenty farmers in Qacha's Nek, a poor, remote district in the mountain kingdom of Lesotho, had no market for their surplus corn in 2007 until the WFP stopped by while looking for food amid a severe drought. The farmers had worked hard using conservation farming methods such as terracing their hillside land to better retain precious water, and, somewhat miraculously, they grew more corn than they themselves could eat. Eight tons more. Isolated from bigger markets, and lacking facilities for long-term storage, the farmers feared their surplus would go to waste. Then the WFP arrived and bought the corn for $2,800, its first-ever direct purchase from peasant farmers in Lesotho. It was a minuscule transaction for the WFP but a huge one for the farmers; for some, it would be their only income of the year. The WFP used the corn for feeding programs in local primary schools, and it promised the farmers it would buy again, should they produce a surplus in the next harvest. The farmers of Qacha's Nek accepted enthusiastically, promising the WFP in return: If you buy it, we will grow it.

It was, in effect, the WFP's first futures contract. The next year, the farmers of Qacha's Nek and two other villages quadrupled their harvest and sold thirty-two tons to the WFP. "Even a small market," said Sheeran, applauding the transaction, "can have a huge impact on the lives of Africa's farmers."

In September 2008, Purchase for Progress was launched with a target of benefiting 350,000 farmers over five years. The Gates Foundation would invest $66 million to begin the program in ten African countries: Ethiopia, Burkina Faso, Kenya, Malawi, Mali, Mozambique, Rwanda, Tanzania, Uganda, and Zambia. The foundation of farmer-philanthropist Howard Buffett would contribute $9.1 million for work in Liberia, Sierra Leone, and Sudan, as well as in the Latin American countries of El Salvador, Guatemala, Honduras, and Nicaragua. The Belgian government chipped in $750,000 to fund the program in one of its former colonial territories, the Democratic Republic of the Congo.

Africa's agricultural value chain, the Gates Foundation believed, would be strengthened at every link: Farmers with access to a reliable market would badger the shopkeepers for the best technology to boost their yields, which in turn would create demand for the scientists to breed better seeds. It was a big step, said Bill Gates in announcing the program at the United Nations, "toward sustainable change that could eventually benefit millions of poor rural households" in Africa.

As the transaction in Qacha's Nek revealed, one of the largest untapped markets for Africa's farmers convened daily under the continent's broad shade trees and in its breezy, ramshackle classrooms: hungry schoolchildren.

In Malawi, one of the Purchase for Progress countries, 430 students of the Magada Primary School gathered under a big *masuku* tree to greet visitors from the World Food Program one cool September morning. Coughs rippled through the dry, dusty air, as if this market segment were clearing its throat in an attempt to get attention: Ahem, feed *us* your crops. There are millions of us across the continent.

"It is difficult to learn on an empty stomach, to sit through the whole day and try and concentrate," said Misheck Chiwanda, a precocious twelve-year-old boy who was chosen to represent his fellow students. He wore the uniform of his school—green shirt, khaki shorts, bare feet—and spoke with proper British English, befitting his ambition to be a news broadcaster.

A group of girls, Misheck's sixth and seventh grade classmates, had picked fresh flowers from the school's garden for their visitors. The girls arranged the pink, yellow, and red blossoms in three plastic cups and placed them on a little wooden table draped with a green and blue cloth sporting silhouettes of purple guinea fowl. The table wobbled in the dirt in the middle of the school yard.

Misheck, steady on his feet, stood at attention. "Your food," he told the WFP guests, "is very important to us."

Just beyond the massive shade tree, smoke billowed from the school's kitchen, which consisted of a wood fire and a ragged thatch roof. Like most of the classrooms at Magada, the kitchen had no walls. A large silver cauldron rested above the fire. A few sticks burned, and the heat was funneled up through a cylindrical metal stovepipe to the bottom of the cauldron. Breakfast porridge was on the boil.

One by one, before and after assembly, children as young as six and as old as sixteen, from first grade through seventh, lined up with red plastic bowls and cups and a metal spoon to receive a ladle or two of porridge. Every day, collectively, they would wolf down 110 pounds of the corn and soybean blend, known locally as *likuni phala*. For most of them, the porridge was the only hot meal they would receive that day, or any day.

Likuni phala was on the boil at schools all over Malawi that morning. Nearly a half-million hungry students waited with their bowls, cups, and spoons at 488 other schools. Throughout the 2007–2008 school year, they would devour more than 15,000 tons of corn and 8,000 tons of corn-soya blend. Almost 80 percent of that food, an amount worth about $4.5 million, was grown by Malawi's farmers, purchased by the WFP, and distributed to the schools. It was one of the single biggest markets for Malawi's farmers, most of whom worked only one or two acres, and helped to absorb the surpluses being produced under the government's program subsidizing the purchase of fertilizer and seeds. Any surplus exceeding demand would drive down prices, sapping farmer incentive.

"The opportunity for our farmers is one of the great additional benefits of school feeding," said Patricia Saukila of the WFP as she waded through the assembly of children at Magada. "It gives them incentive to grow as much as they can."

School feeding programs in Africa, first begun by mission churches and international charities and taken up by the WFP when it was founded in 1963, had always served a dual purpose: feed the children and increase school attendance. The daily meal provided desperately needed nutrition in food-scarce regions, and was a lure that attracted children to school, and kept them there. The feeding programs gave a huge incentive to poor parents to send their children to school rather than keeping them home to do household chores, particularly the girls. It meant fewer mouths to feed. In Malawi, where malnourishment had left nearly one-quarter of the children underweight and nearly half with stunted growth, some of the poorest were also given take-home rations of corn, which made school attendance an economic asset for a family. Attendance at the Magada school had doubled since school feeding began.

As with other food programs in Africa, though, markets were an afterthought. School feeding was viewed as a hunger-relief operation, part of the international food-aid effort. Most of the food served in Africa's schools was grown by farmers elsewhere.

Purchase for Progress would give school feeding a new purpose by having African farmers feed their own hungry schoolkids. Instead of a relief crutch, school feeding would become a development tool. It would also make the WFP a more reliable buyer; rather than stepping in and out of the market depending on the severity of a particular hunger emergency, the WFP would constantly be needing food to supply the school feeding programs. It was also a market that would grow itself. The more children it attracted into school, the bigger the market for Africa's farmers.

And that market is vast. In 2007, WFP school feeding programs were serving about 10 million children in Africa (that's about half the number of children it served in poor countries around the globe). The agency estimated that another 10 million African children were being fed by programs run by national governments or international aid organizations and charities. Together, those 20 million children ate 720,000 tons of grains and beans.

But that's only a slice of the potential market for Africa's farmers. UN organizations estimated there were still 23 million primary school–aged children on the continent going to school hungry; the WFP says it would need $1.2 billion to buy food to give each of them one meal a day. Beyond them, the UN believes there are another 38 million children who don't even go to school.

This enormous potential market has grabbed the attention of Africa's leaders plotting to boost agricultural production. The New Partnership for Africa's Development, or NEPAD, an organization set up by the African countries themselves to promote good governance, economic development, and self-reliance, has set a target of feeding 50 million schoolchildren with homegrown food. And it called for local governments or private companies to take ownership of the feeding programs so they could be sustained beyond the goodness of charities and relief organizations. NEPAD calculated that the provision of one meal a day plus monthly take-home rations would create a demand of 5 million tons of food a year that could be supplied by up to 2 million peasant farmers.

Margrate Ositeni began to hope that she, one day, could be one of them. She had come to the Magada morning assembly with her two daughters, fourteen-year-old Grace and twelve-year-old Tomaida, to thank the WFP visitors. Her girls, she said, wouldn't be in school if they weren't getting a daily meal there. "They would be working, doing odd jobs to earn money to buy food," the mother said, noting that her corn harvest rarely fed her family for a whole year. "I couldn't feed them otherwise."

But, thanks to the homegrown school feeding program, other Malawi farmers could. She was grateful, and inspired. Watching the assembly under the *masuku* tree, Ositeni for the first time saw a market for her labors. It gave her an idea: If she could increase her harvest using better seeds and fertilizer, there was money to be made. And she too could help feed the country's hungry children. "I didn't know that was possible," she said.

Across Malawi's southern border, in Mozambique, another group of farmers, in the village of Nhazombe, had taken the marketing of their main crop into their own callused hands. They had developed a clothing line. They had concocted recipes. They had even written the promotional jingles. Like Eleni in Ethiopia, they knew the importance of building a market while building up production. While Eleni rang an opening bell, these farmers chanted an opening refrain: "Always give orange sweet potatoes to your children if you love them. They are good for their health!" a chorus of women sang as they greeted visitors to an orange sweet potato–growing demonstration. They wore the green tendrils of sweet potato vines in their hair, like olive wreaths, and they wrapped wide swaths of bright orange cloth around their waists, like a skirt. The singing and clapping reached a crescendo in the second verse: "The orange sweet potato gives us better breast milk for our children. We grow the orange sweet potato. It is good for our health!"

Rich in vitamin A, the orange sweet potato, that icon of American Thanksgiving dinners, was certainly good for health. Tens of millions of children in Africa suffered from blindness, stunted growth, and weakened immune systems because of severe vitamin A deficiency. It had long been a noble pursuit of nutritionists and others in the battle against hunger to propagate the orange sweet potato. But in Africa, potatoes had always been white or yellowish. Putting orange-colored food on the table was like putting a blinking neon light in a cemetery. Most people wouldn't go there.

Thus did the continent's standard practice of "produce first—sell later" fail the orange sweet potato. An early attempt by one community of Ugandan farmers to grow the crop sputtered when two-thirds of the harvest never made it to market for a lack of buyers. Disillusioned, the farmers shaved their rotting sweet potatoes into orange chips and fed them to their chickens and pigs.

So when an organization called Harvest Plus introduced new varieties of the orange sweet potato in northern Mozambique, it set out to create the demand as well as the supply. Harvest Plus is a venture of the International Center for Tropical Agriculture and the International Food Policy Research Institute and is funded by the national development agencies of the United States, the United Kingdom, Denmark, and Sweden, as well as the Gates Foundation. Its mission was to breed micronutrients such as iron, iodine, zinc, and vitamin A into crops such as wheat, corn, beans, rice, cassava, and sweet potatoes. The others were staple foods already widely consumed throughout Africa. The orange sweet potato needed a marketing campaign.

"Right here, the healthy sweet!" shouted Eusebio Costa, a vendor in the central market of Milange, Mozambique.

"This potato is healthy! It helps prevent disease!" bellowed his partner, Agustin Nkhwangwa.

The two hawkers wore orange baseball caps sporting a logo of a sweet-potato stick figure riding a bike. They stood inside a new concrete kiosk glowing in bright-orange paint. Out front was an orange sign: "We sell the orange sweet potato. Rich in vitamin A."

Harvest Plus had painted the town of Milange orange. Community theater troupes clad in orange roamed the area, popularizing the orange potato through drama and comedy. Radio ads stressed the need for better nutrition. Orange murals painted on walls depicted families gathering to eat orange sweet potatoes. Orange became the color of health and good nutrition. "Being orange is an advantage. To have a non-visible trait would be more difficult," said Richard Dove, an aid worker with the humanitarian group World Vision who was coordinating the sweet potato campaign on the ground along with the International Potato Center and Helen Keller International. Dove wore an orange T-shirt and drove an orange truck.

The orange campaign was working. By the beginning of 2008, the Milange region was awash in orange food: orange sweet potato fries, orange rolls, orange cake, orange sweet potato juice. The singing ladies of Nhazombe chirped of their favorite recipes: sweet potato porridge, sweet potatoes and eggs, sweet potatoes and coconut milk, sweet potatoes and peanuts.

In the Milange central market, vendor Costa couldn't keep enough sweet potatoes in stock. "It's eight in the morning," he said, "and we're almost sold out." He had started at dawn with four 110-pound sacks of sweet potatoes purchased from local farmers. Two hours later, he was reaching to the bottom of the fourth sack and had sent his partner bicycling away to get a fifth.

Up the street at Rosa Sozinho Duarte's little grocery store, her homemade orange sweet potato cupcakes were selling like, well, hotcakes. "As soon as I make them, they're gone," she said on a Saturday morning. Her little electric oven could bake seven at a time. "If I start early enough," she said, "I can make between sixty and one hundred. People put their names on a waiting list."

She used about sixty pounds of orange sweet potatoes a week, buying directly from farmers when they came to town. Given her location on Milange's main street, on the way to the town's schools and hospital, she believed she could double or triple her sales if she had a bigger oven. A sign—orange, of course—in front of her store beckoned to customers: "Here we sell orange sweet potato cakes, rich in vitamin A for good vision and health."

Duarte winked and said not everyone bought her cakes for the nutrition. "A lot of people," she reported, "say they like them better than cakes made from wheat."

Another shopkeeper, Aissa Soares, fired up a large earthen oven behind her store. Inside the store she sold seeds, hoes, watering cans, machetes, stationery, notebooks, and soap. Out back, she baked orange sweet potato bread—"golden bread," she called it—about nine hundred pounds of it a week. "Business is really good. I'd like to open another shop," she said. "But I'll need a steady supply of orange potatoes."

The market was ripe to ramp up production. On the outskirts of town, Dove's team cleared five acres of scrub brush for the cultivation of orange sweet potato vines. Small fires smoldered at the edges, burning back the bush and driving out mice and other vermin. A battalion of boys crouched at the edge of the fire, poised to pounce on the mice, impale them on sticks, and roast them over the flames—mouse kebabs, a local delicacy! The goal of the Harvest Plus workers was to distribute starter vines to 10,800 farm families, who would then begin their own sweet potato production.

Farmer Tomas Gastin wanted as many vines as he could get. He had seen a performance of the orange campaign theater troupe and found the health promise enticing. But he was hooked when the performers suggested that orange sweet potatoes would become the next big thing in the market. He opened up an extra acre of land on his small farm and began to cultivate orange sweet potatoes alongside his cabbage, onions, lettuce, and corn. After his first harvest, he sold 1,100 pounds of sweet potatoes, and he heard the market clamoring for more. "It is a gold mine," he said, standing in his field. He was barefoot, and he wore a black-and-white-striped beret, which made him look as if he were balancing a skunk on his head. He was clearing more brush, another two and a half acres, to plant more orange sweet potato vines. After all, he was eating up some of the profit himself. "It's not breakfast without the orange sweet potato," Gastin said. "I'm fifty-two. And when I'm eating it, even I feel strong." He held up his arms, posing like a muscleman. It was a good sales pitch. Growing food wasn't enough, he knew; he needed to grow a market, too.

It was the kind of basic business know-how that was beginning to come to the aid of Africa's hungry and malnourished.

CHAPTER 15

Getting Down to Business

DAVOS TO DARFUR

"One . . . two . . . three . . . four . . . five . . ."

Peter Bakker, chairman of the huge Dutch express delivery company TNT, was counting.

"We live in a world where every five seconds a child dies from hunger," he said.

He fell silent. He stared at his feet. He counted in his head. One . . . two . . . three . . . four . . . five.

He looked up. "I've been silent for five seconds," he said. "Another child has died."

Squirming through every second of silence were some of the high and mighty gathered at the World Economic Forum in Davos, Switzerland, in January 2008: The secretary-general of the United Nations. The president of the World Bank. The executive director of the UN's World Food Program. A head of state or two. A dozen or so CEOs and presidents of multinational companies. Members of the royal families of Belgium and the Netherlands.

They had gathered in a most incongruous setting on the Alpine slopes of Davos. Snow crunched beneath their feet as they trudged up a sharp incline and entered a scene out of Africa. TNT engineers had built a Tanzanian

schoolhouse—the Nabererra School, they named it—using plywood for
the walls and corrugated iron sheeting for the roof. Behind that structure,
they erected a white refugee tent, the ubiquitous symbol of disaster scenes
throughout the developing world. For the Swiss winter setting—and for
the hoity-toity clientele—they added heating and indoor toilets. But those
were the only concessions to comfort. Upon arrival, the guests were served
a red plastic cup full of corn-soybean porridge, the standard fare of an
African school feeding program, and a heaping plate of humility.

Bakker was looking to enlist—or gang press, if he must—big business
in the fight against hunger.

One . . . two . . . three . . . four . . . five.

Another child gone. The CEO bared his own conscience, and culpa-
bility: "How could I look at this problem—and how it could be prevented
if we could get the food to the children—and not do anything about it, say
it wasn't our business?"

For that, precisely, *was* his business, getting things to people in a hurry.
He was a logistics problem solver. And here was a problem, a horrible problem. The world had enough food, yet people were still starving. And what
was he, as chairman of a shipping company, doing? "We were sponsoring
a golf tournament—3 million euros for four days of golf," Bakker confessed, "and dreaming of sponsoring an F1 car." Bakker was a big sports-
man, like many of his countrymen. What, he was debating, was the better
fit for one the biggest Dutch companies: hosting the Dutch Open golf
tournament or plastering logos all over a race car?

He was pondering these options on a flight from Amsterdam to Sydney
in November 2001. "It was a long flight, I was reading all the papers and
magazines," Bakker recalled. "There was one story asking, Why did September 11 happen? It talked about the divide between rich and poor creating a fertile ground for fanatics. The story asked, 'What are you going to
do about it?'"

Bakker checked his watch. Another ten hours of flight time. The question
kept gnawing at him: What are you going to do about it? Does a golf tournament help? A race car? He began doodling and drawing up some ideas.

Bakker landed in Singapore for a layover of several hours. He unpacked
his laptop and commenced sending e-mails to his colleagues at the head office in Amsterdam. "How can we sponsor the world?" he asked.

Ludo Oelrich, who was heading up TNT's sponsorships, opened his in-box on the other side of the globe and scratched his head. "Is he crazy?" Oelrich wondered. "What's he mean, sponsoring the world?"

Bakker explained: "Why don't we become a partner with someone involved in helping the world?"

Oelrich and the TNT staff started searching, thinking big as the boss ordered, reviewing the work of more than sixty organizations. Bakker suggested that the right fit for TNT needed to be politically neutral, global in aspiration, and working on a problem that could be helped with TNT's logistical expertise. The list narrowed quickly. A group of TNT executives visited a refugee camp in Tanzania—logistical nightmares abounded in refugee camps—and saw several UN organizations at work. One stood out, its workers scurrying to dispatch food arriving from various points of the globe to swelling colonies of the hungry arriving in various states of distress.

A recommendation slid across Bakker's desk: the World Food Program. The more he read, the more Bakker believed it was the perfect pairing. The WFP, he thought, was the TNT of food. He met with the head of the WFP at the time, Jim Morris, who, coincidentally, had been pondering the need to link up with private partners to diversify its support base, which relied almost 100 percent on donations from world governments. The two men shook hands. TNT would donate its business skills to the WFP to help solve one of the world's greatest tragedies and one of its greatest conundrums: how to move food from areas that have too much to areas that have too little. "We deliver things from A to B," Bakker said at the time. "It's a simple thing that we see can help save the hungry. What we're trying to do is crack the logistics nut of getting food surpluses to the hungry."

It was a partnership that broke the old mold of corporate social responsibility and created a new model for how businesses can take a greater role in shaping the societies around them by using their expertise to help solve some of the world's biggest problems. Although corporate philanthropy had been around for many decades, the movement for corporate social responsibility picked up steam in the 1980s. American and European companies operating in apartheid South Africa were coming under intense pressure to do more to improve the living conditions of their black and "colored" employees. Apartheid's masters had embedded racial discrimination in the country's laws, and multinationals pulling profits out of South Africa were seen to be complicit in that violent and dehumanizing system.

A code of conduct was developed for Western corporations—called the Sullivan Principles after American antiapartheid campaigner Reverend Leon Sullivan—that compelled businesses to get involved in social justice and community-improvement activities for their employees that the government ignored. Corporations built housing and schools, funded development projects like water purification and health clinics, and addressed everyday needs like food and clothing in the regions where they operated. While shareholders and protesters called on U.S. and European companies to disinvest from South Africa, those corporations argued they could do more good by staying and carrying out the Sullivan Principles. Eventually, those principles became expected corporate behavior across the developing world.

But what TNT embarked on when it created its partnership with the WFP went far beyond helping its own employees or residents of the countries in which it operated. TNT didn't just write a holiday-time check from its philanthropy fund; it wove helping the WFP into its business strategy. Bakker established a separate business unit called Moving the World. Oelrich became its director and was given start-up funding of 5 million euros. Bakker pushed the money from sports sponsorships, which included local soccer teams and recreation clubs, to Moving the World. It raised a lot of eyebrows, and prompted more than a few angry voices at home. But Bakker pressed forward on a bigger stage.

One of the company's first tasks for the WFP was doubling the capacity of the agency's supply warehouse in Brindisi, Italy. When a food crisis erupted anywhere in the world, the relief often began in Brindisi. The WFP had budgeted $12 million to expand and streamline its warehouse operations. TNT warehouse experts studied the flow of inventory in and out of Brindisi and were able to double the capacity for less than $3 million. That was a savings of more than $9 million.

Bakker the businessman ran the numbers. "For $35 you can feed a child in a school feeding program for one year. For $9 million–plus, you can feed almost 300,000 children," he calculated. Solving that one logistics puzzle—the core of TNT's business—saved both money and lives. The company had never done *that* before.

On December 7, 2003, TNT operated the first privately funded airlift in the history of the WFP, loading up one of its Airbus 300 planes with thirty-three metric tons of emergency supplies to help feed starving Sudanese refugees in Chad. In 2005, after the tsunami in the Indian Ocean, the first trucks the WFP used to reach the devastated region of Banda Aceh, Indonesia, were from TNT's fleet. In the first five years of the partnership, TNT had rushed to assist in more than thirty hunger emergencies and carried out more than ten emergency airlifts.

Beyond the equipment contributions, TNT employees freely shared their logistics knowledge with WFP field-workers. TNT air operations experts trained dozens of WFP staffers to be air traffic controllers in Kabul, Afghanistan, when the food airlift was in high gear in 2003. Trucking managers traveled to the Ivory Coast and other African hunger spots to reorganize the WFP's fleet logistics and reduce the downtime of the trucks. Warehouse experts helped the WFP establish humanitarian response depots in key areas of the world, such as Ghana and Dubai. The company deployed its global positioning system techniques to map the coordinates of warehouses and schools in Liberia to reduce costs and more efficiently deliver food to more than 2,000 school feeding programs across the country. All this work was financed by TNT, adjusting Moving the World's budget to meet emergency needs; some years the financing more than doubled the original start-up funding.

TNT also encouraged the UN agency to adopt corporate approaches to accountability, transparency, and risk management. That led to questions about Bakker's own fiscal responsibility in sponsoring the WFP. "The skeptics want to know how much the share price has grown, or how much revenue is up," he said in Davos.

His bottom line: The WFP partnership had enhanced TNT's reputation and motivated the company's employees. He cited the annual ranking of corporate reputations in the Netherlands: "In 2001, we were number twenty-six. In 2008, we are number four." An internal survey of one-quarter of the company's 160,000 employees reported that 78 percent of the respondents said they were more proud of the company because of its work with the WFP, and more than 50 percent of them had personally contributed to the partnership. Total employee donations to the WFP in the first five years of the partnership topped 8 million euros, including 17,000 euros raised by ten employees in the United Kingdom who rounded up sponsorships to perform an aerial stunt: They strapped themselves to the wings of biplanes and cruised over the English countryside. That money, along with corporate contributions, provided 58 million school meals.

Dozens of employees had also volunteered to work on the ground with WFP school feeding programs in Malawi, Tanzania, Cambodia, Nicaragua, and Gambia. There they created school gardens, dug latrines, designed water-collection systems, and built storage rooms—and they regularly shared their experiences with colleagues across the globe through blogs and articles in the company newsletters. "They are very good storytellers," noted John Powell, the WFP's deputy executive director. "We find they describe what we do in ways that we've long forgotten. One of their employees talked about an AIDS patient in one of our feeding programs, a woman weighing just thirty kilograms [about sixty-six pounds]. He said, 'That's less than our check-in luggage.' All of a sudden, you could see people thinking of their luggage and this woman. It's all about seeing what we do, and who we work with, with fresh eyes."

At the beginning of the partnership, Bakker worried that he was seeing the corporation's mission through rose-colored glasses. "For one or two years, we were wondering if we were doing the right thing," he admits. "Other companies were looking at us, asking, Is it too idealistic?"

Jan Willem Maas, though, caught on immediately. A senior partner and managing director at the international Boston Consulting Group, Maas, based in Amsterdam, was reading a Dutch newsmagazine in November 2002 when he spied a story on Bakker's new venture. "Peter was saying, 'We're not sponsoring Formula One or a golf tournament, we're working with the WFP.'" Bakker's passion jumped off the page, inspiring Maas to write a letter to the TNT boss asking how BCG could help.

BCG became the second WFP corporate partner, and promptly set out to enlist more companies in the cause, because that's part of what it does as a consulting company. "We're not developing new vaccines. But we can help groups get together better," Maas said in Davos.

The company teamed up with TNT to develop WFP's fund-raising strategy for the corporate sector. The idea, Maas explained, is to build corporate partnerships with companies whose products or services would benefit the WFP's work. Among the WFP's target industries are advertising, automotive, beverages, computer hardware and software, credit cards, hotels, Internet networks, airlines, financial institutions, food producers, insurance, oil and gas, pharmaceuticals, shipping, and telecommunications.

Unilever and DSM, two big Dutch food and nutrition companies, were among the first to enlist. "We sell food and hygiene. We're in nearly every country in the world," noted Paulus Verschuren, senior director of partnership development at Unilever, which makes products ranging from salt and spices to soap and shampoo. "We have an institute with 150 people constantly working to make food more nutritious," like fortifying its Blue Band/Rama margarine with additional nutrients for the WFP's school feeding program.

Unilever saw the world's bottom billion—the poorest of the poor living on less than a dollar a day—as a potential market someday. "But you can only access that if you have healthy societies," Verschuren said. Like TNT, Unilever formed a separate business unit to manage the WFP partnership, which it dubbed Together for Child Vitality. "Historically, corporate philanthropy gave money to organizations. But that's not sustainable," Verschuren added. "The wife of the next chairman might have other causes. To be sustainable, you have to embed it in your business."

DSM, the world's largest producer of vitamins, figured it was a natural to match up with the largest distributor of food aid. "Our goal is to make sure that food aid is enriched in vitamins and minerals," said Fokko Wientjes, manager of DSM's partnership with the WFP. "In the past, the focus of the food aid has been on providing calories. We want to make sure the best science is in the food, to provide good nutrition as well."

The company set out to draw up specifications and standards for fortifying WFP food, and it developed a daily vitamin and mineral supplement for children called Sprinkles. One gram of powder contained vitamins A through E, plus folic acid, zinc, copper, and iodine. Packaged in small sachets, like packets of sugar, it can be sprinkled over the standard serving of porridge in school feeding programs.

At the Davos gathering, DSM chairman Feike Sijbesma jumped from his seat and waved some of the confetti-colored sachets. "We'll give you 20 million of these," he told WFP executive director Josette Sheeran. He moved to sit down, then straightened up again. "You can't be successful in a society that fails," he told his fellow business chiefs.

Peter Bakker smiled. He was making progress. Three years earlier when he first built the African schoolhouse in the snow, only two people accepted his invitation. The corporate world didn't want to have anything to do with the hungry. In 2008, nearly eighty people packed the schoolhouse and counted silently with him.

One . . . two . . . three . . . four . . . five.

"All we want to achieve here is to change your life," Bakker told his guests. "I'm not asking you for money. But we want you to think and ask yourselves, 'What can I do to end child hunger in the world?'"

Vittorio Colao, the CEO of European operations for mobile telecommunications giant Vodafone Group, PLC, had an answer: "We can accelerate the flow of information, put scarcity of food into contact with abundance." The evening—"inspiring!" he said—had him thinking of signing up Vodafone as a WFP partner, which he later did. His company, he explained, could help the agency quickly establish emergency communication networks in hunger hot spots.

"This has me thinking about technology as an equalizer, how it equalizes opportunity," Colao said. Everybody, he was thinking, should have an equal opportunity to eat.

Colonel Sanders was thinking the same thing.

The white-goateed icon of fast-food nationhood was raising money the old-fashioned way, pleading for donations for the hungry while posing for pictures with customers at a Taco Bell–KFC restaurant in suburban Chicago. He held an empty cardboard bucket emblazoned with his famous slogan, "It's finger-lickin' good."

"You don't know how fortunate we are in this country. We can just come in and eat," the Colonel told three women from an accounting firm down the street who had indeed just come in to eat. Each dropped a one-dollar bill into the bucket and threw their arms around the Colonel. A Polaroid flashed. "Thank you," the Colonel said, shaking the money in his treasure chest. "This will put food in the mouths of several people who can't get any themselves."

The Colonel—real name Bob Thompson, a former IBM programmer and mayor of Lawrenceburg, Kentucky, and a doppelganger of the original Colonel, Harland Sanders (his business card proclaims: "World Chicken Festival's reigning Colonel Sanders look-a-like")—was the star of the inaugural World Hunger Relief Week of Yum! Brands, Inc., the world's largest restaurant company, with 1 million employees working at such properties as Taco Bell, KFC, Pizza Hut, Long John Silver's, and A&W All-American Food. The company that popularized stuffed burritos and extra crispy chicken around the globe was now trying to do the same for the World Food Program.

Yum had enlisted as a WFP partner to commemorate its tenth anniversary in 2007. "We were looking for a unifying big idea to galvanize the whole organization," said David Novak, Yum's chairman and CEO.

For a company that feeds people—some would say too well—the world's growing hunger problem was a flashing neon billboard of irony and embarrassment. Yum was already a large donor to U.S. food banks, sharing its restaurant leftovers. But it didn't grasp the global scale of hunger until Jonathan Blum, Yum's head of public affairs who was leading the search for the big idea, happened across a newspaper interview with the WFP's Morris. "I wrote him a letter," Blum recalled. "I said, 'I don't know you, you don't know me. You're the largest feeding organization in the world, we're the largest restaurant company.'" He suggested they talk. A meeting was arranged. "It was in New York, at an airport hangar. We rented a conference room," Blum said. "After one hour, we walked out of the meeting saying, 'Wow, that's who we want to partner with.'"

First, though, Blum wanted to see the WFP in action. He set off for Sudan. In one village in the southern part of the country, ravaged by a war that had raged for two decades, Blum peered into a dark hut. "I saw a woman starving to death," he said. "In another village, I saw a mother with newborn twins who were malnourished, dying. She had no mother's milk, she was also malnourished."

From village to village he went, looking into the eyes of the hungry. "I could have been extremely depressed coming back home," Blum said, "but I was uplifted, because I realized I could help do something about it. As a company, *we* could do something about it."

Back home at Yum's headquarters in Louisville, Kentucky, Blum told his colleagues what he had seen, and he outlined the world's hunger problem. Jaws dropped; heads shook. "I wasn't aware that hunger killed more people than war, AIDS, malaria, tuberculosis, all of them combined," Novak said. "A lot of huge problems are invisible until they stare you in the face and ask, 'What can you do about it?'"

The CEO took executives of the various Yum divisions on a trip to see WFP operations in Guatemala. As a clincher, Novak invited Morris to the company's tenth-anniversary celebrations in Hawaii in January 2007. The WFP executive director spoke emotionally about how little it takes to feed a child and change a life. There wasn't a dry eye in the room.

Then the CEO spoke. "We've never saved a life," he said. "I never have." By teaming up with the WFP, he suggested, "We can save a lot of lives."

In mid-October 2007, Yum launched World Hunger Relief Week at its 35,000 company and franchised restaurants in 112 countries to coincide with international World Food Day. The business skill it contributed to the WFP? Marketing. All its restaurant brands, which usually run their own advertising campaigns, joined together in one common campaign. "We told our franchises that we're going to leverage our network to spread awareness of the world's largest problem," Novak said. "We've never done anything where we put all the brands together. Usually, we sell just Taco Bell, KFC." In this campaign, he noted, "We sold hunger relief."

Some in the WFP were wary, trying to figure out Yum's angle. The company, after all, had grown rich off of eating. "Initially," Blum recalled, "there was a healthy dose of skepticism in the WFP about our motivation. Are they trying to sell fried chicken, tacos, and pizza off of us? But we were careful, we didn't tie it to any purchases whatsoever. It was never a percent of sales. It was all about donations."

Fast-food critics also charged that Yum was trying to score some public relations points to counter accusations that its restaurants' fare added to the world's rising obesity problem. Novak bristled at those suggestions. He pointed out that Yum had 2 percent of a global food-service market that totaled more than a trillion dollars. "To think that we're the cause of obesity in the world is the most ridiculous thing," he said in an interview.

Yum reported that its inaugural World Hunger Relief Week generated awareness of hunger among 1.5 billion people, and that its own employees chipped in nearly 4 million hours of volunteer work on various money-raising projects. All told, Yum figures the campaign raised $16 million, most of it going into the WFP's school feeding programs. In 2008, the week was expanded to a month—and longer in some countries—and raised about $20 million in donations as the awareness campaign spread from billboards and in-store posters to Facebook, MySpace, and YouTube. Yum became the largest corporate contributor to the WFP, larger even than some Western countries.

"Gee, when you think that one child dies every five seconds from hunger," said Debera Johns, director of operations at twenty-one Yum restaurants, including the combined Taco Bell–KFC in Wheeling. "How many children were in here this afternoon?" Fifty or sixty, at least. In Africa, twelve of them would have died in the minute it took for their Polaroid image with the Colonel to appear.

"This makes you think of the hungry, when you're here stuffing your face," said a woman named Jeanne, who donated a dollar for her picture with the Colonel before tucking into a plate of tacos.

"This makes me feel guilty," added a friend from work. She wrapped a taco in a napkin and stuffed it in her purse; she would eat it later in her office, she promised.

"We throw away tons and tons of food every day," volunteered an office worker named Devon as he settled down to a lunch of chicken wings with honey barbecue sauce after his picture with the Colonel. "We're an obese country. There shouldn't be any hunger in the world."

His wife, Donna, joined him. "The corporations have a big influence and big voices. If they step up, something can be done," she said. "Much more can be given, not less."

By late in the afternoon, the restaurant walls were plastered with hundreds of postcards depicting a WFP burlap bag filled with wheat. Every person who made a donation could sign a card, which trumpeted that they have "joined the movement to stop world hunger."

The Colonel, posing with another customer, said, "More than 850 million people are hungry every day and we throw away so much. Think of that and think of all the hungry kids in the world."

Four-year-old Sadia Mohamed Yousif had been one of those hungry children. She was near starvation when her family arrived at the Krinding refugee camp on the hem of the Sahara Desert outside El Geneina in West Darfur, Sudan. They had walked twenty-five miles—Sadia nestled in her mother's arms once she could no longer stand—after being chased from their home in Darfur by the Janjaweed.

Aid workers from Save the Children immediately swarmed to Sadia and began feeding her from a silver-and-red foil packet. They snipped off a corner of the sachet and squeezed at the bottom. Out oozed a sweet-tasting peanut butter paste enriched with various nutrients. After several weeks on a steady diet of this paste, Sadia was able to once again stand and walk—and talk. One morning, when she spied the packet in her mother's hand, she stepped precariously out of their refugee hovel made of sticks and plastic sheeting and reached out her hands. "Plumpy," she said.

Her mother, Fatma, embraced her with a broad smile. "Plumpy saved her," she rejoiced, clapping her hands.

Plumpy is what the hungry of Africa call Plumpy'nut, a whimsically named and serendipitously discovered product made in the lush countryside of Normandy, France. There, in a country known for its haute cuisine, a small private company called Nutriset SAS churns out nutritionally fortified food to be used only for humanitarian relief. In contrast to TNT and Yum! Brands, which use their wider commercial base to help feed the hungry, Nutriset is one of a handful of companies in business solely to serve the starving. Its customers aren't big retailers like Wal-Mart and Carrefour, but humanitarian agencies like the United Nations Children's Fund, Save the Children, and Doctors Without Borders. Its products may be unknown to consumers in the rich world, but they are household names in the world's hunger zones.

Nutriset revolutionized the treatment of severely malnourished children with the invention of Plumpy'nut, which first gained serious notice in the 2003 Ethiopian famine. Unlike the powdered-milk formulas that had been the standard treatment for severe malnutrition, Plumpy'nut doesn't need to be mixed with clean water, a rare commodity in famine-stricken regions. Medical officers aren't needed to be on hand to mix ingredients and guard against contamination; a mother simply snips a corner of the packet and squeezes the paste into her child's mouth. Plumpy'nut allowed nutritionists, for the first time ever, to take treatment beyond crowded emergency feeding centers and hospital settings, where disease can spread rapidly, and into the communities and homes where malnourished children live.

This shift from emergency treatment to more routine community care made possible by Plumpy'nut "has long been a Holy Grail of humanitarianism," said Dr. Steve Collins, a director of Valid International, a UK agency specializing in hunger relief. "It's an amazing breakthrough when it comes to therapeutic feeding."

Entrepreneurs mixing capitalism and humanitarianism—doing well by doing good—have developed a number of breakthroughs in the push to end hunger. For example, cheap and simply designed human-powered water pumps, contraptions that operate like a Stairmaster exercise machine, have enabled hundreds of thousands of small-scale farmers to irrigate their crops and greatly boost yields and income and pull themselves out of hunger. Two organizations that popularized these pumps—KickStart International and International Development Enterprises—hope that an entire private-sector industry will arise to satisfy the vast need for basic irrigation systems throughout the developing world. "Our mission is to bring millions of people out of poverty," says Martin Fisher, cofounder of KickStart, whose top-selling pump is called the SuperMoneyMaker. "The best way is to have the technology available to everyone."

Nutriset wishes the same thing for Plumpy'nut. Plumpy's origin lies in the African hunger crises of the early 1980s, including Ethiopia's epic famine of 1984. The standard feeding regimens at the time, which grew out of efforts to rescue malnourished survivors of World War II, were overwhelmed by the demands of Africa. They involved various levels of protein, fat, and nutrients that in some cases made things worse by putting excessive demands on a malnourished person's already weakened digestive organs. They were particularly harsh on children. And in the African famines, the little bodies piled up at unprecedented rates.

Michel Lescanne was toiling in a research laboratory of a French dairy company. He stared at the television images of starving children and quickened his experiments to deliver the needed nutrients in an enriched, child-friendly chocolate bar. But the product never made it beyond the lab. "The taste wasn't good," Lescanne recalled, making a sour face, "and it was expensive to produce."

The company dropped the project, but Lescanne pushed on with his research, tinkering in his spare time at home. In 1986 he bought some scales and blenders and founded Nutriset in his kitchen.

At the same time, nutritionists fresh from the hunger fields were furiously working their drawing boards, scheming to come up with new treatment combinations. In the early 1990s, they developed a set of formulas for therapeutic milks that were dubbed F-75 and F-100. Lescanne and his fledgling company then developed a way to deliver these treatments to the field, turning the drawing-board formulas into a powdered mix laden with nutrients. "Very simple. Just open the package and add some water. Voilà!" Lescanne said, waving his hands with the flourish of a French chef.

This product did catch on. The powdered-milk mix became the accepted way to treat malnutrition. And Nutriset found its niche, marketing to relief agencies that, in turn, deployed the mix in the field.

But Lescanne wasn't satisfied. He and other nutritionists knew that the powdered-milk mix had its limitations. Milk-based products can be breeding grounds for bacteria, either when mixed with contaminated water or when left out in the open. So the mix could be used only in clinical settings, either in established hospitals or in therapeutic feeding tents set up at the onset of a famine. This meant malnourished children were crowded together, aiding the spread of illnesses such as diarrhea and measles. It also required mothers to stay with the sick children during treatment. Nutritionists wondered: Would the health of siblings left behind at home deteriorate? What about those who never reached the treatment centers?

"It became a fixation for me to come up with another way," André Briend recalled. He was a specialist in pediatric nutrition at the French government's Institute of Development Research before joining the World Health Organization in Geneva. After many years working in the developing world, he had returned to France in the early 1990s and began consulting with Nutriset. He and Lescanne obsessed over finding an alternative to the powdered mix. Briend tried using pancakes and doughnuts as the delivery vehicles for the nutrients. He tried a chocolate bar, as Lescanne had done a decade before, but it melted at high temperatures, making it unsuitable for use in desert famine zones. Besides, as Lescanne had discovered, adding the necessary minerals ruined the taste.

One morning in 1997, while eating breakfast, Briend noticed a jar of Nutella, the chocolate-hazelnut spread particularly popular in Europe. He had seen it on breakfast tables, including his own, for years. But the light-bulb never went on. Now, on this morning, he smacked his head as he was struck with a eureka moment. "Of course!" he thought. "That's it!"

Briend hurriedly called Lescanne. "Why not a spread?" he blurted out.

"A spread?" Lescanne wondered. Then the lightbulb went on in his head, too. "Of course, a spread!" Forget the solid delivery mechanism, like a candy bar. A spread just might work.

Briend, fed up with his chocolate experiments, considered other spread-able foods. He explored his kitchen shelves. What about peanut butter? When the ingredients from the F-100 milk formula were added to peanut paste, it tasted like peanut butter, only sweeter. The taste wasn't ruined, it was enhanced. And since peanuts are a staple food in most African coun-tries, it was already a familiar taste to the children.

During field trials, Briend and Lescanne watched severely malnourished children gobble up the healthy paste. "The children cried when we took it away in order to weigh them," Briend recalls.

Nutriset devised new machines to process the paste, and the new prod-uct went into production. But what to call it? Nutriset executives pored through a dictionary trying to come up with a name that would conjure up a whimsical personality rather than a clinical, scientific term. Coming across the *P* section, they combined *plumpy*, which is how they would like to see the children once they recover, with *peanut.* They dropped the *pea*, kept the *nut*, and used a drawing of a peanut for the apostrophe. Plumpy'nut. Voilà!

When the massive Ethiopian famine of 2003 struck, Plumpy'nut was ready for deployment. Relief organizations hit the hunger zones and, fol-lowing standard practice, erected a network of feeding centers to adminis-ter milk-based treatment. Countless lives were saved, but medical workers were overwhelmed by the crush of children filling the centers. Aid work-ers using Plumpy'nut were able to relieve the pressure by returning children to their homes and treating them there.

Darfur, in 2004, was the first large-scale deployment of Plumpy'nut. "When we got the first order for Darfur, our initial reaction was, 'It's a pity, it's happening again,'" said Isabelle Sauguet, Nutriset's sales and development manager. The second reaction was to scramble the staff into around-the-clock production at Nutriset's small blue-and-white factory in Malaunay, France. In that bucolic setting, surrounded by green pastures and grazing cows, Nutriset cranked out about 2,700 metric tons of Plumpy'nut in 2005.

Armed with the sweet paste, aid agencies like Steve Collins's Valid International, the Irish group Concern, and the U.S.-based Save the Children began popularizing a new treatment method centered on caring for severely malnourished children at home: "community-based therapeutic care." Nutritionists found that a steady diet of Plumpy'nut—three or four sachets a day for several weeks, or a total of about ten kilograms per child—will usually bring recovery for most malnourished children. In 2007, about 7,000 tons of Plumpy'nut was distributed, saving 700,000 young lives. By the end of 2010, Plumpy production could be more than 50,000 tons.

To reach these ambitions, and to speed delivery and lower costs—Plumpy goes for three euros per kilogram, or thirty cents per one hundred–gram sachet—Nutriset has established partnerships with local manufacturers in Malawi, Niger, and the Democratic Republic of the Congo. In 2007, the Hilina Enriched Food Processing Center on the outskirts of Addis Ababa began producing for the Ethiopia market; its clean-as-a-whistle factory has the capacity to produce twelve tons of paste a day. At the beginning of 2008, Nutriset was also in talks with partners in Ghana, Madagascar, the Dominican Republic, and Cambodia. In most cases, Nutriset provided the technology and the mineral supplements, while the local manufacturers supplied the peanuts.

Still, this production was meeting only a tiny fraction of the worldwide demand. Collins estimated that 1 million tons would be needed worldwide if severe malnutrition was to be effectively treated and prevented. So he set up a not-for-profit company, Valid Nutrition, to work with local businesses in Africa and other developing countries to produce Plumpy-like foods with whatever local crops are most abundant and affordable, be it corn or chickpeas or sesame. "We want to engage business in reducing malnutrition," he said. "The motivation is the same as any business: achieve revenues."

With his overstuffed backpack and hiker wardrobe, Collins always looks like he's just emerged from the African bush. Still, he moved deftly in a boardroom as he pushed a strategy with Nutriset to establish both production standards and ethical standards for a new line of what has been called Ready-to-Use Therapeutic Foods, which would be marketed to the world's humanitarian aid agencies fighting malnutrition. Flashing a series of PowerPoint slides, he boiled down his business model to this: making profits, not off the hungry, but to help feed the hungry. "We'll make a profit, but those profits will all go back into the business," he said. "Research and development, expanding to different areas, lowering costs, increasing accessibility. We'll look like a company and act like a company. Except for this: The goal is not to pay shareholders. The goal is to alleviate malnutrition."

As businesses big and small broke old molds and set new ones to achieve that goal, individuals guided by a moral compass to do the right thing were rallying around an old standby: Every little bit helps.

CHAPTER 16

Small Acts, Big Impacts

KENYA, OHIO, AND MALAWI

The Mercy of God Dam stretching across the Ikiwe River in Machakos, Kenya, wasn't much to look at. As dams go, it was a modest edifice, maybe one hundred feet wide and ten feet deep, crudely made of cement, boulders, mud, and sand and shaped by the unskilled hands of local villagers. But it beautifully did its job, which was to capture the water during the region's two brief rainy seasons, one in the spring and the other in the fall. Before the dam was completed in September 2006, the rainwater would quickly wash away, and the Ikiwe, after flowing wildly for a couple of weeks, would become a dry bed of sand. The dam held the rainfall for months, giving two hundred peasant farmers a reliable water source for their cattle and enabling them to irrigate twenty-five acres for the first time and grow vegetables for their families and for the market.

"We're not so hungry anymore," declared the Reverend Cosmas Mwanzia, pastor of the Redeemed Gospel Church, who had christened the dam with its ecclesiastical name. Mercy of God, indeed.

But now he was considering giving it a new name. He was standing beside the dam in the company of Jim and Linda Rufenacht, cattle farmers from the small town of Archbold, Ohio. For four years the Rufenachts had rallied the townsfolk of Archbold to raise calves that were sold for the benefit of struggling farm communities in this arid region of southern Kenya. Here, holding back the water of the Ikiwe, was one of the projects they had financed.

"Mercy of Archbold Dam, that's what we should call it," Reverend Mwanzia suggested. It had a good ring to it, he said, better certainly than the unintended profanity, when you said it quickly, of Mercy of God Dam. The villagers rarely spoke the English name. Mercy of Archbold Dam sounded better and better—and very appropriate. "It is here because of you," he told the Rufenachts.

The Archbold donations had provided $3,000, and the farmers of Machakos built the dam themselves. They used the money to hire a Kenyan engineer to design the dam and to buy the cement. The farmers themselves supplied the sand, rocks, and labor. Within twenty-five days, just before the rains came, the dam was finished.

As the Ikiwe filled with water, the farmers bought a small pump with the Archbold money and laid some pipes from the river to the parched, scrubby field on the left bank. Several months later, when the Rufenachts visited, there were acres of tomatoes, peppers, chilis, and watermelons. Susan Kanini, one of the farmers, leaned on her cane and triumphantly picked a green pepper from her first harvest. She presented it to Jim. "Thank you," she said, "for all you have done."

"Oh, it's nothing special," Jim replied, his voice choking up. Tears formed behind his sunglasses. "We're just farmers like you."

The dam stood as a monument to the big impact of small projects: how one family and one community can often do more than a big international agency to spur agricultural development and alleviate hunger. The Archbold initiative was part of the Foods Resource Bank (FRB), a U.S.-based hunger-fighting organization financed by churches and other donors that connects urban congregations with farming groups. The churches help fund the growing of crops or the raising of cattle that are dedicated to a particular agricultural development project in Africa, Latin America, Asia, or eastern Europe. Rather than send the food as aid, it is sold on U.S. markets and the profit is then dispatched abroad, where the recipient farmers decide how best to use the money to boost their own production. Since 2000, FRB growing projects in twenty-two states had raised more than $10 million for rural communities in about three dozen countries, mostly in Africa; through 2008, that amount had been supplemented by more than $3 million from the public-private partnership initiative of the U.S. Agency for International Development.

The farmers in the Machakos district were particularly in need of help. Recurring drought had left thousands of families scratching for food and walking ever-longer distances for water. "It was very bad," Reverend Mwanzia recalled. "If I think about it, I cry."

He had tried to comfort his hungry parishioners with his preaching. "One day we'll all be in heaven," he would say. "And in heaven, there will be no shortage of water. In heaven, there will be no famine."

"But pastor," came the cry from the congregation, "what are we supposed to do before we get there?"

Reverend Mwanzia began distributing food aid provided by relief agencies at his church. But that, he knew, was no solution. "After the first year, I worried we had become dependent on handouts," he said. "That wasn't right."

He summoned the community leaders to a meeting, and together they formed the Machakos Rural Development Program to fight back against the drought. Their top priorities were water and seeds for drought-resistant crops and money to get started. They wrote to various international aid organizations, asking for help. The Foods Resource Bank, hearing about the plea from one of its member organizations, embraced the cause, and it brought Elizabeth Kamau, one of the Machakos leaders, to the United States to put a face on the farmers' struggles.

Kamau told gatherings at churches and schools how she and her children would trudge farther and farther for water as the drought tightened its choke hold, lengthening the quest from six to twelve miles. She and her four oldest children would set out at nine and return home at four the next morning, walking and lugging the water during the relative cool of the night. Her children would get only two hours of sleep before they rose and prepared for school. The next night, they would make the same trek.

Her plight struck a chord in Archbold, where the Mennonite church worked with the FRB. "The thing that got to us was that there were people in the world who have to walk seven miles one way for water. If we had to walk that far for water, we wouldn't get anything else done," said Cork Rufenacht, Jim's brother. "We're in a very blessed area of the world here, and we know it. When you know it, some generosity comes out of your heart."

The Rufenacht brothers decided to dedicate several dozen calves each year to be sold for the farmers of Machakos. But they knew the project would be more successful if the entire town would get involved. Archbold, population 4,500, is a quintessential middle-American farming town of sturdy houses, steepled churches, and steady commerce, surrounded by green fields and red barns. The village was settled by Mennonites and Lutherans, who tamed the wilderness in the first half of the nineteenth century, and it still reflects their earnest, hardworking, salt-of-the-earth nature. A blue-and-white sign on the main street leading into town greets visitors with a slogan from the Archbold Character Council. Every month, a new admonition appeared: "Self-Control: Having a Life Purpose Bigger than Self," "Enthusiasm: Being an Energy Giver, Motivate and Uplift Others," or "Gratefulness: Showing Appreciation in Word and Action."

When the Rufenachts spread the word about the cattle-raising project, the town jumped into action. "I would talk at a church and say we need more feed for the calves. And by the time I got to the back of the church, there'd be several bales of hay waiting for me," Cork recalled.

Darlene Polasek and Louise Short donated a barn to hold the calves. "We have it, it's empty, why not use it?" Darlene reckoned.

John Poulson, an agricultural science teacher at the Pettisville Local School, which runs from kindergarten through high school, volunteered his older students to help with the bookkeeping. "It's good practice for the kids," he said.

Cecily Rohrs, the local social worker, raised the alarm. "You can make a difference in our unsettled world!" trumpeted a flyer she printed. "Not one church. Not one school. Not one community group. But all of us—together!"

Charlie Beck, a retired farmer, stepped forward to look after the calves. Archbold's churches hosted an annual Burger Bash in a city park to add to the pot of money.

By the end of 2008, the project had raised $130,000, which had helped the farmers of Machakos construct about five hundred small-scale dams and water-retention ponds, delivering more than 5,000 families from drought and hunger. In Kenya, the visitors from Archbold were hailed as saviors. "We ain't done anything special," Jim Rufenacht said over and over in his aw-shucks manner. "We all just gave what we had."

Edwin Onyancha, standing beside the Mercy of God Dam, begged to differ. "What you have done is very special," said the eastern Africa director for Dorcas Aid International, a development agency working with FRB member Christian Reformed World Relief Committee to channel the Archbold money to Machakos. "For years, we have been ignored by the World Bank and other big agencies who build big projects. We didn't matter. But now we have learned that small projects like this are very important. A big dam would be very intimidating. The local community would worry, 'Now how do we repair that if something happens?' With this one, it was built by their own hands and it can be repaired by their own hands."

Rufenacht and his wife had set out for Africa with Jon and Sharilyn Grushkin of a Foods Resource Bank growing project in Illinois and FRB President Marv Baldwin to see for themselves what their donations had wrought. They often rubbed their eyes like disbelieving kids on Christmas, making sure that the lush fields they were seeing weren't mirages. A man of few words even in his most loquacious moments, Jim's mantra through the Kenyan bush became "Awesome."

No sooner were they back on the dirt roads, having left the dam, when Peter Mutiso, a small, wiry man with big ambitions, pedaled his bicycle alongside their rambling safari van. On the back of his bike balanced a pump and a mechanical motor.

"What's with the pump?" Reverend Mwanzia asked.

"Improving my irrigation," Mutiso said, a smile filling his face. The FRB traveling party piled out of the van to listen as the farmer related his remarkable climb out of hunger.

Two years earlier, he was a hardscrabble subsistence farmer, growing crops like corn and beans to feed his family and selling whatever surplus he had. In good years, which were few, Mutiso estimated he made about eighty dollars. In bad years, which were plenty, his parched soil didn't yield enough to satisfy his family. Like many of his neighbors, he choked down his pride and accepted food aid.

With the aid and advice of Reverend Mwanzia's Rural Development Program, Mutiso bought some shovels and dug a water-retention pond to collect the rainwater that falls during the region's two annual rainy seasons. He also bought a simple manual pump, called the SuperMoney-Maker, designed by KickStart International to work like a Stairmaster. For several hours a day, he or his wife or their children would step up and down on the pump, drawing water from the pond to his fields. It was hard work, but it utterly transformed his two-acre plot. In addition to the staple foods, he used the water to expand into market crops like chili peppers, green peppers, watermelon, and fruit trees. In 2007, he earned about five hundred dollars selling his produce at the nearest urban market.

Mutiso said the extra money bought more food for his family. And he took about one-third of his profit to buy the generator and pump. The new pump would spare his family the hours of stepping, hours that could be more productively used to double the size of their cultivated land. Mutiso said this would allow him to further diversify his crop to provide better nutrition for his family and more variety for the market. He had already planted four hundred new mango trees.

"That is my story," Mutiso said. He doffed his cap, emblazoned with the black-and-red logo of English soccer club Manchester United, and profusely thanked his visitors for their help.

Reverend Mwanzia swelled with pride, and the Rufenachts' eyes lit up. "Progress!" shouted Jim.

Mutiso excused himself, for he was in a hurry to pedal over to the neighboring village, where he hoped to find someone who could show him how to connect the pump to the generator. The parts didn't come with instructions, and the shopkeeper who sold them to him had no clue. He pointed ahead down the dirt road to where the visitors would find his house and his fields.

As they climbed back into the van, the traveling party joked that, given Mutiso's accelerated rate of progress, their next visit would find him sitting in a reclining chair and watching English soccer on a big-screen television. For the moment, though, the van was a time machine, transporting its passengers back to an earlier time in agricultural history. The quantum jumps in farm production in Machakos made possible by the availability of water and hybrid seeds "must be like the U.S. in the 1940s," Jim said. "Farmers used their own stores of seeds and then the hybrids came and it was like, boom!" His thoughts drifted to his childhood on the family farm in Archbold as the latest seed technology was applied in the mid-1960s. "It was BOOM, this is unbelievable! I can even remember the field, it was that pronounced. I'd never seen corn like that. The yields were 20% to 25% better."

The van stopped suddenly, two hundred yards short of Mutiso's round mud-brick hut, and the Rufenachts were jolted back to Kenya in the twenty-first century. In the distance, they saw three women pounding the ground with giant sticks. They were Mutiso's wife and two daughters, beating a pile of dried bean pods to husk the beans. Reverend Mwanzia led the way across a grassy field, warily stepping past two Zebu bulls, African humpbacked oxen that pulled Mutiso's plow. The retention pond was still full with water two months after the rains stopped.

The women flailing at the beans spotted Reverend Mwanzia and put down their sticks. Mutiso's wife approached her guests and escorted them to the fields. It was just like Mutiso had described: row after row of peppers stretching westward to the end of the clearing. Mango, papaya, and orange trees embroidered the edges of the field. It was a lush oasis amid the sunbaked, tangled brush of the African bush.

The irrigation system had changed—no, had saved!—their lives, Mutiso's wife said. Reverend Mwanzia told her that the Rufenachts and their neighbors on the other side of the world had made it all possible. She clapped her hands. "We were dependent on food aid until we got the water," she said. "Thank you."

Rufenacht, wading through the chilis and other vegetables, struggled for the right words. "Awesome," he said.

Back in the van, the FRB party headed to the village of Ngangeni and Reverend Mwanzia's church. The dirt roads of Machakos were brutally bad, subjecting the travelers to miles of bouncing over washboard terrain. On one narrow pathway, the van slipped into a rut and tilted so far to one side the door wouldn't slide open; everybody crawled out through a window and then leaned together on the back bumper to push the van free.

As Ngangeni drew nearer, the bouncing suddenly stopped. The ride became stunningly smooth. The dirt hadn't magically become pavement. It was still dirt, but now it was leveled dirt. "Because the farmers don't have to walk so far for water anymore, they have more time to do other things," Reverend Mwanzia explained. "So now they volunteer one day a week to improve the roads." Villages took turns removing rocks, filling in potholes, clearing away brush.

The poor roads had been preventing farmers from bringing their produce to market, from going to health clinics, from visiting relatives. As the road conditions worsened, as each rainy season brought deeper gullies and ruts, the villages became more and more isolated. With the improved roads, commerce flourished. A bike ride—the main mode of transportation—that once took more than two hours was now down to thirty minutes. And the price of renting bike transportation to haul farm produce over that route had fallen in half, to three dollars. "You can imagine what that savings means," Reverend Mwanzia said. "Three dollars is a lot of money here."

When the bumps returned, the pastor quickly noted that it was by design. Farmers had built up a series of small ridges in the road. The ridges would catch the rainfall and guide it to a trench, which in turn channeled the water to a retention pond. If a village worked together, Reverend Mwanzia said, it could create this water-catchment system in four or five days.

In Ngangeni, several chairs and benches awaited the visitors in the shade of an acacia tree, the flat-topped, thorny icon of the African bush. As a cooling breeze stirred, Reverend Mwanzia described how the water projects had even refreshed his church: "During the years of drought, my people were coming to church late, they were coming at noon. I'm waiting at the pulpit to preach, but the people spent the cooler morning hours getting water. Now that they can draw water very near to their houses, they come to church on time to hear me preach." And, feeling more prosperous, they put more money in the collection plate. "Before the water," the pastor said with a giant smile, "I couldn't afford a tie. Now look." He puffed out his chest. Hanging down over his ample belly, a blue-and-yellow necktie clashed gloriously with a red-and-black-checkered shirt. "We pray for you," he told his visitors. "Tell the farmers of America we love them."

"It's very difficult to help people you haven't seen," Edwin Onyancha of Dorcas Aid said. "Sometimes you wonder, am I making a difference? But then you see change, and you see that you are making a difference. If your country got developed, I am sure people like us can make it, too."

Yes, you can, urged FRB's Marv Baldwin. "What we have seen today," he said, "is that a lot of little things together make a big thing."

Jim Rufenacht, a rugged six-footer, rose to speak under the acacia tree. His eyes watered. "Bear with me," he said. His voice trembled. He bowed his head to compose himself. "This is one of the best days of my life," he began slowly. "We need to recognize we are equal, we are on the same plane as you, we want to be a part of you." He removed his sunglasses and wiped his eyes. "We, as farmers, we raise cattle to make money. It's nothing special, it's what we do. You are very valuable to us."

Now his wife, Linda, was dabbing her eyes, too.

"I wish I could have brought all the people who helped us, 2,000 to 3,000 people," Jim said. "They have no idea what you're doing here. It's super. It's great, guys. It's worth everything."

Back in Archbold, the Rufenachts gathered with hundreds of their neighbors under the maple and oak trees in Ruihley Park for the annual community Burger Bash. Astonished at the tales of Africa told by the Rufenachts since their return, enthusiasm was high for another year of cattle raising.

"It's a complete cycle," said Jon Lugbill, the proprietor of Brookview Farm, a country store and butcher shop in Archbold with the slogan "Let Us Barbecue for You." "What's neat about this project is it's giving independence to the people over there in Africa. Independence from having to walk so far for water, independence to spend more time on their farming."

Lugbill was a businessman who clearly appreciated time-saving innovations. As he spoke, he was loading seven hundred hamburgers on a giant rotating grill set in a chrome oven—a Ferris wheel for burgers. After several minutes riding around the contraption, the burgers were grilled to perfection.

"What's exciting and encouraging," Lugbill said about the Africa project, "is you can see the benefits. Sometimes, sitting here, you wonder what aid money is being used for."

Cork Rufenacht's Sunday-school class set up the long tables in the park's pavilion. The Lutherans manned one serving line, the Catholics the other. The Reformation wouldn't stand in the way of dishing out the baked beans and coleslaw. Harold Plassman, the town's veteran attorney, kept an eye on the collection box and handed out the ice cream tickets.

The guests arrived in waves as the Sunday church services let out: first the Methodists, then the Catholics, the Lutherans, and finally the Mennonites. Shouts of "Hi, neighbor!" echoed around the pavilion.

"Isn't this terrific?" Harold said. "It's a real sign of this community."

John Poulson, after cooking the baked beans, finished calculating proceeds from the previous year's steer sales, Burger Bash, and other donations and waved a check for $29,493. It was presented to Marv Baldwin, who promised the money would soon be on its way to Africa.

Before the crowds arrived, Cecily Rohrs had arranged dishes of ketchup, mustard, pickle relish, and onions on all the tables. She also placed a yellow half-sheet of paper every couple of chairs. It was a thank-you note, and a summary of what the Rufenachts saw in Machakos. It quoted Jim: "It's not what we have done for them. It's what we can do together. They are just in a different place on the development cycle. We can learn so much from each other. They live with very little of what we consider necessity!"

Archbold mayor Jim Wyse picked up the paper, stained with ketchup, and read it with relish while finishing his hamburger. "A lot of people may not know exactly what we're raising money for here, but they know it's helping others and that's all they need to know to contribute," he said. "We were raised with a culture of service. It's been that way for generations."

For three generations, the Sauder family had operated Sauder Woodworking Company, the country's largest manufacturer of ready-to-assemble furniture, and Sauder Manufacturing, a leading manufacturer of church furniture, like pews. The family's name was all over Archbold, including the Sauder Village, a living-history experience that harks back to Archbold's beginnings. Maynard Sauder, the current woodworking chairman, never missed a Burger Bash. "I liked the concept of this project right from the start. There's a direct connection between the giver and receiver," he said. "Everyone wants to feed the hungry and give a drink to a thirsty person. But how do you know it's happening? Well, in this project, we know." Sauder turned to the man sitting next to him at the picnic table. "Vernon," he said, "this is a great thing you got started."

Vernon Sloan and his wife, Carol, stalwart Methodists, were among a group of representatives from seven church-related agencies who founded the Foods Resource Bank in 1999. Concerned about hunger in the developing world, the Sloans set aside some of the corn harvest from their fields

in Stryker, Ohio, just down the road from Archbold, for those in n
abroad. It became the model for the many growing projects today.

As the park benches filled, Vernon said he finally discovered what he
was put on the earth to do. Events that he thought were random strokes of
luck he now interpreted as destiny, like the day he broke his collarbone in
a football game in 1944. "I was supposed to go to the war that year," he
said. "That probably saved me from the Battle of the Bulge," where thousands of American soldiers died. He did enter the army the next year, and
was dispatched to the Philippines, where he survived the fierce fighting in
the Pacific theater. "A lot of boys didn't get to come back," he said. "I got
to come back."

Vernon, in his eighth decade now, began to weep softly. Through watery
eyes he looked around the park pavilion, at Jim and Cork Rufenacht and
at all his friends and neighbors who came to help hungry farmers in Africa.
"I know why I got to come back," he said. "I got to come back for this."

Francis Pelekamoyo was also finding his life's meaning in small acts that
were having big consequences for Africa's farmers.

For six years, Pelekamoyo had been Malawi's central reserve bank governor. He controlled his country's purse strings, monitored the ebb and
flow of precious foreign currency, and modulated inflation and interest
rates. He traveled in the pin-striped circle of the world's central bankers.
When he retired, he retreated to his farm outside the capital, Lilongwe.
He kept busy by overseeing the small national airline. But he rebuffed all
other overtures to get him back into pinstripes.

One day, an American businessman named Larry Reed came calling
with an offer: Would he join an outfit called Opportunity International, a
provider of financial services to entrepreneurs and farmers in the developing world, and open a microfinance operation for the poor in Malawi?

Pelekamoyo chuckled. He had just turned down political suitors pressing him to become finance minister. Why would he do anything micro
after doing so many things macro? Why lend pennies when he had once
controlled billions?

He politely said he would think about it, though he wasn't really interested. But the idea seemed to have a life of its own. It nagged him relentlessly, particularly during his regular Bible readings. Pelekamoyo, a devout

Presbyterian, found himself returning over and over again to the Gospel of Matthew, chapter 25, where Jesus spoke of the Last Judgment: "For I was hungry and you gave me food, I was thirsty and you gave me drink, I was a stranger and you welcomed me in. I was naked and you clothed me, I was sick and you visited me. . . . 'Truly I say to you, as you did it to one of the least of these my brethren, you did it to me.'"

Psalm 116 was also working on his mind: "What shall I render unto the Lord for all His benefits toward me?" Pelekamoyo's pondering went into overdrive. "God looked after me," he thought. "I had a good life, I was central bank governor. What do I do after that, to give back?"

Feed the hungry? Clothe the naked? But how, as a banker?

As a lender to the poor. "This work, transforming people's lives, is something I can do," Pelekamoyo told himself.

He called Larry Reed at Opportunity International. "OK," Pelekamoyo said, "I'll give it a try."

Within three months, leaning on his old central bank colleagues, Pelekamoyo had obtained a license to open a new bank. He drafted a business plan. He hired staff. He found an office, a nondescript curbside cubbyhole looking out on a parking lot filled with ragged vendors hawking wooden carvings. In May 2003, he opened the microfinance bank, Malawi's first for the poor, specializing in loans of as little as $50 or $100—enough in Africa to stock a small shop or buy better seeds and fertilizer—that other banks wouldn't bother with.

The client lines started forming the first day—farmers, teachers, entrepreneurs, anybody with a dream to improve their income—and haven't diminished since. By the end of 2008, Opportunity International Bank of Malawi had opened 195,007 savings accounts with an average balance of about $128 and totaling about $25 million, had 33,835 active loans with a value of about $22 million, and had extended crop insurance to more than 2,500 peanut and corn farmers. And Pelekamoyo himself had become chairman of Opportunity International's operations in Malawi, Mozambique, and Rwanda, all of which were bringing capital to agricultural projects and to farmers who had long been starved of financing and, therefore, starved of food. Throughout Africa, near the end of 2008, the agency had opened 285,604 savings accounts totaling nearly $40 million and had made 306,714 active loans for about $138 million.

"When you see the economic growth of our clients, the first thing you see them buy is food. You see them eating better, looking better nourished," Pelekamoyo said from his little office. A photo from a recent newspaper, tacked to the wall, captured his transformation. Once regularly pictured in Malawi's newspapers shaking hands with heads of state and government ministers, Pelekamoyo was now photographed smiling broadly while he handed out bags of fertilizer to winners of one of the bank's regular savings contests. To achieve true success, he confessed, "I had to remove my necktie and go to the poor people."

Pelekamoyo's journey from central banker to micro banker was a trademark odyssey of Opportunity International employees. Since the dawn of the millennium, the nondenominational Christian microfinance organization had become a magnet for baby-boomer business professionals from many countries and many pedigrees who had achieved dazzling career success and amassed staggering fortunes only to find true significance by putting their talents to work for their faith. Near the end of 2008, Opportunity was servicing 1 million active loans to entrepreneurs and farmers and was covering 3.5 million lives with microinsurance. Its ambitious goal: touching 100 million lives by 2015.

"We are at a significant turning point in history," Dale Dawson, a gregarious Texan, told his fellow Opportunity International board members and donors at a meeting in Bonita Springs, Florida, in early 2007. As he spoke, he waved a small book, *William Wilberforce: A Man Who Changed His Times*, about the nineteenth-century slavery abolitionist in England who had inspired the Jubilee 2000 debt-cancellation campaigners. "With affluence, technology, and extended life expectancy, our boomer generation is uniquely positioned to change the world," Dawson said. "In increasing numbers, our generation is beginning to ask the question: 'To what end?' We want our lives to make a difference. We want them to have meaning, purpose, and significance. Over my career I have known many who are rich and successful and one truth that I have learned is that it is easier to make a fortune than to make a difference."

And fortunes he had made. Dawson had been a deal maker and entrepreneur all his life. He was a partner and national director at the global accounting firm KPMG, and then became head of investment banking at Stephens, Inc., in Little Rock, Arkansas. He then set out on his own, rolling together a number of truck-parts companies into TruckPro. When that company became the largest of its kind in the United States, racking up annual sales of about $150 million, Dawson sold it to AutoZone in 1998. The sales price wasn't disclosed, but it was enough for Dawson to retire. He was forty-six.

His retirement didn't last long. Through friends, Dawson had met Rwandan Anglican bishop John Rucyahana, who told him of the desperate need for business skills to help rebuild the country devastated by genocidal warfare. Other friends introduced him to Opportunity International, and he began learning all he could about microlending, a financial instrument for the poor popularized by Muhammad Yunus, who founded the Grameen Bank in Bangladesh and was awarded the 2006 Nobel Peace Prize. "It's a divine calling," Dawson concluded. Like Pelekamoyo, he had come to believe that big advances against hunger and poverty could come with the smallest actions.

He told Opportunity President and Chief Executive Chris Crane that he wanted to build a bank in Rwanda. Crane, himself a Harvard MBA who cashed out an Internet venture at forty-eight and then joined Opportunity International, said it would take about $5 million to begin operations. The deal maker got busy. In four months, working with Opportunity fund-raisers, he had commitments for the entire amount.

Dawson headed to Rwanda and in August 2007 opened the Urwego Opportunity Microfinance Bank of Rwanda. People could start a savings account, their first ever, with as little as $2, or get a loan of $50. *Urwego* means "provide a ladder."

Meanwhile, in Malawi, thousands of farmers were using Pelekamoyo's banking ladder to climb out of the chronic hunger that had plagued the country in the early years of the millennium.

"The children and old people were dying," remembered Gelesom Chimpopi, a peanut and corn farmer in Malawi's Mchinji district west of Lilongwe on the road to Zambia. "I lost a grandparent."

"I lost two children," volunteered farmer Henry Kangwelema, who joined a conversation at a peanut-sorting warehouse. "They were four and ten."

"I lost my four-year-old child and my grandmother," added Gerald Abudu, a third farmer.

The farmers didn't have enough to feed their families, let alone a surplus to sell to pay off their debts. Amid the dying, the creditors—the seed and fertilizer suppliers and the government-owned credit agency—came around and started dismantling houses. "They took the iron sheets from my roof," said Chimpopi. "They even took my kitchen utensils, and my blanket!" He flashed a macabre smile, showing nothing but gums where his front teeth on both the top and the bottom should be.

That's when Opportunity knocked on their doors, or what was left of them. Loans of $50 or so enabled the farmers to buy hybrid, drought-resistant seed and, combined with new government subsidies, more bags of fertilizer. To lessen the risk to farmers, the bank also lent to commodities firms so they could buy the farmers' harvest. This ensured a market for the farmers, who would have money to pay off their loans. And, for further protection, the bank began offering crop insurance, a first for Malawi. Pegged to rain levels recorded at a nearby weather station, the insurance would protect the Mchinji farmers from losing everything in the event of another drought.

This injection of credit into the countryside accelerated the farmers' recovery. "We planted the best seed, we applied fertilizer and the rains were good," said Kangwelema. Harvests of peanuts and corn doubled and tripled. Surpluses were sold; profits were reaped. Mchinji's farmers opened their first-ever savings accounts when Opportunity's mobile bank came to town. They returned to three meals a day.

"We are able to buy meat for the first time in a long while," Kangwelema said at the warehouse. He raised his arms and, like a preening body builder, showed off his muscles. "We are doing fine." Everyone laughed, an emotion that had all but vanished during the years of hunger.

Back in Lilongwe, in his cubbyhole of an office, Francis Pelekamoyo smiled too, as his loan officers told him about the three ever-more-robust farmers. Rarely had he received such a joyous progress report when he was central bank governor. The news from Mchinji was Matthew 25 come to life. The least of his brethren were no longer so hungry.

CHAPTER 17

"We Must Not Fail Them"

WASHINGTON, D.C.

Late one evening in a time of world crisis, the president addressed the nation: "Hungry people in other countries look to the United States for help. I know that they will be strengthened and encouraged by this evidence of our friendship. I know that they will be waiting with hope in their hearts and a fervent prayer on their lips for the response of our people. . . . We must not fail them."

That was Harry Truman, speaking on October 5, 1947, in the first-ever televised speech from the White House. The trauma of World War II was still fresh. Economies and societies were in ruins. The peace in Europe was fragile. Fascism had been vanquished, but now hunger loomed as a major threat to democracy. Truman's speech set the table for the Marshall Plan, a blueprint for the recovery and reconstruction of Europe that would begin the following year.

Sixty-two years later, in another time of world crisis, another president spoke: "To the people of poor nations, we pledge to work alongside you to make your farms flourish and let clean waters flow, to nourish starved bodies and feed hungry minds. And to those nations like ours that enjoy relative plenty, we say we can no longer afford indifference to the suffering outside our borders, nor can we consume the world's resources without regard to effect."

That was Barack Obama, speaking just after noon on January 20, 2009, shortly after being sworn into office. Prosperity was threatened by a world economy in deepening recession; peace was under assault from "a far-reaching network of violence and hatred," as the president put it. "The time has come," he urged his fellow Americans, "to reaffirm our enduring spirit, to choose our better history."

One of the best episodes of American history was the Marshall Plan, with its cornerstone of feeding desperate Western Europeans. Now it is the hungry of Africa who are longing for a bold plan, a new Green Revolution uniquely tailored to the conditions of that continent and mindful of the mistakes of the past, that could indeed help their farms flourish. Substitute the word *Africa* for *Europe* in President Truman's speech, and President Obama would have a ringing call to action for the twenty-first century:

> The situation in Europe is grim and forbidding as winter approaches. Despite the vigorous efforts of the European people, their crops have suffered so badly from droughts, floods, and cold that the tragedy of hunger is a stark reality.
>
> The nations of Western Europe will soon be scraping the bottom of the food barrel. They cannot get through the coming winter and spring without help—generous help—from the United States and from other countries which have food to spare.
>
> I know every American feels in his heart that we must help to prevent starvation and distress among our fellow men in other countries.
>
> . . . We have dedicated ourselves to the task of securing a just and a lasting peace. No matter how long and hard the way, we cannot turn aside from that goal. An essential requirement of lasting peace is the restoration of the countries of Western Europe as free self-supporting democracies. There is reason to believe that those countries will accomplish that task if we aid them through this critical winter and help them get back on their feet during the next few years. They must do most of the job themselves. They cannot do it if thousands of their people starve. We believe they can—and will—do the job if we extend to them that measure of friendly aid which marks the difference between success and failure.

Their most urgent need is food. If the peace should be lost because we failed to share our food with hungry people there would be no more tragic example in all history of a peace needlessly lost.

If sufficient food was deemed to be the most elemental need for the development and political stability of Western Europe in 1947, surely it is also so for Africa, and the other hungry areas of the world, today. After World War II, eliminating hunger was seen to be a bulwark against the extremism of the day: international communism. Today, eliminating hunger would be a bulwark against the extremism of the twenty-first century: global terrorism.

"Hunger," said another former president, Herbert Hoover, as he helped to bring relief to Europe after World War II, "brings not alone suffering and sorrow, but fear and terror. He carries disorder and the paralysis of government, and even its downfall. He is more destructive than armies, not only in human life but in morals. All of the values of right living melt before his invasions, and every gain of civilization crumbles. But we can save these people from the worst, if we will."

As Truman recognized, America itself had much to gain—"a battle to save our own prosperity," he said—in heading the effort to conquer hunger. It was true as America sought to lead a divided world after World War II, and it would be true today in a world fractured along ideological and religious lines. Rallying a divided world to defeat hunger would help to restore America's moral standing and leadership after a period of go-it-alone policies in the war on terror battered its image abroad. It would unite a grassroots movement that has been gaining momentum in disparate points across the globe.

For Americans, such a campaign would be the grand gesture suggested by Obama's inaugural call to "reaffirm the greatness of our nation," and by his exhortations for individuals to embrace a cause greater than themselves. "What is required of us now is a new era of responsibility," he said, "a recognition on the part of every American that we have duties to ourselves, our nation, and the world."

As the new administration took office, Americans were poised to act on hunger. Momentum had been gathering in churches, universities, charities, and in discussions around family dinner tables. More than 100,000

members of the ONE Campaign, which grew out of the grassroots debt relief and AIDS efforts, signed a petition to Obama asking him to make a
strong statement about global poverty in his inaugural address; once he
did, they flooded the White House with encouragement to make good on
that statement.

Polls commissioned by the Alliance to End Hunger, an offspring of
Bread for the World, during the 2008 election campaign indicated that
the country was awaiting action on hunger by their politicians. The research was led by pollsters Thomas Freedman, who served as a senior adviser to President Clinton and a consultant to Democratic elected officials,
and Jim McLaughlin, who has worked for the national Republican sena-
torial and congressional committees. They battled against each other in
the 1996 presidential campaign—Freedman for Clinton, McLaughlin for
Bob Dole—but they have joined forces to show each party how important, and ripe, the hunger issue is.

Freedman-McLaughlin charted the emergence of a constituency they
call Do Right voters, who urgently want policies enacted to help solve problems like poverty and hunger. They also identified a category of Fed-Up
voters who care strongly about issues of helping the least fortunate but are
skeptical of the government's ability to solve them. And they found wide
support in the electorate for a reordering of America's moral priorities.

The pollsters asked the question, "Which one of the following do you
think is the biggest moral issue?" Fighting hunger and poverty registered
41.8 percent; protect the environment, 23.1 percent; abortion, 16.7 percent; gay marriage, 12.8 percent. Among Republicans, hunger was in a
statistical tie with abortion and substantially exceeded gay marriage. Democratic voters chose fighting poverty and hunger (48 percent) as the biggest
moral issue over protecting the environment (30 percent).

In another poll conducted on the night Obama won the election,
Freedman-McLaughlin found that 60 percent of surveyed voters wanted to
hear more from the presidential candidates about reducing hunger, and 69
percent supported the United States spending an additional 1 percent of
the federal budget in aid to address the needs of the world's poorest people. On a question the pollsters have been tracking over time, those who
said the United States spent too little to reduce world hunger increased to
44 percent in 2007 from 27 percent in 2003. The pollsters concluded at

the outset of the election campaign: "The country is missing an opportunity to turn an emerging consensus about poverty and hunger into political action. Now is the time to act."

Norman Borlaug, a lion in winter, had primed Washington for action on a new Marshall Plan when he received the Congressional Gold Medal in the summer of 2007. His warning from thirty-seven years earlier at the Nobel Peace Prize ceremony had come to pass; it was high time, he said, for the United States to reverse the world's neglect of the hungry:

> My plea today to the members of Congress and to the administration is to re-commit the United States to more dynamic and generous programs of official development assistance in agriculture for Third World nations, as was done in the 1960s and 1970s. Ever-shrinking foreign aid budgets in support of smallholder agriculture . . . are not in our nation's best interest, nor do they represent our finest traditions.
>
> As you chart the course of this great nation for the future benefit of our children, grandchildren, and great-grandchildren, I ask you to think more boldly and humanely about the Third World and develop a new version of the Marshall Plan, this time not to rescue a war-torn Europe, but now to help the nearly one billion, mostly rural poor people still trapped in hunger and misery. It is within America's technical and financial power to help end this human tragedy and injustice, if we set our hearts and minds to the task.

In that task, the United States would enjoy the support of many governments, particularly Ireland. In contrast to the United States, where action against hunger would connect back to an era of greatness, Ireland's inspiration flows from a time of tragedy. "Because of our history, Ireland can rightly claim to empathize with those who are suffering from disease, poverty, and hunger every day around the globe," said Bertie Ahern, the Irish *taoiseach*, or prime minister, in 2006 when he unveiled a government white paper on the future of Irish overseas aid. "But empathy is not enough," he continued. "Our actions must speak louder than our words."

The white paper led to the formation in 2007 of a hunger task force, which went to work carving out a leading role for Ireland in a global assault on hunger. From the outset, its ambitions were immense. "Ireland should aim to be the Norway of Hunger," insisted Tom Arnold, a member of the task force and the chief executive of Concern, the Irish aid organization. Norway, he noted, was also a small country that had assumed an outsized role in peace building and conflict resolution around the world. Brokering peace had become a priority of Norway's foreign policy and an area of expertise in its universities and institutions. Oslo had hosted numerous peace summits between warring factions. The country's diplomats led peace delegations to trouble spots. It hosted the awarding of the Nobel Peace Prize. Ireland, he said, would do for hunger what Norway had done for peace.

In September 2008, the task force recommended that Ireland target its international development aid and diplomacy in three areas: increasing the productivity of Africa's small farmers, reducing maternal and infant malnutrition, and prodding governments in Africa and beyond to deliver on their commitments to reduce hunger. It suggested the appointment of a hunger envoy to coordinate and spread Irish know-how: agricultural experts sharing practices from Ireland's transformation from famine to surplus, universities becoming centers of agricultural and nutrition research, food corporations tailoring products for the malnourished, Irish politicians rallying the international political will to conquer hunger that hasn't existed since the Green Revolution. Above all, Ireland would keep alive the ancient emotion of hunger, making sure the rich world wouldn't forget the awfulness of starving to death, which Ireland has felt so deeply.

Arnold noted that a campaign against hunger would create common cause not only between the Irish people so long riven by sectarian violence, but also among the peoples of the entire world. Ending hunger is both a moral issue held sacred by all the major religions as well as a matter of international security—to alleviate tensions between rich and poor and to stabilize economic disruptions.

The scramble to feed the hungry during the food crisis of 2008 proved the unifying potential of an end-hunger campaign. As the rising food prices ripped a huge hole in the World Food Program's budget, Executive Director Josette Sheeran traveled the globe to round up $755 million in donations. Everywhere she went—the White House, Congress, parliaments in countries big and small, the Chicago Board of Trade, Oprah—Sheeran held out a little red plastic cup, the symbol of the WFP's school feeding programs. Within a few months, thirty-one countries contributed to fill the cup. The biggest donation of all came from the Kingdom of Saudi Arabia—$500 million. The Saudis, who traditionally hadn't donated large amounts to UN operational organizations, suddenly became one of the WFP's biggest patrons. "This is an example of what humanitarians around the world can do when we come together to address problems that affect us all," Sheeran said.

That rising hunger is a collective failure in need of a collective solution was one of the lessons of the 2003 famine and then the 2008 food crisis. Another lesson was this: The world needs Africa to produce as much food as possible. In 2008, food prices soared, triggering riots and economic distress in more than one-quarter of the world's countries, because the world's farmers couldn't keep up with the demand for food, be it from the burgeoning middle class in nations like China and India or from rich nations mandating the use of crop-derived alternative fuels. The global economic slowdown curbed some of this demand and brought down commodity prices in late 2008. But when the economies of the world recover, the crisis will reappear. Only next time there will be even more mouths to feed. Africa is the world's final frontier of agriculture, a rare place with room to dramatically increase production and meet the rising demand. If the neglect of Africa's farmers continues, we all will suffer.

It is easy to look at the hunger crisis and be overwhelmed. But the vast scope of the hunger problem is equaled by the vast possibility for solution—and the vast opportunities to jump in and help, be it governments, corporations, universities, philanthropists, or concerned individuals. To conquer hunger and carry out a revolution in African agriculture, there are some things that must be done, as addressed in the following sections.

Keep Promises to Expand Development Aid

The global financial meltdown at the end of 2008 plunged many countries into deep budget crises. And as richer governments introduced bailout plans to aid their distressed economies, a new moral calculus emerged. If these countries can come up with hundreds of billions of dollars to take care of those who had the most (and lost it), surely they can come up with a tiny fraction of that for those who have the least.

Even before the financial crisis hit, the G8 countries—the United States, United Kingdom, Canada, France, Germany, Italy, Japan, and Russia—had fallen woefully behind on their commitment at the 2005 Gleneagles summit to increase their annual development assistance to Africa by $25 billion by 2010. In 2008, DATA, the watchdog group closely tracking the promises, reported that the countries had delivered only an additional $3 billion through the halfway point. The U.S. commitment would increase its aid to Africa by $4 billion (to a total of $8.8 billion) over those five years. At halftime, the increase was only $581 million.

How much would an African agricultural revolution cost? The Gates Foundation estimates that currently about $9 billion annually flows to agricultural development on the continent from African government spending, foreign government aid, private-sector investment, and philanthropic donations. The foundation calculates it will take an additional $9 billion to $12 billion of annual spending from all sources to triple the incomes of 60 million households in sub-Saharan Africa—for a total cost of about $20 billion a year.

This sounds like a lot of money, but when placed on the new moral scale of the world financial crisis, these efforts become a great bargain, and the argument that there's not enough money vanishes. The Gates amount is less than the bailout of Citigroup, Inc. The $4 billion needed to meet the U.S. commitment at Gleneagles is a trifle compared to the rescue of the auto industry. And then there's this comparison from America's obesity front: The Gates estimate to eliminate hunger in 60 million African households is just over half of what Americans spend to counter their overeating. The market for weight-loss treatments in the United States, including diet programs and herbal products, has been estimated to be worth some $33 billion a year.

Create a Global Fund to Aid Small Farmers in Africa

Just as the Global Fund to combat AIDS, malaria, and tuberculosis funneled billions into the assault on Africa's most serious health problems, a global fund for agriculture would channel these increases in aid to Africa's small farmers, who make up a large majority of the continent's population. As organizations from the UN Millennium Villages to the Foods

Resource Bank have discovered, the most efficient way to fight hunger and boost rural economies is first to help these poor farmers grow enough to feed themselves. For many of them, it can be accomplished with simple investments that raise their yields: harvesting rainwater with small dams and ponds, conserving that water with no-till practices that keep the moisture in the ground, planting with better seeds that better cope with the elements and small dabs of fertilizer. The next step is to help them grow surpluses that can feed their countries—and help meet the increasing global demand for food.

Invest in Infrastructure

After years of retreat, international institutions such as the World Bank and the African Development Bank should expand their financing of large-scale projects to improve Africa's agricultural infrastructure, such as roads, rural electrification, and irrigation. The needs are vast, and shameful. Only one-third of sub-Saharan Africa's rural population lives within one and a half miles of a paved road, less than 4 percent of its cropland is irrigated, and only 8 percent of rural households have access to electricity, according to a report on infrastructure investing by Michael Taylor of the Partnership to Cut Hunger and Poverty in Africa, a Washington, D.C.–based advocacy group.

In particular, the continent's great water resources, such as the Nile River basin in the East (including Ethiopia's Blue Nile) and the Niger River basin in the West, are crying out to be harnessed so Africa's fields can blossom. When World Bank President Robert Zoellick traveled to Addis Ababa in early 2008 for a summit meeting of African heads of state, he brought a pledge to double the bank's spending on African agriculture, to $800 million a year. He was bombarded with requests from the African leaders to finance everything from tractor factories to port rehabilitation.

There is also plenty of opportunity for corporate investment. Chinese companies are thick on the ground, particularly building roads to transport the raw materials needed to fuel their factories back home. But those same roads should be maintained to also benefit farmers moving their produce to market. European horticultural companies are erecting greenhouses to grow flowers for export and also establishing irrigation links; phone companies have been expanding communication networks, which help farmers gather price and market information. Norway's Yara International ASA, a leading supplier of mineral fertilizers, is widening its distribution network in Africa. U.S. companies like Cargill and Dunavant have been investing in African cotton operations. These actions are only the tip of what should be a far bigger movement involving companies big and small. Venture capitalists should back social entrepreneurs eager to bring simple, affordable technology to Africa, like the manual irrigation pumps. And representatives from the world's commodity exchanges should lend a hand to budding Eleni's across the continent to foster more orderly market conditions for African farmers.

For their part, African governments are wary of a new colonization, this time at the hands of multinational corporations. And rightly so, given the track record of some multinational oil and mining companies that have extracted raw material and left little benefit behind. Governments should work with farmer associations that are gaining strength in many countries to protect farmers' rights and to ensure the sanctity of contracts. The foreign investors should adhere to the principles of social responsibility first established in South Africa, so that a percentage of profits are reinvested in their host communities. Civil society organizations in the countries must hold the companies accountable for their behavior.

Africa Takes Responsibility

African governments need to hold true to their promises, too. Of Africa's fifty-three nations, only seven had reached the goal of investing 10 percent of their national budgets in agriculture by 2008: Burkina Faso, Cape Verde, Chad, Ethiopia, Mali, Malawi, and Niger. Another thirty had managed to spend between 5 percent and 10 percent, according to the scorecard of the New Partnership for Africa's Development. Top priorities for the spending should be scientific research, extension services to get the latest technology out to the farmers, and incentives to help them grow as much as possible.

African governments also need to allow more land to be privately owned. In many countries, most of the land is controlled by some level of administration, be it the national government or a tribal chief; one reason often cited is that public ownership keeps bigger interests from buying up all the land from peasant farmers, who would be forced into the cities. But this prevents small farmers from using their land to secure credit, which is the lifeblood of farmers the world over. Outright ownership, or at least ninety-nine-year leases, would also give farmers the confidence to make improvements to their property, such as irrigation systems.

Above all, the continent's wars need to stop. Two of Africa's largest and potentially most fertile countries—Sudan and the Democratic Republic of the Congo—have been tortured by years of conflict, and farming has become too dangerous over vast stretches. Rather than devouring a large amount of international food aid every year, these two countries—along with Zimbabwe, once a breadbasket of southern Africa—should be feeding themselves, and even exporting food.

Plant New Seed Technology

The dispute between the United States and Europe over the use of genetically modified (GM) seeds has largely kept that technology out of Africa, at least north of South Africa. African countries fear that if they use these seeds, then markets may close to them in Europe, which has resisted acceptance of genetically modified food that is widespread in U.S. supermarkets. African governments should engage in vigorous debate and decide for themselves based on their domestic needs whether to embrace certain GM crops. If they do, they should develop rigorous regulation for policing the testing and safety of those crops. And if they do, they should focus on crops that are specifically bioengineered to be more nutritious and easier for small farmers to grow— crops that are bug resistant, tolerant of weed killer, or better able to efficiently mine nutrients from the soil. Ugandan researchers have already developed a strain of banana plant that is resistant to a deadly leaf disease; in some quarters, it is viewed as a matter of national security, since Ugandans eat more bananas than any other people in the world. But the dispute between the United States and Europe over GM technology has made some Ugandan officials nervous and delayed the deployment of the new banana plant. In Kenya, a roundtable of farmers assembled by the World Food Program to discuss the role of African farmers in food aid soon led to clamoring for GM seeds. Most beneficial for a number of African countries, including Kenya, would be the development of new drought-tolerant crops.

The United States, European Union, World Bank, and other donors should increase funding of the Consultative Group on International Agricultural Research, and the funds should be unrestricted so the scientists can develop what they think would be most beneficial for peasant farmers. These research institutes are geared toward poor smallholder farmers and were instrumental in the success of the original Green Revolution. In the past, even U.S. farmers depended heavily on breeders working at public universities to provide new crop varieties, such as wheat. But in recent years public researchers have fallen behind as companies with seed operations, such as Monsanto, DuPont, and Syngenta, race ahead to patent genes as well as the steps in the process of transplanting those genes. Conducting cutting-edge research has become increasingly expensive; Monsanto, for instance, spends $2 million a day on research and development. (That cost propels them to protect their right to patent their products; without it, they argue, there wouldn't be any incentive to pursue the research.) Western biotech companies should see it is in their interest to share their breakthroughs with poor farmers on a royalty-free basis. Some have already begun sharing their drought-resistant genes. If these seeds help millions of farmers lessen their poverty, those farmers will eventually become customers who can afford to pay for commercial seed. This technology will also be important in helping Africa adapt to the impact of climate change by uncovering strains able to flourish in drier, hotter regions.

Separate from the gene transplanting, Africa should jump on board the newest branch of crop biotechnology called molecular breeding. In this field, scientists are discovering important traits they didn't know existed in certain plants, and often had to look for in other species. Rather than transplant a gene from another source, molecular breeding finds traits in a plant's own DNA that had been lost over time or ignored by crop breeders who had focused on other traits. Molecular breeding is cheaper and quicker, and, since it doesn't involve gene transplants, it avoids many of the emotional issues surrounding current biotech efforts.

Find an Alternative to Turning Food into Fuel

Not only are the economic benefits of turning food into fuel in doubt, as we have shown, but it has ignited moral consternation at a time of growing global hunger. If there are no other alternatives to petroleum-powered engines at hand, then the government should launch an effort to make biofuel from plants we don't eat, or the parts of plants we throw away. In India and Africa, biofuel efforts are focusing on a plant called *jatropha*, which grows like a weed and is inedible for both humans and animals. In the United States, researchers are already working on making biofuel from the cellulose in everything from switchgrass and wood to the inedible parts of corn plants. Some entrepreneurs are even trying to cultivate oil-making algae.

Consider an International Grain Reserve

It's time to seriously explore the idea of setting up an international grain reserve, which would have food at the ready to meet hunger emergencies. In 2008, it could have alleviated the food shortages that shook many countries when the prices for staple commodities such as corn, wheat, soybeans, and rice skyrocketed. At times, the World Food Program couldn't find available food for purchase as countries raised protectionist barriers to preserve their strategic stockpiles.

The idea of a grain reserve has been shot down in the past for several reasons: Wealthy countries want to be seen as rising up to feed the hungry in times of crisis by summoning emergency donations, storage costs would mount, and exporters fear that food in the reserve could interfere with markets. But the food in the reserve would be for emergency use only, and not for commercial sale or price stabilization. It could be stored in places such as the WFP's prepositioning depots in Italy, Ghana, and Dubai. And wealthy countries could rally to crises by restocking the reserve.

Level the Plowing Fields

Just as farm subsidies were vital for the development of modern agriculture in the United States and Europe in the last century, so are they crucial for the successful development of African agriculture in this century. As Malawi has shown, smart subsidies targeted to help farmers obtain seeds and fertilizer, while also boosting the business of private-sector traders who carry those items, have led to vast improvement in production and encouraged the development of self-sufficient agriculture. Producing food is a matter of national security; each country should be able to feed its own people. And subsidies have been a historically important tool in achieving that objective.

The issue is how to subsidize farmers. When most of a country's farmers are poor, it makes sense to subsidize production by the bushel or with cheap seeds and fertilizer. It's a relatively easy formula for a government to impose, and it encourages the production of much-needed food. In nations where agriculture has modernized, however, subsidizing production puts money into the hands of people who don't need it.

The subsidies of one country shouldn't hurt farmers elsewhere. When a country produces more food than it needs, it should change the way that it subsidizes its farmers so that its financial support doesn't encourage the production of price-depressing gluts that then must be dumped onto the global markets. While cheap food is good for the urban poor, their food security is undermined if their country's farmers lose the incentive to grow as much as they can. Thus, U.S. and European subsidies should be decoupled from production as much as possible. If taxpayers want to continue to subsidize agriculture, the incomes of farmers could be supplemented with government payments for following environmental practices that maintain green spaces for society, prevent erosion, encourage wildlife habitat, and conserve water.

An alternative would be to offer a buyout to growers of crops that the United States already produces in excess: a onetime payment in exchange for permanently withdrawing land from the subsidy program. Washington's decision to scrap tobacco subsidies in 2004 shows that retiring a crop from the subsidy program can be done without destabilizing a regional economy.

If eradicating farm poverty is still Washington's goal, the solution is simple. A groundbreaking study conducted in the mid-1990s found that what the United States typically spends on crop subsidies is just about what it would take to once again directly attack poverty on the farm. The federal government spent $43.4 billion on farm subsidies between 1993 and 1997. As it turns out, that amount is a little bit more than it would have cost the federal government to give poor farm families enough money to ensure a minimum standard of living. According to an October 2000 study issued by the USDA, it would have cost $42 billion to raise the incomes of about

530,000 farm households to 185 percent of the poverty line during that period. (At the time, the USDA's school lunch program was targeted at families with incomes below 185 percent of the poverty line.) Under a safety-net approach, a farm family of four would have been guaranteed an income of $30,040 at that time. Under the prevailing U.S. system, subsidies are doing more harm than good at home and abroad.

Give U.S. Food Aid the Flexibility for Local Purchase

The United States should use up to 50 percent of its food-aid budget to buy crops in the regions closest to the hunger areas rather than only sending U.S.-grown food. Or increase the food-aid budget by at least 50 percent and use the new funding for local purchase. Not only will the food arrive to the hungry quicker and cheaper—transportation time and costs will be greatly diminished—but it will also create another market for African-grown food. Still, it is always good to have American grain ready to be shipped out, which is why the United States shouldn't go to all cash, as the Europeans have done.

It is time to put to bed the old argument of the Iron Triangle of agricultural interests that Americans support food aid only because the money stays in America. In the new millennium, the most forceful argument for a cash component of food aid is also the simplest: It's the right thing to do.

Get Involved

Follow the examples of Pat and Elaine in Alabama, the Rufenachts in Ohio, Gregory Wayongo and Dr. Mamlin in Kenya, the students at Wheaton College, Eleni in Ethiopia, Francis Pelekamoyo in Malawi, Peter Bakker in Holland. Enlist in the war on hunger—where individuals can make a big difference—at a church or a charity or a university or a business. Norman Borlaug wants you.

At ninety-three, the father of the Green Revolution was still at it, returning to the fields of Ciudad Obregón, Mexico, where it all began and where new recruits awaited. On unsteady legs, he gingerly waded into an ocean of waist-high wheat, the descendants of the plants he had designed by hand nearly a half-century earlier. A breeze from the Gulf of California rippled the golden stalks and lifted a few strands of his snow-white hair. Squinting through thick glasses, he could see the Sierra Madre shimmering in the distance. "This is my favorite place in the world," he said, savoring it all with a deep breath. "Here I can see how much can change, and it gives me hope. It even gives me optimism about feeding Africa."

Borlaug could see his legacy all around him reflected in the agriculture-based prosperity he had initiated. New pickup trucks sped over blacktop roads past grain silos poking into the sky. Billboards touted the latest in American tractors. At night, teenagers in their cars cruised the four-lane boulevard named for him. His arrival from his modest two-bedroom home in Dallas on the corporate jet of an American admirer was front-page news in the local paper. At an elaborate barbecue, an elderly farmer offered a toast and compared Borlaug's good deeds to those of the Pope, making the guest of honor blush.

In the city hall, a mural wrapped around a stairwell depicted highlights of the region's history. Alongside scenes of marching peasants and a dam supplying water for crops, a well-tanned Borlaug appears within a halo of golden wheat stalks as he scribbles notes in a crop-breeding book, a microscope by his side. The inscription borrows a line from his Nobel Peace Prize lecture: "If you desire peace, cultivate justice, but at the same time cultivate the fields to produce more bread, otherwise there will be no peace."

Borlaug himself was not at peace, for in 2007 there was still much work to be done. Global hunger was on the rise again. There was a new generation of disciples to inspire. Cancer had begun to bend and hollow his body. Yet his passion and determination were undiminished as he talked with colleagues over dinner in a motel restaurant. "It's criminal what is happening. The West just isn't doing enough to fight hunger," Borlaug said. "I am not satisfied with how far the Green Revolution has gone."

Suddenly, blood spurted from his nose, a side effect of his cancer treatment. Borlaug was so caught up in conversation that he wasn't aware of the blood soaking the front of his plaid shirt until he noticed the startled looks of his companions. He snatched paper napkins from the table and dabbed. A look of fear and then anger flickered across his blue eyes as he cursed his cancer. "This damn thing. I don't have time for it," he said as he stood up from the table and walked to his room.

At dawn, though, Borlaug was back pacing in the motel lobby. He was anxious for a ride to his old research station to see the latest experiments and encourage the newest crop of researchers. Angela Dennett, a petite Australian college student in jeans and a T-shirt, stood shyly to the side as Borlaug walked slowly through her plot of grain, peering closely at individual plants. "It's amazing what one person can do," she said.

Sensing a teaching moment, an instructor began to tell the story of how Borlaug had invented a new way of breeding wheat in these fields. Borlaug turned around, chuckling. "Permit me to interject," he said. "Perhaps you don't know I was worried I could get fired if I didn't come up with something fast."

It would have to be fast now, if he were to see it. As he left his fields, Borlaug didn't know if he would ever return. He was preparing for the end of his days. But that didn't mean his dream had to die, too. "Hunger isn't an insurmountable problem," he said as he stared out the window of the airplane, watching the fields of the verdant Yaquí Valley grow smaller and smaller. "I have big faith in the judgment of common people if they get the facts. When change comes, it can come quickly."

Hagirso

In the final room of the Famine Museum in Strokestown, Ireland, on the very last wall, the eyes of the hungry stare out at visitors in two haunting photos. One, from India, dated 1876, is a portrait of several skeletal famine victims, adults and children, arranged in a macabre group pose. The other photo is from Sudan, 1985, in what was perhaps a camp for Ethiopians who fled their famine only to end up in another land that had nothing to eat. A stick-figure child sits alone in the sand, while, in the foreground, a couple of photographers ready their cameras.

John O'Driscoll, the museum's general manager, pulled his jacket tight against the chill as he entered this last room. It was autumn, the tourist off-season, so the heating was turned down in the museum. But even in the summer, a shiver is common for those in the presence of these final powerful exhibits, looking into the eyes of the starving. "You should hear the reaction to these photos, particularly the reaction of the children," O'Driscoll said, noting that schoolkids make up a large portion of the 60,000 annual visitors to the museum. "Shock. Anger. And the questions."

Always questions.

"Why?"

"What happened to the children?"
"Did they die?"

What happened to Hagirso, the starving Ethiopian boy in the emergency feeding tent up in the Boricha highlands? Did he die?

There had been little improvement to the road climbing from the lowlands to the plateau since the relief trucks carrying food and medicine rumbled over the dirt and gravel in 2003. For six miles it spiraled upward, following the contours of a corkscrew, past the mud-brick *tukuls* of the peasant farmers. On top of the plateau, the road leveled off and provided relatively smooth passage to the small shops and densely packed neighborhoods of the region's main town. The health clinic was still operating, but the emergency feeding tents were gone. Weeds had overgrown the field of stones.

"Another fifteen kilometers or so," said Nega Ambago, the World Food Program field officer for the Boricha area.

The dirt pathway was choked with the usual market-day travel. There were some trucks and cars and motor scooters, but mainly people traveled by donkey-drawn wagons, some of which transported a dozen passengers at once. A few of the fancier wagons had a cloth awning to provide a little shade. Most, though, were open to the blazing sun. It was one of these basic versions that had carried starving Hagirso, cradled in the arms of his father, Tesfaye, to the emergency feeding center five years earlier.

The market traffic thinned as the road left the town behind. Vegetation thickened, and Nega intensified his lookout. A cluster of huts appeared on the left side of the road. "Stop here," Nega said. The WFP's white Toyota Land Cruiser rolled to a gentle halt. "Tesfaye should be here."

What seemed to be the entire population of the little village, children and adults alike, immediately surged to the vehicle, propelled by curiosity. The crowd parted as a tall, thin man came striding out of the settlement, a silver sickle in hand. "There he is," said Nega.

A broad smile stretched across Tesfaye's face. Still hanging on to the sickle, he bear-hugged each of his visitors. "I remember you," Tesfaye said. "I was in the feeding center. We were sitting on the floor. You took some pictures. You asked how my child came to be sick. You asked my name, my child's name."

He remembered everything.

What about Hagirso?

"Come," Tesfaye said, leading the way to a clearing between the huts. "The doctors told me he wouldn't live."

After a few steps, a little boy came running to Tesfaye.

Hagirso! He had survived.

He was wearing a ragged brown polo shirt but no pants and no shoes. On the pocket of the shirt—a typical piece of the secondhand clothing that circulates through Africa—was stitched the word *Winner*. These rich-world slogans often look so out of place on the bodies of the poorest in Africa. But this shirt was appropriate. Hagirso was a winner. He had beaten starvation; the therapeutic feeding regimen had returned him to life.

His eyes, so empty and resigned back in 2003, bidding farewell, were now brighter, more joyful, mischievous even. His father told him to put on some pants, and he scampered away.

But clearly all was not well.

"He's been a little bit better," Tesfaye said. "He looks fine, but I can see some symptoms that he's not quite well. I can see from his color that he's not fine. I can see from his growth he isn't so good. He hasn't grown."

Hagirso was very small, perhaps no bigger than in 2003. He was nine or ten now, but he stood little more than three feet tall. He was stunted.

"I know he didn't grow well," Tesfaye said. "I wish I could find more nutritious food. But that is my problem. I can't afford it."

Tesfaye led the way past a row of tall, green cacti serving as a picket fence until he came to a giant shade tree. The crowd of curious children followed. A few women stood on the edge of the gathering, breast-feeding their babies. Some men joined the group. They carried small three-legged wooden stools, which they set down on a level patch of dirt under the tree. Tesfaye took one of the stools and motioned that his visitors should sit on the others.

Hagirso returned, now wearing brown pants that ended above his ankles and a dirty white jacket with yellow flowers embroidered on the ripped pocket. The visitors gave Hagirso a box of chocolates. He put the box on the ground beside his father's stool and sat on it. The crowd convulsed in laughter. The WFP's Melese Awoke had to explain to him what the chocolates were, since Hagirso had never had any; they are very tasty, Melese said, and he should cherish them and eat them later. Hagirso smiled, gave the box to his father, and sat on the ground.

Under a high blue sky punctuated by a few billowy clouds, Tesfaye recounted what had happened the past five years. Melese translated from Tesfaye's Amharic.

The famine, Tesfaye said, had claimed all his material assets, as he sold them one after another to stave off starvation as long as possible. The drought had ended, and he and his countrymen were reaping higher yields. But Tesfaye was still crippled by the aftereffects. He said he hadn't yet been able to save enough money to replenish the livestock he had lost then. Without an ox to help him plow, he had cut back on his corn planting and sowed just a small area. Feeding his eight children (he had four with his first wife, who died some years before the famine) was still difficult. He harvested the false banana plants growing near his *tukul*—those plants don't yield fruit, but the pulp inside the trunk is used as a potato-like staple. He also nurtured a small patch of sugar cane, and grew some beans and cabbage as well. And he tended to a field of *khat* bushes. Khat produces leaves and stems that are chewed as a mild narcotic; Ethiopia exports it to neighboring Arab countries. The khat was Tesfaye's lone cash crop. "I can harvest it three times a year, and each time I get between fifty and sixty birr." That was six or seven dollars. Sometimes he could grab a day or two of work plowing fields for other farmers in the area, which might pay five birr a day. His wife also worked for others, using a large mortar and pestle to pound false banana pulp into a kind of flour. "We buy some corn, maybe some cooking oil and salt and spices," Tesfaye said.

His older children had dropped out of school. The oldest had made it to seventh grade; one completed fourth and one third. Hagirso never started school, and now, Tesfaye feared, he was also stunted mentally from the malnourishment. "I can't afford the fees, or books, or proper clothes," Tesfaye said. He himself could barely read and write. "I'd love to see my children go to school and be educated. But this is my life. All our money goes for food, and maybe some clothes."

Tesfaye was asked the same question he had wrestled with in 2003 in the emergency feeding tent: What happened to cause such misery?

He said he had never forgotten the question. "I have thought about that. What did I do? Nobody came to my land and stole my things. The rains didn't come. I don't know who is to blame. I think God was angry with us."

In the years since the 2003 famine, Ethiopia's agricultural production had been steadily increasing. The rains were good, and relief agencies and companies had made seeds and fertilizer more available. Irrigation projects began. Up north near the Blue Nile River, Takele Tarekegn, who as a boy in the 1960s had watched Americans survey the land along the Koga River while he led his family's cows to drink, finally saw the strangers return. Now a gray-bearded elder leaning on a wooden shepherd's staff, Takele watched the new interlopers—Ethiopians and other Africans, bankers and engineers—bring to life the old American plans to construct an irrigation project along the Koga. He was told it would bring water to 15,000 acres and benefit 6,000 families, including his. It was a $50 million project backed by the African Development Bank and, most important, the Egyptians, who had decided to approve it after the Ethiopians had pointed out the devastation of famine on the entire Nile River basin. Other projects in the region would follow, giving Ethiopia's farmers hope that they could finally use some of the water flowing past their feet.

The Ethiopian government and international donors had also woven a post-2003 safety net to keep peasant farmers fed during the annual hunger season, which usually lasted several months from the time food stocks from the last harvest ran out to when the new harvest would come in. Under the safety net program, farmers worked on communal land reclamation projects like field terracing and tree planting, or road repair, and then would be paid cash to purchase food in the local markets. The payments were thirty birr per month per household member; that would buy about fifteen kilograms of corn or wheat. It also generated a market for the growing grain surpluses.

But in 2008, the early rains failed. And then the global food crisis hit; the soaring prices roiling the rest of the world arrived in Ethiopia. The safety net was ripped to shreds. The monthly payments could buy only five kilograms of corn or wheat per household member, barely enough to feed a child for a week. To counter the higher prices, the donors to the safety net program increased the work payments to forty birr per month. But that modest boost was overwhelmed by a tripling of grain prices. In the country's markets, merchants introduced smaller measuring containers to sell tinier portions to meet consumers' tightened budgets.

"We have gone from three meals a day to two. Then it will be one meal. Then we will die," said Yoseph Yilak, the manager of the Addis Ababa Grain Traders Association who had railed against the country's antiquated marketing system back in 2003. Now he cursed the rising worldwide demand that had driven up prices. The people in China and India who were eating better couldn't be blamed, he said; Ethiopians hoped to one day do likewise. His fury was focused on those in faraway lands who were converting food into gasoline for their cars. "Why is the world taking corn for fuel?" he asked. "It will mean the death of many people."

By the summer of 2008, as the hunger season arrived, the country's malnutrition levels were on the rise again. Tesfaye said the World Food Program had been delivering food to Boricha. His family and two others shared a monthly ration of fifty kilograms of wheat. Other families were worse off than his, he said. So many, he noted, that he wasn't even part of the safety net program; he was on a waiting list.

Beyond the shade tree, an ox was tied to a stake in a little patch of grass. It belonged to a friend in town who had asked Tesfaye to watch over it and feed it. Tesfaye laughed at the irony: His family hadn't eaten meat for months, yet he was fattening an ox for someone else's feast. Nor could he use it for plowing, lest it grow too tough and lessen the value. He had been promised one hundred birr to look after the ox for a couple of months; he hoped it would be enough to stretch until his corn was ready for harvest.

Tesfaye rose from his stool and walked to his field. First, he showed off his one-room house. He had built it fifteen years earlier by arranging long poles in a round teepee style and then covering the gaps with a mud-and-grass plaster. Over the years, the elements had taken their toll. There were holes in the wall where the recent rain had pounded. Inside, illuminated only by the sunlight squeezing through the cracks in the wall, the dirt floor was pocked with holes and crevices. Banana leaves and cow skins were strewn over the floor in the sleeping area. Several gourds and calabashes, the family's only eating utensils, hung from the center pole. Outside, Tesfaye had begun stripping a tall cactus with his sickle; he would shape it into a pole to give added support to the leaky wall.

Tesfaye led the way through a thicket of false banana plants to his field where corn and khat and beans grew. Hagirso followed, chewing on a raw stem of sugar cane. In a clearing in the field, Hagirso said something to his father that made Tesfaye laugh. "He says he has chosen you to go home with," Tesfaye said, still chuckling. "I explained to him he is staying here. I told him it was you who wrote down his name when he was starving and now you are here to see how he is."

Tesfaye put his hand on his son's shoulder, and together they walked back to find relief in the shade beneath the big tree. "You asked me how life is. We are doing better compared to when I last saw you. But not much better," Tesfaye said. "Now I will tell you this: We don't ever want to be so hungry again. Everything is in the hands of God. And you."

Tesfaye and Hagirso in front
of their tukul, 2008.

ACKNOWLEDGMENTS

To all those in Africa who welcomed us into their homes, their fields, and the shade of their trees and told us their stories, thank you. This book wouldn't have been possible without the narratives of their lives in the hollow of plenty. Many of their stories are in these pages; we hope we have done them justice.

The African reporting was helped immensely by a multitude of people who pointed the way, and then helped us get there. Government ministers, aid workers, fellow journalists, drivers, interpreters, bartenders. And in the capitals of Europe and many points in the United States, there have been countless experts on international agriculture and the hunger issue who shared their analysis, facts, documentation, and passion. Thank you in particular to Chris Dowswell, Norman Bolaug's aide-de-camp; Julie Howard at the Partnership to Cut Hunger and Poverty in Africa; Max Finberg of the Alliance to End Hunger; Gary Toenniessen at the Rockefeller Foundation; Ann Tutwiler at the William and Flora Hewlett Foundation; and Marshall Bouton of the Chicago Council on Global Affairs.

Many of the episodes in this book began as stories in *The Wall Street Journal*, so we are grateful to our past and present colleagues who supported our reporting sojourns around the world, among them: Bryan Gruley, Lee Lescaze, Karen House, Fred Kempe, Paul Steiger, Ken Wells, John Brecher, Mike Miller, Marcus Brauchli, and Kevin Helliker. There has been a battalion of editors who sharpened our copy, and a legion of reporters who shared their knowledge and opened their notebooks to us. Our thanks and appreciation to all of them. We are particularly grateful to our current colleagues in the *Journal*'s Chicago bureau who cheered us to the finish line.

It was Ken Wells, an ace foreign correspondent, editor, and author himself, who helped us hatch the idea for this book. From his post overseeing the *Journal*'s book division, he shepherded our proposal to PublicAffairs, where it was embraced by founder Peter Osnos, publisher Susan Weinberg, and senior editor and marketing director Lisa Kaufman. Lisa shared our vision for the book from the outset and provided invaluable advice. Meredith Smith and Annette Wenda deftly guided the production and editing. And publicity director Whitney Peeling has spread the word. Rose Ellen D'Angelo, director of the *Journal*'s books and special projects realm, kept the faith and the good humor. Anne Thurow and Patricia Callahan read many drafts of this book and detected wayward passages big and small.

Above all, our deepest gratitude goes to our families for their love, encouragement, and steadfast belief in our work.

NOTES

Preface

Precisely calculating the number of hungry people in the world is difficult.

Experts disagree over how to define undernourishment. One rough measure is to count people who consume less than 2,100 calories daily, but the minimum nutritional requirement of people varies by their age and how much physical labor they do. The United States isn't nearly as strict when trying to gauge food insecurity within its own borders. The U.S. government counts households that don't have enough money or resources to get adequate food at times during the year.

Estimates of the undernourished population are generated by the United Nations' Food and Agriculture Organization (FAO), which publishes *The State of Food Insecurity in the World*. In December 2008, the FAO released a preliminary estimate of 963 million undernourished people. The U.S. Department of Agriculture issues an annual *Food Security Assessment*. The 2007 edition, which was issued in July 2008, put the number of food-insecure people in seventy poor nations at 982 million.

Another way to look at hunger was developed by the International Food Policy Research Institute in Washington, D.C. Its Global Hunger Index is based on the proportion of the undernourished population, the prevalence of underweight children under the age of five, and the mortality rate of children under the age of five. The results released in October 2008 were based on data that ended in 2006, at which time nine of the ten countries with the highest hunger index were in sub-Saharan Africa.

Chapter 1

This chapter is based on interviews with Norman Borlaug, his family and colleagues, and with farmers and scientists in the Yaquí Valley, where he started the research station that operates still. Borlaug as a young man and the scene in which he learns he won the Nobel Peace Prize are portrayed in Leon Hesser's, *The Man Who Fed the World: Nobel Peace Prize Laureate Norman Borlaug and His Battle to End World Hunger* (Dallas: Durban House Publishing, 2006). Some material was also collected from Dr. Borlaug's speeches and essays.

Information on Henry Wallace came from John C. Culver and John Hyde, *American Dreamer: A Life of Henry A. Wallace* (New York: W. W. Norton, 2000.) We also used archival material from *Wallaces' Farmer* of Urbandale, Iowa, and Pioneer Hi-Bred International Inc., now a unit of DuPont Co.

Information on the Rockefeller Foundation's agricultural work in Mexico was gleaned from E. C. Stakman, Richard Bradfield, and Paul C. Mangelsdorf, *Campaigns against Hunger* (Cambridge: Harvard University Press, Belknap Press, 1967), as well as material from the foundation.

Chapter 2

The Soviet Union's purchases of U.S. wheat is described in Clifton B. Luttrell, *The Russian Wheat Deal: Hindsight vs. Foresight* (St. Louis: Federal Reserve Bank, October 1973).

The impact of the Soviet purchases on U.S. consumers is explained in Dan Morgan, *Merchants of Grain* (New York: Viking Press, 1979), 39.

The early 1970s food crisis and the position of the Ford administration at the 1974 World Food Conference is described by D. John Shaw in chapters 10 and 11 of *World Food Security: A History since 1945* (New York: Palgrave Macmillan, 2007).

The comment by John Block, the U.S. agriculture secretary during the Reagan administration, is from "Cakes and Caviar: The Dunkel Draft and Third World Agriculture," *Ecologist* (November–December 1993): 220.

The impact of the structural adjustment policy is described in Max Lawson, *Death on the Doorstep of the Summit*, an Oxfam briefing paper published in August 2002.

The quote by former Haitian agricultural minister Philippe Mathieu is from Joel Millman and Roger Thurow, "Food Crisis Forces New Look at Farming: Poor Nations, and Their Donors, Now Rethink Emphasis on Free Trade," *The Wall Street Journal*, June 10, 2008, A1.

The decline in development assistance for agriculture is charted in *World Development Report 2008: Agriculture for Development*, 41. The report, which was issued by the World Bank in October 2007, was prepared by a team directed by Derek Byerlee and Alain de Janvry.

The drop in U.S. bilateral aid for agricultural development is detailed in chapter 12 of *Agricultural R&D in the Developing World: Too Little, Too Late?* Edited by Philip G. Pardey, Julian M. Alston, and Roley R. Piggott, the report was published in 2006 by the International Food Policy Research Institute, a research center primarily supported by the Consultative Group on International Agricultural Research.

Chapter 3

Part of this chapter expands on an article in *The Wall Street Journal* by the authors about Borlaug's work in Africa: "Diminishing Returns: Africa Could Grow Enough to Feed Itself; Should It?—Issue Pits Rich Donor Nations against Man Who Sowed Green Revolution in Asia—In Ghana, a Legendary Harvest," December 3, 2002, A1.

Africa's early food production is described in the National Research Council report *Lost Crops of Africa*. Vol. 1, *Grains* (Washington, D.C.: National Academy Press, 1996).

Evolutionary biologist Jared Diamond explains why agriculture arose in Asia and Europe before Africa in "The Shape of Africa," *National Geographic*, September 2005.

Chapter 4

Parts of this chapter expand on these *Wall Street Journal* articles: "Hanging by a Thread: In U.S., Cotton Farmers Thrive; in Africa They Fight to Survive," by the authors, June 26, 2002, A1; "Bittersweet: How an Addiction to Sugar Subsidies Hurts Development," by Roger Thurow and Geoff Winestock, September 16, 2002, A1.

The comments from President Bush at Monterrey come from the *New York Times*: "Bush, in Monterrey, Speaks of Conditional Global Aid," by Elisabeth Bumiller, March 23, 2002; "More Aid, More Need: Pledges Still Falling Short" by Tim Weiner, March 24, 2002.

Chapter 5

Parts of this chapter expand on an article in *The Wall Street Journal* by Roger Thurow: "Road to Hunger—Behind the Famine in Ethiopia: Glut and Aid Policies Gone Bad—Fledgling Free Market Failed as Surplus Battered Prices; Farmers Slashed Planting—Then the Drought Took Over," July 1, 2003, A1.

Chapter 6

Part of this chapter expands on an article in *The Wall Street Journal* by the authors about food aid: "Seeds of Discord: As U.S. Food Aid Enriches Farmers, Poor Nations Cry Foul—Sending Crops, Not Cash, Eases American Gluts, Ignores Local Surpluses—A Pitch from Raisin Growers," September 11, 2003, A1.

Chapter 7

Part of this chapter expands on a story in *The Wall Street Journal* by Roger Thurow: "Changing Course: Ravaged by Famine, Ethiopia Finally Gets Help from the Nile—

For Generations, Politics Kept Tributaries Flowing by, Bringing Bounty to Egypt—Parched Corn, Rushing Water," November 26, 2003, A1.

Chapter 8

Parts of this chapter expand on the following stories in *The Wall Street Journal* by Roger Thurow: "Empty Fields: In Africa, AIDS and Famine Now Go Hand in Hand—As Farmers Die in Swaziland, Their Plots Lie Fallow; Bush Visits the Continent—Five Orphans in a Mud Shack," July 9, 2003, A1; and "Rapid Reversal: Once a Breadbasket, Zimbabwe Today Can't Feed Itself—Politics, Drought, AIDS Bring a Severe Food Shortage; Aid Is Coming Up Short—Caterpillars Become a Staple," December 24, 2003, A1.

Chapter 9

Information on Ireland's agricultural history comes from "Europe and the Revolution in Irish Agriculture," by Tom Arnold of Concern Worldwide.

Information on Bono's early musical influences comes from an interview in *Rolling Stone*, November 3, 2005.

Chapter 10

Information on the Gates family conversations on global health and the Foundation's philosophy come from the Foundation's Web site, www.gatesfoundation.org.

The Bill Gates Sr. comment regarding IAVI comes from "From Rags to Riches," by Amanda Ripley, *Time*, December 26, 2005, 83.

Chapter 11

Parts of this chapter expand on a story in *The Wall Street Journal* by Roger Thurow: "Full Treatment: In Kenya, AIDS Therapy Includes Fresh Vegetables—Indiana's Dr. Mamlin Prescribes Food, Drugs; Patients Learn to Farm," March 28, 2007, A1.

Stephen Lewis' comments are from his forward to *Poverty, AIDS, and Hunger: Breaking the Poverty Trap in Malawi* by Anne C. Conroy, Malcolm J. Blackie, Alan Whiteside, Justin C. Malewezi, and Jeffrey D. Sachs (New York: Palgrave Macmillan, 2006).

Chapter 12

Information on Liberia's president growing rice came from Natalie Obiko Pearson, "Africa Looks for Silver Lining in Food Crisis—International Aid, Other Resources Flow to Ailing Farm Sector," *The Wall Street Journal Europe*, June 20, 2008.

Much of the section on food aid expands on articles in *The Wall Street Journal* by the authors, including: "Pork Chops: In Fight against Farm Subsidies, Even Farmers Are Joining Foes—A Snowballing Movement Draws Churches, CEOS; Huge Hurdles in Congress—A Bolster to WTO Pressures," March 14, 2006, A1; and "Meal Ticket: Farmers, Charities Join Forces to Block Famine-Relief Revamp—Bush Administration Wants to Purchase African Food; Lobby Says Buy American—Proposal Is Stuck in Congress," October 26, 2005, A1.

Information on fertilizer consumption by major U.S. crops came from Keith Wiebe and Noel Gollehon, eds., *Agricultural Resources and Environmental Indicators*, Economic Information Bulletin No. 16 (Washington, D.C.: U.S. Department of Agriculture, Economic Research Service, July 2006).

Information on subsidy payments to U.S. farmers came from Ron L. Durst, *Effects of Reducing the Income Cap on Eligibility for Farm Program Payments*, Economic Information Bulletin No. 27 (Washington, D.C.: U.S. Department of Agriculture, Economic Research Service, September 2007); U.S. Department of Agriculture Economic Research Service Web site, "Farm and Commodity Policy Briefing Room: Government Payments and the Farm Sector," www.ers.usda.gov/Briefing/FarmPolicy/Gov-Pay.htm; and Edwin Young, Victor Oliveira, and Roger Claassen, *2008 Farm Act: Where Will the Money Go?* (Washington, D.C.: Amber Waves, U.S. Department of Agriculture, Economic Research Service, November 2008).

Information on the financial condition of U.S. farmers came from Craig Gundersen and others, *A Safety Net for Farm Households*, Agricultural Economic Report No. 788 (Washington, D.C.: U.S. Department of Agriculture, Economic Research Service, October 2000); *Agricultural Income and Finance Outlook* (Washington, D.C.: U.S. Department of Agriculture, Economic Research Service AIS-86, December 2008); as well as updated estimates released by the USDA in February 2009.

Information on the permanent U.S. farm subsidy legislation came from "The Effects of Failure to Enact a New Farm Bill: Permanent Law Support for Commodities and Lapse of Other USDA Programs" (March 2008), a miscellaneous report for the farm policy briefing Web page maintained by the U.S. Department of Agriculture, Economic Research Service.

Information on ethanol's share of the U.S. motor fuel market came from *Monthly Energy Review* (Washington, D.C.: U.S. Department of Energy, Energy Information Administration, January 2009).

Information on the amount of U.S corn used to make ethanol came from *World Agricultural Supply and Demand Estimates*, a monthly report issued by the World Agricultural Outlook Board (Washington, D.C.: U.S. Department of Agriculture).

Information on the corn use to fill an SUV gas tank came from an interview with Robbin Johnson, a University of Minnesota lecturer and retired Cargill, Inc., executive.

Chapter 13

Warren Buffett's philosophy about passing on wealth to descendants is described in Roger Lowenstein, *Buffett: The Making of an American Capitalist* (New York: Random House, 1995), and Alice Schroeder, *The Snowball: Warren Buffett and the Business of Life* (New York: Bantam Books, 2008).

Chapter 14

Part of this chapter expands on a story in *The Wall Street Journal* by Roger Thurow: "Ethiopia Taps Grain Exchange in Its Battle on Hunger," February 27, 2008, A1.

Chapter 15

Part of this chapter expands on a story in *The Wall Street Journal* by Roger Thurow: "Famine Relief: In Battling Hunger, a New Advance: Peanut-Butter Paste—Plumpy'nut Doesn't Use Water and Is Easily Distributed; Big Deployment in Darfur—Balancing Profits with Aid," April 12, 2005, A1.

Chapter 16

Part of this chapter expands on a story in *The Wall Street Journal* by Roger Thurow: "A Dam Connects Machakos, Kenya, to Archbold, Ohio—As Development Aid in Rural Africa Dwindles, American Farmers Pitch In," April 23, 2007, A1.

Chapter 17

President Truman's speech can be found in its entirety online: John Wolley and Gerhard Peters, "The American Presidency Project," www.presidency.ucsb.edu.

Information regarding the market for weight-loss treatments in the United States came from "Inside Drugmakers' War on Fat," *BusinessWeek*, March 17, 2008, 41.

INDEX

Anne Thurow   Patricia Callahan

Roger Thurow has been a *Wall Street Journal* foreign correspondent for twenty years. He was based in South Africa from 1986 to 1991, an assignment during the last-gasp years of apartheid and the early days of reconciliation that ignited a passion for writing about humanitarian and development issues. His reporting has taken him to more than sixty countries, including two dozen in Africa. **Scott Kilman** has covered agriculture at the *Journal* for much of the past two decades, chronicling the actions of the U.S. government and agro-industrial sector that impact farmers and consumers worldwide. He writes about trade, biotechnology, food safety, subsidies, and the rural economy. Over the past seven years, Thurow and Kilman have teamed up to produce a stream of page 1 stories in the *Journal* that have broken new ground in our understanding of famine and food aid. Their stories on the 2003 famines in Ethiopia and southern Africa were a finalist for the 2004 Pulitzer Prize in International Reporting. The series, Anatomy of Famine, was praised by the Pulitzer board for "haunting stories that shed new light on starvation in Africa and prompted international agencies to rethink their policies." In 2005, Thurow and Kilman were honored by the United Nations for their reporting on humanitarian and development issues. They are both based in Chicago.

PublicAffairs is a publishing house founded in 1997. It is a tribute to the standards, values, and flair of three persons who have served as mentors to countless reporters, writers, editors, and book people of all kinds, including me.

I. F. STONE, proprietor of *I. F. Stone's Weekly*, combined a commitment to the First Amendment with entrepreneurial zeal and reporting skill and became one of the great independent journalists in American history. At the age of eighty, Izzy published *The Trial of Socrates*, which was a national bestseller. He wrote the book after he taught himself ancient Greek.

BENJAMIN C. BRADLEE was for nearly thirty years the charismatic editorial leader of *The Washington Post*. It was Ben who gave the *Post* the range and courage to pursue such historic issues as Watergate. He supported his reporters with a tenacity that made them fearless and it is no accident that so many became authors of influential, best-selling books.

ROBERT L. BERNSTEIN, the chief executive of Random House for more than a quarter century, guided one of the nation's premier publishing houses. Bob was personally responsible for many books of political dissent and argument that challenged tyranny around the globe. He is also the founder and longtime chair of Human Rights Watch, one of the most respected human rights organizations in the world.

·   ·   ·

For fifty years, the banner of Public Affairs Press was carried by its owner Morris B. Schnapper, who published Gandhi, Nasser, Toynbee, Truman, and about 1,500 other authors. In 1983, Schnapper was described by *The Washington Post* as "a redoubtable gadfly." His legacy will endure in the books to come.

Peter Osnos, *Founder and Editor-at-Large*